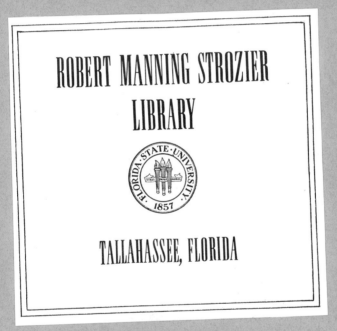

Panama to Patagonia

A Mountain Bridge

Panama to Patagonia

The Isthmian Canal

And the West Coast Countries of South America

By

Charles M. Pepper

Author of "Tomorrow in Cuba"

With Maps and Illustrations

Chicago

A. C. McClurg & Co.

1906

COPYRIGHT
A. C. McCLURG & Co.
1906

Entered at Stationers' Hall

Published March 24, 1906

THE UNIVERSITY PRESS, CAMBRIDGE, U. S. A.

THIS BOOK IS AFFECTIONATELY DEDICATED

TO

𝕸𝖞 𝖂𝖎𝖋𝖊

KITTIE ROSE PEPPER

AND TO

𝕸𝖞 𝕯𝖆𝖚𝖌𝖍𝖙𝖊𝖗

NORITA ROSE PEPPER

COMRADES IN MANY TRAVELS

PREFACE

MY purpose in this work is to consider and describe the effect of the Panama Canal on the West Coast countries of South America from the year 1905. At this period its construction by the United States may be said to have begun. If my own deep conviction that this influence makes powerfully for their industrial development and their political stability be an illusion, the pages which follow may afford the disbelievers grounds for pointing out wrong premises or false conclusions. "We doubt" long has been the dogma of the North American and the European in everything relating to the permanency of progress in the Spanish-American Republics. "I believe" is yet only the creed of the individual. A huge material fact obtruding itself may secure a listening ear from the doubters. The Canal obtrudes.

The severely practical Northern mind finds itself in a brain-fog with reference to the Southern Continent. Speculative reasoning regarding new forces of civilization does not appeal to it. It wants the concrete circumstances. Now the Canal is not an abstraction. The industrial and commercial energies which it wakens are not abstractions. The interoceanic waterway is a national undertaking, but it shows the way to individual enterprise. More than the gates of chance are opened to American youth. They are the gates of opportunity. Consequently the need of knowledge.

The number of recent books relating to the history of South America seems to indicate a demand for this knowledge in its primary form. They open the path for a volume which may be limited more strictly to industrial, fiscal, and political information. For that reason, while not overlooking the historical element in the institutions and governmental systems, I have not thought it necessary to consider them chronologically from the colonial epoch or even from the era of independence.

The effort to divorce economic and social forces from places and peoples in order to analyze a principle usually is so barren that I have not attempted it. Places have their significance, and people are the human material. Customs and institutions are only understood properly in their environment. So many excellent descriptive works have been written about South America that I have sought to subordinate these features; yet since the information applies to localities something about them could not entirely be omitted. Moreover, I have that abounding faith which leads me to look forward to the time when the engineering marvels of the Canal construction may prove enough of a magnet to draw thither the travelled American who would know what his country is doing and who, once on the Isthmus, will be likely to continue down the West Coast with a view to determining the relative attractions of the noble Andes and the Alps. Yet I have made no attempt to preserve the form of continuous narrative. The treatment of the subject does not demand it.

To South American friends who may be offended at the frankness or the bluntness of the views expressed, a word may be communicated. The confidences extended me while on an official mission widened my own vision of the aspirations of their public men. At the same time they conveyed the idea that the economic evolution to which all look forward will come more swiftly if reactionary tendencies are combated more openly and aggressively. Opinions on the policy of the United States being uttered with freedom, I have not thought it necessary to adopt the apologetic attitude in regard to other Republics. In seeking the constructive elements in the national life and character of the South American countries, it has been with the undisguised hope that the contact and the impact of North American character may be a reciprocal influence.

Acknowledgment of material for the general map, which amplifies that of the permanent Pan-American Railway Committee, is due its chairman, Hon. H. G. Davis, whose faith in the future relation of the United States to the other American countries is an example to the generation which will share the benefits both of the Canal and of railroad construction.

C. M. P.

Washington, D. C.
January, 1906.

CONTENTS

CHAPTER I

ECONOMIC EFFECT OF THE CANAL

CHAPTER II

TRAVEL HINTS

CHAPTER III

THE ISTHMUS OF PANAMA

CONTENTS

CONTENTS

CHAPTER VII

AREQUIPA AND LAKE TITICACA

CHAPTER VIII

THE REGIONS AND THEIR RESOURCES

CHAPTER IX

WATERWAYS AND RAILWAYS

CHAPTER X

THE PEOPLE AND THEIR INCREASE

CHAPTER XIV

NITRATE OF SODA AN ALADDIN'S LAMP

CHAPTER XV

CHILE'S UNIQUE POLITICAL HISTORY

CHAPTER XVI

PALPITATING SOCIAL QUESTIONS

CONTENTS

CHAPTER XXI

BOLIVIAN NATIONAL POLICY

CHAPTER XXII

NEW BASIS OF THE MONROE DOCTRINE

ILLUSTRATIONS

MAPS

PANAMA TO PATAGONIA

CHAPTER I

ECONOMIC EFFECT OF THE CANAL

Philosophic Spanish-American View — Henry Clay's Mistaken Population Prophecy — The Andes Not a Canal Limitation — Intercontinental Railway Spurs — Argentina and the Amazon as Feeders — Centres of Cereal Production — Crude Rubber — Atlantic and Pacific Traffic — Growth of West Coast Commerce — North and South Trade-wave — Distances via Panama, Cape Horn, and the Straits of Magellan — Waterway Tolls and Coal Consumption — Ecuador and Peru — Bolivia and Chile — Isthmian Railroad Rates — Value of United States Sanitary Authority — American Element in New Industrial Life.

THE effect of the Panama Canal on the West Coast industrial development and the reciprocal influence of this South American progress on the waterway are economic facts. The citizen of the United States who would know the subject in a wider range than the mere gratification of his patriotic impulses and his national pride, should turn to the study of commercial geography, the potential political economy of unexploited natural resources. The European statesman, jealously watchful of trade conditions in the New World and the causes which modify them, will follow these channels without suggestion.

Whether the digging of the Canal take ten, fifteen, or twenty years, does not affect its industrial value. The Spanish-American, with his inherited inertia and his lack of initiative, in waiting for to-morrow would be content if the work consumed half a century. What Humboldt prophesied of the Southern Continent as the seat of future civilization, what Agassiz predicted of the Andean and the Amazon populations, he is sure now will be realized. He even reverts to his favorite method of comparing the square miles of Belgium with the square miles of his own South American country, whichever one it may be, and exhibits the latter's possibilities for the human race by explaining the number of people it can sustain when it shall have as many inhabitants to the square mile as has Belgium. Yet while he believes that the destiny of the Southern Continent is at the threshold of realization, Yankee impatience only would amuse him. Since the interoceanic waterway and all its benefits are to be, what matter a few years? Time, says the Castilian proverb, is the element. This philosophic Latin view may serve as a curb to fault-finding if the construction work on the Canal seems to halt while the engineering obstacles are studied and experiments are made in order to determine the best means to overcome them.

But though the Spanish-American, who is of the race that controls the West Coast countries of South America, is patient in his waiting for ultimate results, he does not fail to grasp the immediate effect. All the processes of the economic evolution unroll before his mental vision. For Colombia, Ecuador, Peru, Chile, and Bolivia, the standard already has been set, and the goal towards which they must work has been fixed. Their national policies and their commercial and industrial growth at once come under the stimulus of the waterway. "The Panama Canal," said the leader of public thought in one of the Republics, "will precipitate our commercial evolution." It is the spring from which will gush the streams of immigration.

In the present volume I shall have little to say of Colombia, for though the Isthmus of Panama is the reception-room of that country, the Canal is to be. considered jointly with relation to the Caribbean and the Pacific shores. I include Bolivia because, while as a political division it is not ocean-bordering, geographically it is a Pacific coast country on account of its outlet through Chilean and Peruvian seaports.

Population in South America is not marked by periods of phenomenal increase. Henry Clay, in his generous pleas for the recognition of the struggling Republics, was led in the warmth of his imagination to foresee the day when they would have 72,000,000 and we would have 40,000,000 inhabitants. The population of the United States was then less than 10,000,000. Clay spoke when the resources of the Louisiana Purchase were still distrusted by many conservative public men, and long before Daniel Webster had delivered his celebrated philippic against the Oregon region as a worthless area of deserts and shifting sands. Mindful of the slow growth in the Southern Hemisphere, I make no predictions of sudden leaps, but merely seek to indicate what proportion of the present and future inhabitants comes within the sphere of the Canal.

The population of western Colombia and of Ecuador, Peru, Chile, and Bolivia is approximately 11,000,000, dwelling chiefly along the seacoast. It has been assumed that only this long slope of almost continuous mountain wall from Panama to Patagonia is subject to the direct influence of the Canal, and that the barrier of the Andes makes all the rest of the South American continent dependent on Atlantic outlets. The assumption is presumptuous. It is based on an unflattering lack of geographical knowledge and on a complete ignorance of political and economic conditions.

The primary mistake is in considering the Coast Cordilleras as the principal chain. The great rampart of the Andes in places is hundreds of miles across. Productive plains and fertile valleys lie on the western side of the Continental Divide as well as on the Atlantic slope. Besides, there are many bifurcations of these lofty ranges which must be pierced toward the Pacific. The mineral belt with its incalculable wealth, after centuries only partially exploited, has its basis of profitable production and export by means of the water transport of the Pacific. And greatest of all the facts is the certainty that railways will bore through the granite ramparts in a westerly direction. The central spine or backbone of the Intercontinental or Pan-American trunk line is not all a dream, and from its links spurs will shoot out toward the Pacific. It would have been as reasonable to imagine that the Rocky Mountains could forever shut in the region between them and the Sierra Nevadas, barring all outlet to the Atlantic and the Gulf of Mexico, as to suppose that the Pacific Ocean from Panama south is everlastingly restricted to the fringe of coast for its commerce. This is in the industrial sense and aside from the reasons of national polity which by railway enterprises on the part of the various governments are causing the Andes to disappear.

The grain fields and pastures of Argentina lie close to the Pacific. How close? Within less than 200 miles. The pampas of the western and northwestern provinces are from 500 to 1,200 miles distant from the Atlantic seaboard. The pressure of the agricultural population is westward. A generation — perhaps a decade — will bring it to the slopes of the Andes. The first railway to join the Atlantic and the Pacific, that from Buenos Ayres to Valparaiso, will be completed by means of a spiral tunnel long before vessels are propelled through the Canal.

But Valparaiso is far south, so far that, in the opinion of some authorities, it is the limit of the Canal radius. Let this be granted momentarily while the map is scanned. Place the thumb on the Chilean port of Caldera, 400 miles north of Valparaiso; the index finger on Tucuman, and the middle finger on Cordoba. The lines forking from these Argentine cities forecast the next chapter of railway expansion. Let it be known also that Nature, in kindly mood, has formed a saddle in the mountain range in this section, and that engineering surveys of routes through the depression are the basis of projects which only await a larger agricultural area under cultivation in order to become railway enterprises with an assured commercial basis. Both Cordoba and Tucuman will be in rail communication with the Pacific coast some years before the waterway is finished. Nor are these the only

trans-Andine lines in prospect. They serve the purposes of illustration, so that a description of the others
may be omitted. I cite the first two in order that it
may be known there is an Argentine relation to the
Canal, and a highly important one as to population
and as to the exports and imports which are the
foundation of maritime and rail traffic.

If this suggestion is new and strange, I follow it by
a more startling proposition. As one result of the
Panama Canal, a measure of Amazonian commerce
will flow to and from the Pacific.

To begin with, there is the nearness. By several
trans-Andine routes the navigable affluents of the Amazon are less than 300 miles from the coast. Steamships of 800 tons navigate as far as Yurimaguas on
the Huallaga River, which was the historic route of
the Spaniards over the Continental Divide. Steam
vessels also go up the Marañon from Iquitos, 425 miles
to the Falls of Manserriche, which by several practicable railway routes are within less than 400 miles of
the Bay of Paita. Minor Peruvian ports below Paita
are able to offset its shipping advantages by shorter
trails. Not more than 225 miles of difficult railway
construction are necessary to open to a large section
of the vast Amazon region the commerce of Callao,
Peru's chief port.

In relation to the Amazon as a feeder, it has to be
recognized that the Andes form a greater obstacle than
in Argentina, and that the river basins will be populated much more slowly and never so densely as the
Argentine pampas and sierras. But the mighty stream
is within the sphere of the Canal, as I shall have occasion to explain more fully in subsequent chapters.

For the present purpose a single illustration, perhaps fanciful, will answer.

It may seem a far cry from the 200,000 telephones used by the farmers of Indiana, the trolleys which tangle their way through that State, and the automobiles and bicycles which traverse the country roads, to the gum forests of South America. But the world's hunger for crude rubber is a growing one. Bicycles, the infinite variety of motors, electric lighting, and telephones, all demand more of this article; and the 55,000 tons, which was substantially the world's production in 1905, is insufficient for future needs. This increasing demand will stimulate the rubber production of an extensive region in northeastern Peru, and Peru has imperative reasons of national policy for wanting to turn that traffic down her own rivers, and across and over the Andes to the Pacific, instead of letting it flow out through Brazilian territory. Iquitos, the centre of this commerce, is 2,300 miles up the Amazon from Para, and Para is 3,000 miles from New York, a total of 5,300 miles by the all-water route. By river and future rail Iquitos is, at the furthest, 800 miles from Paita, and Paita, via Panama, is a little short of 3,100 miles from New York; so that the total distance is less than 4,000 miles. New Orleans by the isthmian route is within 3,300 miles of the Peruvian rubber metropolis.

Instead of the Pacific commerce being limited to the seashore strip after the Panama Canal is dug, the view which receives attention in South America is the probable influence of the waterway in diverting traffic from the Atlantic to the Pacific. Trade may not be turned upstream, and commerce is slow to leave established lines of transportation, but trade-waves are not so fixed as isothermal lines. They may show variations until the current finds its natural course to the newer markets created.

I do not mean from this to infer that the aggregate commerce of the Atlantic coast countries of South America will be lessened by the Panama Canal. Tropical Brazil, for an indefinite period, will continue to supply the bulk of the coffee consumed, and the maritime movement will follow the existing courses of navigation. Temperate Brazil, the Argentine Republic, and Uruguay will develop as the granary and the grazing-ground of the world in proportion as the United States consumes its own wheat and beef. Their exports increase with the widening of the market for these staple products. Political economists and crop statisticians have been slow to perceive that the extension of the area of agricultural cultivation and the growth of population in this great cereal region depend more on the ability of Europe to take the surplus grain, beef, and mutton than on the demands for home consumption. Public men, especially in the Argentine Republic, in their measures for encouraging immigration also have neglected to take into account this overshadowing economic factor. But it explains why during certain periods immigration has been almost stationary, while at other periods the incoming of settlers for the field and farm has been a rushing one. As a natural balance, therefore, for the diversion of traffic to the Pacific coast through the agency of the artificial waterway, the Atlantic slope has the certainty of steadily growing exports of agricultural products.

As regards Argentina, the coming railways to the Pacific, of which I have made mention, mean that a quantity of the cereals, wool, and hides will find their outlet by these routes; and a larger volume of the exchange for them — farm tools, cottons and woollens, mineral oils, and miscellaneous merchandise — will obtain the cheaper and shorter transit through the Canal and down the West Coast. Thus, without damage to the Atlantic commerce, the Pacific coast traffic will form a larger proportion in the total of South American commerce than in the past. This is especially true with reference to the United States. The tradewave north and south may be accounted one of the phenomena of international intercourse. It is not tidal, but a brief comparison shows its growing volume. In 1894 Argentina took from the United States goods to the value of $4,863,000, and sent in return products worth $3,497,000. In 1904 the exports were $10,751,000, and the imports $20,702,000, and in the following year they were increasing.

The commercial relation of the West Coast countries may better be exhibited by tabulation in the following form:

	Exports to United States [1]		Imports from United States	
	1894	1904	1894	1904
Chile . . .	$3,536,000	$10,685,000	$2,272,000	$4,880,000
Peru . . .	491,000	3,008,000	591,000	3,961,000
Ecuador . .	816,000	2,347,000	761,000	1,354,000
Total . .	$4,843,000	$16,040,000	$3,624,000	$10,195,000

[1] See *Foreign Commerce of the United States, Annual Review, 1904.*

Here, within the extremes of the eleven years, is an increase in the foreign commerce between the West Coast countries named and the United States from $8,467,000 to $26,235,000 as measured by the annual volume. The growth continued in the subsequent twelvemonth. It is a forcible illustration of the north and south trade-wave movement. Under the further stimulus of the Canal for industrial development and commercial growth the contribution to traffic for the waterway will be not inconsiderable.

An analysis of the West Coast foreign commerce for a given year shows it to have exceeded $211,000,000, with a rising tendency. The intercoast trade, which is included under the foreign head, may be placed at $11,000,000 to $12,000,000. There is left, therefore, approximately $200,000,000 of international traffic for Europe and the United States.

If the international traffic were to remain stationary, the amount that would be diverted from the Cape Horn or the Magellan route through the Canal would be important, but the overshadowing element in the waterway as an economic factor is the certainty of an increase in the foreign trade. The marked feature of the West Coast countries in recent years is the growth in consumptive capacity as shown by the imports, for the increase in population has not been large. Oriental trade may be diverted from other channels through the Canal, but western South American commerce may look for growth in volume on account of internal development of the countries which are tributary to it. In this view it may be doubted whether the estimate that 75 per cent of the Canal traffic will be between ports north of the same parallels of latitude will prove

Swamp Section of the Canal — The Atlantic Entrance to
the Canal — Scene on the Chagres River

correct. The north and south trade-waves may be
watched for an indication of the proportion of waterway freight that will go south, keeping in mind that
New York is almost on a direct line north of the
western South American ports.

These West Coast markets may be studied with reference to the shortening of distance. We may take
the fact that from Colon to New York is 1,981 miles,
and from Colon to New Orleans 1,380 miles; add the
48 miles of future waterway and then make our comparisons of the ports along the coast — Guayaquil,
Callao, Valparaiso — with the distance through the
Straits of Magellan or around Cape Horn. We
also may figure on the national policy of the United
States, which will not be to treat the Canal as strictly a
commercial proposition. The fixing of the toll rates
is not near enough to furnish the basis of definite
calculation any more than is the possibility of estimating the total prospective tonnage each year, though
the guesses have ranged from 300,000 to 10,500,000
tons.

The steamers which ply between New York, Hamburg, or Liverpool and the Pacific coast ports vary
from 3,000 to 6,500 tons. That hardly may be taken
as the measure of carrying capacity of the major part
of the vessels which will pass through the Canal, but
on such a basis the estimate may be made of the saving in coal consumption, and the radius within which
it will be cheaper to use the Canal than to double
Cape Horn or thread the difficult and dangerous passage through the Straits. For New Orleans, Mobile,
and the other Gulf ports, the element of distance is
not comparative, because heretofore no direct maritime

movement between them and the West Coast of South America has been maintained. With the waterway once open the whole Mississippi Valley becomes the beneficiary. Nor does the talk of carrying coal and other cargoes from Pittsburg through Panama to Patagonia without breaking bulk appear fantastic.

Variations in the steamers' courses are responsible for the differences in the tables of distances usually given, but they are not important.[1] The relation in nautical miles of the chief shipping-ports on the West Coast to trade centres may be set forth as follows :

	MILES		MILES
New York to Colon . . .	1,981	Panama to Mollendo . . .	1,928
Colon to Panama	48	" " Arica	2,161
Panama to Guayaquil . . .	835	" " Iquique	2,267
" " Paita	1,052	" " Antofagasta . .	2,418
" " Callao	1,569	" " Valparaiso . . .	3,076

This brings Valparaiso within 5,100 miles of New York by way of Panama ; but with the omission of all the intervening ports except Iquique, Callao, and Guayaquil, it would be less than 5,000 miles. By way of the Straits the distance from Valparaiso is usually accounted 9,000 miles, touching at Montevideo and the Brazilian ports. When the Straits are avoided and Cape Horn is doubled, from the Cape to Pernambuco is 3,468 miles, and from Pernambuco to New York 3,696 miles. Either by the Straits or around the Cape the total is almost twice the distance via Panama.

Colon is 4,720 miles from Liverpool, and the relative advantages of the West Coast ports between Valparaiso and Panama may be calculated in the

[1] See Appendix for tables of the Hydrographic Office of the United States Navy.

proportion of their respective distances. From Valparaiso to Liverpool via Panama is 7,600 to 7,800 miles according to the vessel's schedule of wayports on the Pacific. From Valparaiso to Liverpool, through the Straits of Magellan, is 9,800 miles, touching at the Falkland Islands, and about 300 miles shorter by omitting them.

For Hamburg the saving in distance by the isthmian route may be placed at 2,400 miles. Proceeding north from Valparaiso, the loss by Cape Horn is in inverse proportion. Fifteen hundred miles north of Valparaiso is the central Peruvian port of Callao, which therefore has 3,000 miles' gain in distance by Panama to Hamburg instead of by Cape Horn.

I have given these general figures before reciting details on the maritime commerce of the various countries. They show how the economic value of the Canal to them is primarily a question of subtraction, — the difference between the coal needed on the longer sea voyage and the Canal tolls. But the question of the return cargo also enters into the calculation and is distinctly in favor of the waterway, as is also that of the duration of maritime insurance.

No statistics are available which show the commerce of the western departments of Colombia; and the unsettled state of that country for years past gives no index of what its potential traffic may be. But the valley of Cauca in its variety of agricultural and mineral resources is a kingdom in itself. It is a future commercial feeder to the Canal.

The foreign trade of Ecuador amounted in the latest available year to $19,000,000.[1] Substantially all of it

[1] Statistics obtained by New York Chamber of Commerce for 1904.

constitutes what might be called light freight, and a part of it now goes across the Isthmus by transshipment. Yet the portion which follows the longer route around Cape Horn or through the Straits is not small.   The traffic flows through Guayaquil as in a single stream. Guayaquil, by way of Panama, is 2,864 miles from New York and 2,263 miles from New Orleans; by the Cape Horn route it is 11,470 miles to New York. The entire foreign commerce of Ecuador in the future is for the Panama Canal, except the excess which follows up the coast to San Francisco and beyond.

The foreign commerce of Peru may be placed above $40,000,000 annually.[1]   The bulk of the traffic is now via the Straits of Magellan and Cape Horn. From Callao to New York, by way of Cape Horn, is 10,700 miles.   By way of Panama it is 3,600 miles, only a little longer than from New York to San Francisco or from New York to Mexico City by the transcontinental railroad lines.   In reference to Peru, it also is to be noted that the heaviest exports are from the ports north of Callao.   Sugar is the largest marine freight in quantity, and this comes from Salaverry and other ports fully 500 miles north.   Much of this raw sugar is now carried around Cape Horn, though some of it is left at the Chilean ports to be refined for the West Coast consumption.   When the Canal is opened, with the exception of this Chilean traffic, all the raw sugar of Peru will be shipped through it to New Orleans, New York, or Liverpool.

Through the port of Mollendo, 360 miles south of Callao, come the ores, the metals, and the wools,

---

[1] Estimated on the basis of the calendar year 1904, when the total was $41,000,000, according to the report of the British Consul General.

both of southern Peru and of Bolivia. Some of the minerals may continue their course around the Horn, and also the guano which Peru in the future may export, but not all of these cargoes will find the longer route cheaper. All the wools will take the shorter route. Some wool is sent up the coast and transshipped across the Isthmus by the railways. This method is also followed in the shipment to Liverpool of some of the raw cotton raised in southern Peru. The whole of this light freight is traffic for the interoceanic waterway.

Bolivian commerce finds its outlet and inlet, chiefly through Chilean and Peruvian seaports, to the amount of $18,000,000 a year. Small as this is, the bulk of it follows the Cape Horn and Magellan routes, though some of the European merchandise is imported on the Atlantic slope through Argentina. The silver and copper ores are transported principally through the port of Antofagasta, which is 650 miles north of Valparaiso. For the mineral freights, Canal tolls may neutralize the advantage of the shortened distance via Panama to Liverpool, or may not compensate for the lessened coal consumption. But whether they do or not, the general merchandise from England and from Germany, not being bulky, will have the shorter course and probably the cheaper one on the return voyage through the Canal.

But Antofagasta, though of growing importance, is not likely to be indefinitely the chief port of export for Bolivia. The building of a railway from the great central plateau to Arica makes it certain that the copper output of Bolivia, much of the tin, and part of the silver product in time will be shipped through that port, while it will be a natural inlet for imported merchandise. Arica is so close to Mollendo — only 233 miles — that with regard to distances it may be considered on the same basis. The mineral and other internal developments, which are to fix the industrial status of Bolivia and which I shall have occasion to discuss in subsequent chapters, have a very direct relation to the facilities that will be afforded by the isthmian waterway.

Formerly it was thought that Chile would be seriously harmed by the Panama Canal. In the commercial sense this supposition does not bear scrutiny. Chile's foreign trade is approximately $130,000,000 annually, with a tendency to reach $150,000,000. By far the heaviest proportion of this commerce is the shipments of the nitrates of soda or saltpetre fertilizers. Iquique is the principal shipping-point. The sailing-ships are the cheapest carriers for these bulky cargoes, and tolls based on tonnage may make it unprofitable to transport a large portion of them through the interoceanic channel. There is also the other consideration that the vessels which bring coal to the Chilean ports from Australia and from Newcastle secure their return cargoes of nitrates. These fertilizers being a natural monopoly, Chile will have the benefit of the industry, and the Panama Canal in no way can lessen this traffic. In its permanent effect the waterway can have little influence on the nitrates, because the deposits will be worked out not many years after its completion. Within a third of a century, or forty years at the furthest, the exhaustion of the saltpetre beds will have begun, and the cargoes of fertilizers will be lessening before that time.[1] In any aspect of the broad future of the Canal and its effect on the West Coast, the nitrates of Chile need not be considered as an influencing factor.

But it may be said that until the interoceanic canal is actually open these subjects are too remote to call for immediate consideration. This view does not hold when analysis is made of the swift recognition of its effect by South American countries. There are present-day influences which are clear enough to be taken into account.

For the entire West Coast there is at once a beneficial result in having the Canal an enterprise of the United States government. This is the equal treatment which must be accorded all the steamship companies in transshipping freight over the Panama Railway. The line was operated in the interest of the transcontinental railroads to prevent competition. Under this arrangement little regard was shown for the traffic from the coast south of Panama. The result of the control of the isthmian railway line by the transcontinental roads was against encouraging the steamship lines to seek to increase their freight between Valparaiso and the intervening ports to Panama for transshipment, because the Panama Railway exacted what it pleased.[2] With the stock of the company vested in

[1] See Chapter XIV, Nitrate of Soda.

[2] In the memorial presented in 1905 to the United States government by the diplomatic representatives of various South American Republics, asking for fair treatment in Panama railroad rates, these statements were made :

It may be calculated that the most distant ports of our respective Republics are from New York, 4,500 miles, via Panama. From those same ports to New York there is a distance of over 11,000 miles, via Magellan ; and, nevertheless, the transportation by this last route and the trans-

the United States, hereafter all traffic agreements must be made on the basis of equality. This is a very important factor in the tendency of the West Coast countries to mould their national policies for industrial development and commercial expansion. It enables them to enjoy some of the benefits of the Canal without waiting for its completion. It means more shipping from the year 1906 on.

An international good also comes from the presence of the United States on the Isthmus in the capacity of a sanitary authority. It will not be hampered, as at home, by state quarantine systems. The example of what it is doing at Panama will be of immense benefit to all the ports south to Valparaiso. Its resources and its assistance will be at the disposal of the various governments which may seek its aid. With them power is centralized, and they will be able to coöperate effectually. The International Sanitary Bureau, with headquarters in Washington, for which provision was made by the Pan-American Conference held in Mexico, may

portation by steamer from our ports to Europe, are on an average from 25 to 30 per cent cheaper than our commerce with New York via Panama.

The Peruvian sugar pays, by the Isthmus, 30 shillings sterling a ton, and 23 shillings sterling a ton via Magellan.

The cacao of Guayaquil, via Panama, pays to Europe from 52 to 58 shillings a ton, and to New York 65 to 68 shillings a ton.

From Hamburg shipments of rice from India are constantly being made to Ecuador, via Panama, at the rate of from 30 to 33 shillings sterling per ton of 2,240 pounds, or, say, from $7.50 to $8 per ton; while the same article from New York pays at the rate of $0.60 per 100 pounds, or, say, $13.20 per ton, — an overcharge of almost 75 per cent. Twelve coal-oil stoves, which in New York, free-on-board, cost from $45 to $48, pay on the coast of Ecuador and of Peru 30 and 37½ cents, respectively, per cubic foot, or, say, $19.20 to $21, which represents 42.66 per cent upon the cost price. The same article bought in Germany would pay a freight of from $6.40 to $6.75.

ABANDONED MACHINERY

become a vital force through this means. Epidemics and plagues, of which the most malignant is the yellow fever, may never be entirely wiped out, but that their area can be restricted and their ravages infinitely lessened will be demonstrated by a few years' experience. Commerce will be immensely the gainer, and the trade of the West Coast may look for a steady and natural growth in proportion as the epidemic diseases of the seaports are controlled.

The influence of the gold standard of Panama will be helpful to commerce, though it will not in itself cause the several Republics which are on a silver or a paper basis to change to gold. But they will be benefited by being neighbors to financial stability. Uniformity of exchange will be promoted, and the inconveniences of travellers will be lessened. The fact that the currency of the United States is legal tender in the Panama Republic will help merchants and shippers at home, who heretofore have had to make their transactions entirely on the basis of the English pound sterling or the French franc.

In an outline of the general subject some attention should be paid to the inevitable overflow of energy and capital after they once become engaged in building the waterway and in supplementary projects. No one who understands the constructive American character doubts that the capitalists and contractors enlisted in the work will fare forth to seek other fields. It happens that coincident with the beginning of the Canal construction by the United States, the West Coast countries are entering upon definite policies of harbor and municipal improvements and other forms of public works, including railway building. There

is also the new era of the mines.   The industrial impulse is one of the immediate economic effects of the
Canal.   It appeals to the American spirit.   It will
find a quickening response.   In subsequent chapters
I therefore venture to indicate its field of activity, with
such suggestions as may be of practical worth.

CHAPTER II

TRAVEL HINTS

*Adopting Local Customs — Value of the Spanish Language —
Knowledge of People Obtained through Their Speech —
English in Trade — Serviceable Clothing in Different
Climates — Moderation in Diet — Coffee at its True
Worth — Wines and Mineral Waters — Native Dishes —
Tropical Fruits — Aguacate and Cheremoya Palatal Luxu-
ries — Hotels and Hotel-keepers — Baggage Afloat and
Ashore — Outfits for the Andes: Food and Animals — West
Coast Quarantines — Money Mediums — The Common
Maladies and How to Treat Them*

TO live as they live; to travel as they travel; — that
is about all there is to living and travelling in
South America and on the Isthmus.

All the customs will not be adopted by Northerners,
nor all the habits followed. More comfort will be
demanded and more cleanliness. But the general fact
holds that the people living in any country have
acquired by experience the knowledge of what is required by climatic and other conditions in regard to
food, drink, dress, shelter, and recreation. There
is reason for all things, even for the adobe tomb
dwellings of the aboriginal Indians of Bolivia, or the
mid-day siesta of the busy merchant of Panama.

First of all, it is desirable to know the language.
Spanish is the idiom of South America, with the exception of Brazil. At the outset let me say that the
chance traveller who wants to go down the coast or

even take an occasional trip into the interior can get along with his stock of English. In all the seaport towns are English-speaking persons, merchants or others. On the ships English is as common as Spanish, and in some of the obscurest places the tongue of Chaucer may be heard. In one of the most out-of-the-way and utterly forsaken little holes on the coast, I found the local official who was sovereign there teaching his boy arithmetic in Eng-lish. He had been both in England and in the United States, and while his own prospects now were bounded by the horizon of the cove and the drear brown mountain cliffs that shut it in, he was determined that his son should have a wider future. There are also many young South Americans who have been educated in the United States and some of whom are met at almost inaccessible points in the interior.

I state this so that no one who contemplates a journey may be turned away from it by any supposed difficulty in getting along through inability to speak the prevailing idiom. He can do very well. Yet with all his faculties of observation alert he will miss much through his ignorance of the readiest mode of conveying and receiving thought. To know any country it is necessary to know the people, and the people are only known through the medium of their speech. Their customs are better understood, their limitations are appreciated, and their strivings for something better, if they have any, are interpreted sympathetically. The paramount local topic becomes a living theme into which the visitor can enter understandingly and add to his stock of knowledge.

Let me say, also, that wherever trade is, there is the

English language, and as commerce grows it will spread. The terse English business letter is the admiration of the Latin-American merchant. Yet there is no wilder notion than that trade will advance itself without the knowledge of the language of the country into which it is pushing. Many native mercantile houses have English-speaking clerks, or occasionally a member of the firm knows the idiom. But the commercial traveller from the United States who does not speak Spanish never will compete with his German rival who talks trade in all known tongues.

This, in brief, is the commercial situation as to the English language. The business man who waits for Spanish America to come within its sphere as the world language, will not achieve success in this generation.

For those who look forward to a future in South America, either in trade or in industrial enterprises, there is only one word of advice to be given: that is, to learn Spanish and to learn it at once. Diffident as the North American is about foreign tongues and badly as he speaks any language except his own, there is little reason why his self-distrust or his contempt for other nationalities should keep him from acquiring Spanish. "It is pronounced as written and is written as pronounced." Colloquially it is the easiest of tongues to master. Since every letter is sounded and is always pronounced the same, there is no trouble with the syllables and there are no such difficult sounds as the German umlaut or the French "en." The high-sounding expressions, while they seem very formal and complicated, are quickly acquired, and the habit of thinking of the greetings of the day and similar commonplace topics in the strange tongue comes more easily than is imagined. With practice any fairly persistent person can get enough of Spanish to avoid the cumbersome process of thinking in English and then translating his thoughts. A vocabulary of 2,000 words is an ample one for the purposes of every-day life.

The oaths need not be learned. The English expletives are expressive enough not to need translation, and they lack the suggestive obscenity of the Spanish objurgations. It is good to learn " *Caramba!* " in all the tones and inflections and to stop there.

The phrase-book may be studied without ridicule, and every opportunity be taken for putting its precepts to the test. I do not mean from this to indicate that a thorough knowledge of Spanish can be gained in such manner, or that the Yankee ever will master the noble and stately literary language of Cervantes, Calderon, and Lope de Vega. He will not need to use the literary language. If he have a chance to secure his first training in Bogota or Lima, that will be an unusual advantage, for it is in those capitals that the purest Spanish of the New World is spoken. But this is not necessary, and if it be his misfortune to learn the rudiments through an uneducated Chilean or Argentine source, even that harsh and choppy Spanish will be understood. By all this I mean the practical tool of the tongue in common use, and not the melodious Castilian that may be desirable in polite society.

It is a very decided advantage to know enough of the written language to read the newspapers, an occasional book by a native author, the steamship schedules, the railway time-tables, the proclamations and

official decrees, and the advertising posters. All
serve their purpose to the man who has business or
who would be in touch with his surroundings. It is
true that in the interior the Indian tribes adhere to
their own dialects and the majority of South American Indians do not understand Spanish. But the
officials everywhere speak it, and in the Indian villages there is a head man, or *cacique*, who knows the
idiom of the master race. If they are not familiar
with Spanish, the sounds of English are even more
strange to them.

Dress for sea voyages is easily determined, but
clothing for land and sea is a more difficult question.
My own experience, and I think it is the experience
of other travellers, has been that woollens are the most
serviceable in all climates. In the cold regions they
are essential. In the tropics, when loosely woven,
they are comfortable. Where the pure wool is disagreeable to the wearer, a mixture of cotton in the
garment may serve. Flannels are the best protection
against an overheated body and quick changes of
temperature. These hints apply to all places, all
times, and all conditions.

For the rest, although the Anglo-Saxon newcomer
sometimes assumes otherwise, the people of all the
West Coast cities are civilized and accustomed to the
usages of polite society. Men wear the conventional
dress suit, or *traje de etiqueta*, on formal occasions. The
six o'clock rule does not hold in Spanish-American
countries. Official functions, weddings, and similar
social gatherings call for the dress suit as early as ten
o'clock in the morning. But the visitor in this matter
may consult his own convenience to some extent,

regardless of local customs. The professional classes, doctors and lawyers especially, have a habit of upholding their dignity by wearing the tall hat and the frock coat in the hottest seasons. It is rather a tradition than a requirement of good breeding. The traveller may ignore it without losing social caste.

In the matter of eating and drinking moderation is a rule which slowly impresses itself on foreigners. As to drinking, the Englishman on the West Coast has not yet learned temperance. He absorbs vast quantities of brandy and soda, or of whiskey and water, with the soda or water always in infinitesimal amounts. He has his excuse for it, — the loneliness of his exile, the climate, and so forth. But he also has a counter-irritant for the drink habit in his fondness for the manly outdoor sports which he practises as regularly as at home.

French wines may be procured anywhere in South America, but it is not always well to trust the labels. A fair native wine is made in Peru, and Chile produces an unusually good article. If the quality of the claret is not quite equal to Medoc, it is good enough for any one except a connoisseur. English ales also are to be had, and of recent years bottled St. Louis or Milwaukee beer can be obtained at all the larger places. I have found St. Louis beer up in the Cerro de Pasco mining regions of Peru. All of the countries have local breweries, but Americans do not like the brew.

Mineral waters, which are to be had everywhere, in time come to pall on the palate. They may be alternated with the wines or other beverages satisfactorily. There is a native drink called *chicha*, a distillation of corn fermented in lye, which is refreshing and strengthening and tastes like fresh cider. The subjects of the Incas refreshed the Spanish conquerors with this drink. It is celebrated in song, — " *O nectar sabroso.*" Yet a word of warning — to enjoy *chicha* a second time and other times, make no inquiry and take no thought of how it is prepared. Always imbibe it from a gourd.

The aboriginal thirst of the Indians and also of the *mestizos*, or half-breeds, is for raw alcohol. This thirst is satisfied by the *aguardiente*, or cane rum. It demoralizes the native population, and is a curse with which the governments are unable to cope. When the rum cannot be obtained, some other form of alcoholic spirits is provided.

The Continental custom as to meals obtains both in the tropical parts of the West Coast and in the colder climates, as in Bolivia and Chile. There is simply breakfast, or the mid-day meal, and dinner. In the morning coffee and rolls — or with most of the Spanish-Americans, coffee and cigarettes — are the sole refreshment which is expected to carry one through till noon. Americans, however, usually procure fruit and eggs. Coffee-making and coffee-drinking are arts unknown to the Yankee. Travel in South America is a liberal and much-needed education in this respect.

The *almuerzo*, or mid-day breakfast, is fully as substantial a meal as the six or seven o'clock dinner. Both begin with soup and fish, the best of the latter being the *corbina*. At the breakfast eggs invariably are served, and usually rice. The latter is prepared as a vegetable with rare art, retaining the form and whiteness of the grain. Meat courses, beginning with the fowl, follow in procession, and a salad always may be had.

The Spaniard and his descendants in South America approach roast pig as reverently as Charles Lamb did. For them it is a poem. A very good dish transplanted from Spain is called the *puchero*, and is something like a New England boiled dinner, having a variety of vegetables cooked with the meats which are its foundation.

In the interior, where reliance has to be had on the Indian population, the standard dish is the *chupé*, though it bears different names. This is a rich soup, highly seasoned by dried red peppers, with plenty of vegetables, and with a meat stock as the basis. Sometimes the meat is the vicuña or llama, sometimes goat, sometimes mutton, and once in a while beef. It is wholesome and satisfying. The only caution to be observed is not to see its preparation by the Indian women.

Two luxuries among the fruits of the tropics make oranges, bananas, and pineapples seem commonplace. These are the alligator pear and the *cheremoya*. The Northern appetite cloys at the preserved sweets which the tropical palate demands, but it never loses the enjoyment of these fruits. The alligator pear (*Guanabanus Persea*) in the West Indies and in Mexico goes by the name of *aguacate* or *avocat*. In South America it is called the *palta*. It is eaten as a salad, and French genius never concocted a delicacy equal to this natural appetizer.

The *aguacate* looks like a small squash rather than a pear. It has a kernel, or hard stone, as big as the fist. The flanks are laid open, the stone removed,

BANANA GROVE

PINEAPPLE GARDEN

and the fruit is ready to serve in its own dressing. Some prefer it with just a pinch of salt. Others add a touch of pepper. Many like a little vinegar with the salt and pepper, and a few even prefer a regular French dressing with oil, though that is apt to spoil the natural flavor. Epicures like it with sugar and lemon juice. The *aguacate* is one of the undisguised palatal blessings of the tropics and the semi-tropics. It should be sought after and insisted on at every occasion. The imported fruit loses the poetic savor. The most careful packing and tenderest care cannot preserve its delicate taste. I tried it once in bringing some from Honolulu to San Francisco. They looked well, but something was lacking in the taste. A similar experience between Jamaica and New York was the reward for my efforts. I was convinced after these experiments that the *aguacate* is one of the real luxuries which it pays to go abroad in order to enjoy. Young persons who travel will be interested in knowing that it is said to germinate the tender sentiment.

The *cheremoya* is not unlike the pawpaw of the temperate climates. The fibre is harder and not so juicy. But the fruit is very rich, so rich that the palate does not crave much. A mouthful lingers like the dream of the poet. The *cheremoya* is called the *anona* in Cuba. Several varieties of it differ from one another only in the delicacy and richness of the flavor. Cracked ice is the complement of the fruit. They should be introduced to each other an hour before serving.

A delusion which the adventuring North American should get rid of is that no decent hotels are found on the West Coast and in the interior. Everywhere are

passable ones and in some of the cities exception-
ally good ones.   In the ordinary coast towns they
are not much more than stopping-places, yet almost
invariably an excellent breakfast or dinner can be
obtained.   As to the lodging conveniences the old
Spanish tradition still obtains that a place to sleep in
is all that is called for, and clean linen and similar
comforts should not be demanded by the traveller
who is moving on.   But even in this respect improvements are being made.

Most of the hotel-keepers are of foreign nationality,
— French, Germans, Italians, and Spaniards.   It is
rare to find anything of a higher grade than an inn
kept by a native.   The best hotels are those under
the control of the Frenchmen, and when a choice is
to be made they should be given the preference, for
there is not only good eating but cleanliness and some
consideration for the conveniences of life.   A Frenchman keeps the hotel at La Paz in Bolivia, and it is
a good one.   Another passably fair house of entertainment in the same place is kept by a Russian.   At the
mining-town of Oruro a North American of German
descent provides excellent accommodations.   In the
remote town of Tupiza in the fastnesses of the Andes,
where of all places one would hardly look for a foreigner, I found a Slav hotel-keeper and a decent kind
of a resting-place.   The proprietor was from one
of the Danubian provinces.   In Lima a very well
appointed hotel is managed by an Italian.   In Santiago the best one is under the control of a Frenchman.

In the interior palatial inns are not to be expected,
though a young French mining engineer who came
out telegraphed along the Andes trail which he was

to follow to have room with bath reserved for him. The telegram is still shown. Such inns as exist are called *tambos.* Even in the poorest of these, while the lodging is wretched, a good meal usually can be had.

The practice obtains nearly everywhere of charging separately for the lodging, but in some of the larger cities the hotels now are conducted on the American plan. The visitor is apt to be puzzled by the annexes. Naturally he assumes that the annexes to a hotel are part of it, but usually they are separate and under a distinct management. In Valparaiso there are a Hotel Colon and a Hotel Colon Annex, a block or two apart and altogether different. In Santiago are the Hotel Oddo and the Annex to the Oddo, and so on. This causes confusion, and the traveller should make inquiry in advance so as to know where he is going. While the sanitary conveniences in most of the hotels are poor, improvements are being made, and there is something of an approach to the demands of civilization.

A simple rule as to baggage holds good. Take as little as practicable and pack it as conveniently as possible. That means a good deal of loose luggage; but since trunks are charged by weight and very few of the railroads make any allowance for free baggage, it is desirable to have one's belongings arranged so that they can be piled up around him. One soon becomes accustomed to this and to providing himself with an armful of rugs and blankets.

Railroad fares are about one-third less than in the United States. The accommodations are not luxurious, but they are fair. Night trips are unknown.

Chile is the only country on the West Coast which provides a through night train with a sleeper. This is on the line between Santiago and Talca.

An addition to the regular expense of travel is that for embarkation and disembarkation. It is not covered in the steamship ticket, and since, with few exceptions, in the different ports the vessels do not go to wharves of their own or put their passengers ashore in lighters, each makes his choice of the small boats and pays the bill. These charges are not high, yet in the course of a long voyage they mount up, and it always is desirable to make the bargain with the boatman in advance.

For travel in the Andine regions it is necessary to provide one's own outfit. For those who have to go about much it is not practicable to have their own pack and riding animals, though occasionally a mining engineer will keep a pair of horses or mules and transport them from place to place. Usually the mules and burros, or donkeys, have to be hired. In every case it is advantageous to own the *montura*, or saddle, and other accoutrements, with especial regard to the capacity of the saddle-bags. Though in the United States the McClellan is the favorite for hard travelling, Americans engaged in mining or in exploration work in the Andes prefer the Mexican saddle. A mining company in southern Peru after various trials discarded everything except Mexican saddles, and had these made especially in San Francisco. In my own experience I found them the most comfortable.

The *petacas*, or leather trunks, are used by all the South Americans. These are small, and a pair of them balance nicely on either side of the pack animal. Yet during a long mountain journey I managed to transport an ordinary trunk. The Andean mule is bred in northern Argentina. It is not the society pet that is its cousin of the United States Army, and it will carry a burden of two hundred pounds in the upper altitudes.

A supply of canned goods and similar provisions is essential, for it is not possible to rely solely on such wayfaring entertainment as may be had at the Indian huts, even when the trip is short enough to keep within the limits of human habitation. *Charqui*, or jerked beef, is the mainstay of the stomach for a long journey, but dried mutton sometimes may be had, and is less likely to become unpalatable. *Chuni*, the dried and frozen potato which nourishes the Bolivian Indians, has nutritive virtues, but palatability is not one of them.

The chief problem in mountain travelling is fodder for the animal rather than food for the man. In the valleys and part way up the *punas*, or table-lands, fresh alfalfa may be had. But in the higher sierras this is lacking, and it is necessary to carry a stock of barley. In some places where barley can be raised it runs to straw and does not mature into the grain, so that the local supply is not to be depended on.

A hammock is useful in the forest regions. A tent and other camping outfit are sometimes desirable, yet where it is possible to keep within the range of population it is better to risk shelter in the Indian huts, the traveller carrying his own blankets or sleeping-bag. A Western frontiersman or miner has little difficulty in outfitting for the Andean regions.

The quarantine is one of the serious annoyances

of travel on the West Coast, though the interruption which it causes often is exaggerated. At times one may have to postpone a landing or a departure because of the restriction, and in that case there is nothing to be done but go on to the next open port and wait in patience. The regulations of the different governments are similar, though they are not always enforced with discretion and common-sense. Yet they are no more severe than the regulations of New Orleans or other Southern ports of the United States. Their purpose of self-protection is justifiable. The objection is that the application of the measures taken is unreasonable. The steamship companies insist on the exaction of charging the passengers an extra sum for the time in which the vessel is held in quarantine.

So many sorts of money are in circulation that it is impossible for the traveller not to lose through exchange. The United States dollar is known well enough, but it has not yet made its way down the coast sufficiently to insure being taken for its full worth. Letters of credit and bank drafts would better be in English money, for the banks and exchange houses insist on counting the $5 gold piece as equal only to the pound sterling, or $4.85. It will take some years for the full result of the Panama money system to be felt on the West Coast, though ultimately that will help to extend the use of United States currency.

A calculation is made every quarter by the United States Mint of the value of the coins representing the monetary units of the various Latin-American countries. This serves as an index of values, though in actual transactions it cannot always be insisted upon.

The universal coin on the West Coast is the Peruvian *sol*, equal to 48½ cents gold. It is the size of the American silver dollar. Since Peru has the gold standard and coins a Peruvian pound called the *inca*, exactly the weight and fineness of the English pound sterling, there is no fluctuation. Ten *soles* make a pound. For local purposes along the coast the Peruvian *sol* is therefore the best medium of exchange.

I have left for separate consideration the subject of the diseases incident to West Coast travel and residence. Their mention frightens. Why, I do not know.

Pneumonia and typhoid in the temperate climates cause greater ravages than tropical diseases in their field, nor is malaria in its manifold manifestations limited to a given area. Fever and ague in the United States, *calentura* in the West Indies, *terciana* in the forest regions of the Andes, — it all is essentially the breakbone fever. Quinine and calomel remain the tonic preventives. Tropical dysentery is to be guarded against by common-sense in diet. The social vices bring their inexorable penalty more swiftly than in the North, but their remedy is the moral prophylactic. Yellow fever, since the demonstration of the mosquito as the active agent in its propagation, is losing its terrors, but its avoidance comes under the sphere of epidemic quarantines rather than of individual measures. The exceptional conditions which will prevail on the Isthmus during the Canal construction and the exceptional means adopted to combat disease are not to be taken as representative of the West Coast. Yet the benefit of this experience will be great. But whether along the coast, on the plateaus of the Andes, or in the tropical valleys, one general rule is more valuable than a medicine chest. It is that of a healthy, fearless mind which does not magnify ordinary ailments and which keeps its poise in the shadow of more serious illness.

CHAPTER III

THE ISTHMUS OF PANAMA

Canal Entrance — Colon in Architectural Transformation — Unchanging Climate — Historic Waterway Routes — Columbus and the Early Explorers — Darien and San Blas — East and West Directions — Life along the Railway — Chagres River and Culebra Cut — Three Panamas — Pacific Mouth of the Canal — Functions of the Republic — Natural Resources — Agriculture and Timber — Road-building — United States Authority on the Zone — Labor and Laborers — Misleading Comparisons with Cuba — The First Year's Experience.

WHEN the Caribbean is restive, restless is the voyager. After tossing in misery one April night I peered through the port-hole of the steamer's cabin at what seemed a cluster of swinging lanterns dipping into the sea. They were the lights of Colon. The vessel was riding at anchor to await the morning hour when the approach to the quays could be made.

Daybreak unfolded through the mist, disclosing green foliage ridges and broken forest-clad hills sloping to a shallow bowl. This circular basin is the island of Manzanillo. The town lies as in the bottom of a saucer. Colon is not a harbor in the usual sense, for the curving Bay of Limon which it fringes is an open roadstead. The improvements by the United States will make it a commercial haven.

For all the years to come the blue horizon will be swept by the eager eye of the traveller for the Canal entrance. Seen from the ship's deck, it is like the smooth surface of a sluggish river, broad and open. The artistic instinct of the French engineers found expression even in the prosaic work of earth excavation. They planted a village in the midst of cocoanut groves, and the palm-thatched cottages charm the eye. The bronze group of Columbus and the Indian, Empress Eugenie's gift, allegorical of the enlightenment of the New World, may be seen through glasses, while the showy residence built for De Lesseps is discerned.

Little is noted of the town till the wharves are approached. There is a group of warehouses, a glimpse of railroad yards, a conglomeration of frame houses with peaked roofs and outside balconies and stairways, and then swamps, marshes, and hills beyond. The great transatlantic liners stretched along the docks are far more imposing than the port town itself.

Ashore, the frame structures give an impression of all that is temporary and unsubstantial. Some have been streaked with deep indigo blue, but the sun and the salt air have worn the pigment to a faded azure. Colon has little that is typically and traditionally Spanish, because when the insurgents burned it in 1885 they left only a few brick and mortar buildings. The town which then sprang up was built with economy in view, though pine lumber was not very cheap. The newer city which gradually will replace the aggregation of shanties will be more substantial and more like a permanent seaport. The Gothic brownstone church in which the Jamaica negroes and the whites who profess the Anglican form of faith worship, is the one edifice in Colon that in the transformation should be allowed to remain.

The cocoanut grove in front of the hotel, facing the Caribbean, is a pretty bit of landscape, and the statue erected to William H. Aspinwall, John L. Stephens, and Henry Chauncey, associates in the building of the Panama Railroad, if not a monument of taste, at least serves a praiseworthy purpose as a tribute to indomitable American enterprise. Ornate homes, tropical in the extreme, line the sea-front, but the residence district is a very limited one and will remain so until the swamp is filled in and the marshes cleared away. Colon may be regarded as in the process of hygienic architectural transition, and its lack of attractiveness need not be deplored. The work of reconstruction would be immensely facilitated if another fire could sweep across the marshes and leave nothing but the brownstone church, the hotel, and the wharves.

Colon is the most typically cosmopolitan place upon the Isthmus, and will continue so until the world's commerce begins to flow through the waterway. Then the city of Panama will share with it in this respect. But Panama does not have in so full a degree the European mixture as Colon, for the crews of the transatlantic vessels seldom get across to the Pacific port. In all the mingling of tongues in Colon — German, Spanish, Italian, French, Chinese, dialect Indian, Greek, Swedish, and many varieties of English — nothing is so mellow and so distressing in whining intonation as the broad cockney accent of the Jamaica blacks.

The work accomplished by the Panama Railroad Company, hygienically and otherwise, serves as a basis for the physical regeneration of Colon which must

accompany the Canal construction. Its provisions
for its employees, its hospitals, and its general sanitary regulations were so well conceived and carried out
that their value as an example and a precedent is very
great. The engineering problem is comparatively
simple. It is to raise the level of the island of Manzanillo, and then to provide sanitary conveniences and
enforce hygienic principles both for the community
and for the individual. The question of water supply
is one of gathering the plentiful showers of heaven
in cisterns and distilling them. A system of waterworks which will bring pure water from the springs
of the Cordillera is not impracticable.

Colon is hot and humid. Its climate cannot be
modified by artificial devices. During the dry season,
which is from April to July, the mean temperature is
nearly 90° Fahrenheit in the shade, while in the sun it
is 110°. The humidity is about 77 per cent. In the
rainy season the mean temperature is 85°, and the
humidity varies from 86 per cent to complete satura-
tion. The annual rainfall is seldom less than 125
inches. A man six feet in stature standing on the
shoulders of another man of equal height, would just
about be able to keep his shoulders above water if the
two were placed in a reservoir which would catch and
hold the entire rainfall of the year. But in spite of
heat and humidity and precipitated moisture, existence
can be made passably comfortable.

As the traveller takes his way across the Isthmus,
he may wish also to view in retrospect the waterways
that have been conceived in the brains of men who
were ahead of their times, and the paths of trade and
travel that have been followed; for now, in the

presence of actual construction along a determined course, these pioneer routes quickly fade into oblivion. The projects have been many. They were to unlock the key of the universe and to throw open a gateway to the Pacific. Columbus explored the Mosquito coast in search of the passage to the Indies, and thought he had found another Ganges, though the strait which he sought was obstinate in hiding itself. He planned colonies at the Gulf of Uraba, or Darien. Balboa and his companions, among whom was Pizarro, from near the same place, 200 miles east of the Chagres, hewed their way through tropical forest jungle and over mountains till they reached the summit of Piuri, from which they saw the Pacific and named the ocean inlet San Miguel Bay in honor of St. Michael. A few years later Balboa had "the little boats" carried over this path from the Atlantic to the Pacific. Long afterward, more than a century and a half, Sir John Morgan led his loyal buccaneers in Balboa's footprints to the bloody sacking of the opulent city of Panama.

But the early Spaniards found a shorter route for their traffic. At different periods the Chagres was followed from its mouth till within twenty miles of Panama, and then the jungle was pierced by paths. Yet this was not the *camino real*, or king's highway. That royal road was a cobble-paved mule trail from Portobello, twenty miles east of what is now Colon, to Santes on the upper Chagres, and thence to Panama. This is the route over which the traffic passed for two centuries. The land trails could be tested. The canal courses could only be dreamed or projected in the imagination.

Of the three interoceanic routes which have become historic, the early explorers, Spanish and Portuguese, thought most of the Darien or Caledonian cross-cut channel.   It was to start north of the Gulf of Darien, near the bay which afterward became known as Caledonian Bay, and follow a general direction southwest to the Pacific.   Señor Don Angel Savedro, one of the first petitioners to Charles V for an interoceanic waterway, had this general direction in his mind.   This was the route advocated by the Scotch banker, William Patterson, in his broad scheme for Great Britain to save control of the Antilles, by seizing Havana, acquiring the Isthmus, and constructing an isthmian canal in order to carry the blessings of commerce and civilization to the Sandwich Islands.

During the nineteenth century the Darien general route was no less earnestly advocated than in the sixteenth and seventeenth centuries, and the mythical low level had many believers.   Frederick M. Kelley, the New York banker, who gave fortune and a life's ambition to the project of an interoceanic waterway, also based his hopes on the Darien route.   It required the explorations of Commander Selfridge and subsequent American expeditions, as well as the investigations of Reclus and Wyse for the French company, to dissipate the unfounded hopes regarding Darien.

The San Blas route, being the shortest, should have had more advocates, for it is only thirty-one miles across from ocean to ocean, but the solid mountain wall of the Cordillera discouraged most of the early explorers.   Its merits and demerits were made familiar to the public through the discussions in Congress.

It was of the upper Chagres route that the intrepid

Frenchman, Champlain, whose voyage to the West Indies and the Isthmus in 1602 seems to be historically established, wrote: "At Panama is a little river which rises in the mountains and descends to Porte Bello, which river is four leagues from Panama . . . and being embarked on the said river there are but eighteen leagues to Porte Bello. One may judge that if the four leagues of land which there are from Panama to this river were cut through, one might pass from the South Sea to the ocean on the other side and thus shorten the route by more than 1,500 leagues; and from Panama to the Straits of Magellan would be an island, and from Panama to the Newfoundlands would be another island, so that the whole of America would be in two islands."

The Raspadura channel, by which the Jesuit Fathers were said to have made the passage from ocean to ocean in canoes with a very short portage, lacks historical verification.

The Chagres route was included in the broad vision of the future which Lopez de Guevara had in the middle of the sixteenth century. The realization of his dreams may be for the twenty-fifth century. He proposed the union of the two oceans by three canals opening in three points, — the Chagres in Panama, Nicaragua, and Tehuantepec.

Before following the jungle-screened railway line or tracing the course of the Canal with its luxurious border of tropical vegetation, it is desirable to clear away geographical confusion. The Isthmus of Panama extends almost directly east and west. It is the contour of the two continents as formed by a neck not simply awry but completely twisted, — in popular

language, a gooseneck. The entire West Coast of
South America, except a slight bulge near the Equator,
lies east of the longitude of Cleveland, Ohio. Panama
City is about on the north and south line with Pittsburg. It is southeast of Colon, and the general direction of the Canal from the Atlantic entrance, therefore,
will be southeast.

The route selected by the French engineers, and
which with some variation will be continued by the
United States, does not need detailed description.
The course of the Canal can be observed in the railroad journey to Gatun, where the first view is had of
the defiant Chagres fed by its twenty-one tributaries.
I have seen the Chagres a tame, sleeping brook, losing
itself in the tropical jungle or the narrow gorges, and
again have looked on it when it was a wild, resistless
torrent. The engineering problems never can be fully
appreciated until one has seen the Chagres sweeping
on in its conquering career.

Native customs and the mixed life of Canal construction are seen at the stations along the railway.
Every village has its collection of parrots and mon-
keys. The sights differ from the scenes in other
parts of the Isthmus, because of this intermingling of
foreigners, largely Chinese and Jamaican. But the inhabitants are so markedly of the local type that they
may be easily distinguished from the foreign mixture.
The aboriginal Indian race, of which there are various
branches, forms a third of the inhabitants. The Pana-
meñan is about three-fourths Indian blood and one-
fourth Spanish, although farther away from the Canal
Zone a very strong negro element exists, due to the
introduction of African slavery by the early Spaniards.

THE DE LESSEPS HOUSE, COLON

CARIBBEAN COCOA PALMS

The natives, from their familiarity with the jungles and their ability to withstand the hardships of the climate and the exposure, are useful principally to the exploring parties and the pioneering expeditions. They are too indolent for the actual work of excavation.

The Culebra Cut is not seen to full advantage from the railway, yet a fair idea may be obtained of the task involved in cutting the spine of the Cordillera or the Continental Divide at this the lowest depression, 272 feet. The excavation and removal of the material from this section is said to be the controlling factor in the Canal construction. The valley with the city of Panama huddled at the foot of Mt. Ancon, and Taboga Isle in the bay, are seen to advantage from Culebra.

There are three Panamas. One is primitive Panama, in jungle-covered ruins, a few miles from the present port. This was the city whose opulence was the envy of the world until its treasures awakened the greed of Morgan and his fellow freebooters and became their spoil. Then the new town was built and fortified. It is gloriously mediæval with all its Spanish and Moorish buildings, its cluster of emerald rocks in the bay, its high tides and its mixed nationalities, with little Italy and modernized China side by side. But the present Panama attracts only at a distance, and will be attractive only at a distance until modern sanitation can be installed and some of its picturesqueness be destroyed in the interests of public and private hygiene.

Rivalry exists between Panama and Colon over their relative climatic attractions. Panama is much drier than the Caribbean seaport, the annual rainfall usually being not more than 70 inches and the humidity of the atmosphere not so great. But 90° Fahrenheit in the shade is the average mean temperature, and the humidity is penetrating enough to serve all practical purposes of discomfort.

The new Panama is at La Boca, the Pacific mouth of the Canal. This is the railway terminus, and it is there the United States authorities created the port of Ancon and then abandoned the plan of collecting customs duties in competition with the Isthmian Republic. Wharves are located there, and for shipping the place offers some advantages over the port of Panama. The present Panama with its population of 25,000 is congested. Its old buildings are overcrowded. They are solid, substantial, and will last for centuries yet; but the natural movement of population, especially in view of the enormous rents demanded in Panama, will be to seek the new city which will grow up as a frame town with elements of stability. Much business is certain to drift to the Canal mouth, some of it in American hands. The mercantile community in the days when Colombia controlled the Isthmus was anything but Colombian. It was West Indian, Italian, Chinese, German, French, American, and English. It is the same to-day and will be the same to-morrow.

The United States is the paramount authority on the Isthmus, the control of the Canal Zone making it such, and its duty to itself and its responsibility to the world could be discharged in no other way. Yet there is also the government of the Republic of Panama, — a protected commonwealth. All that needs to be understood is Article I of the Hay-Varilla

Treaty. This says that the United States guarantees and will maintain the independence of the Republic of Panama.

In its political relations the Spanish term may be adopted, and the Republic may be said to be " in function " within the sphere of the United States. I omit particulars of the governmental system in order to examine the industrial resources and prospects. Details of administration are unnecessary, because the authority exercised by the American officials in the Canal Zone, and the supervising power over sanitation in Colon and Panama, take the subject out of its local limitations. The liberality shown by President Roosevelt's administration in adjusting the jurisdiction of the United States on the broad lines laid down by Secretary Taft, left the Panama government free to work out its commercial and industrial growth through its own measures and to the full extent of its own abilities as a commonwealth. A full account of fiscal policy may be omitted, with the general statement that international traffic in transit as taxed by port dues is not subjected to heavy burdens, while the imposts on domestic trade are not severe. While a tariff in the protective sense may not be said to exist, the system of *ad valorem* valuations secures a customs revenue which places all merchandise under tribute. Internal taxation has many forms, modelled, as it is, after the Spanish system. In addition the income from the $10,000,000 received from the United States assures that the government will continue to be a "going" concern, in practical operation as well as in legal phraseology.

For the student of political institutions the interest

is in the moulding of the inheritance of Spanish laws and Spanish administrative system to American models and the influence of an environment so pronounced as the American control of the Canal Zone. The evolution of the civic spirit, instead of being under the shadow of an unfriendly Power, is in the sunshine of a big genial Republic.

In its soil of decayed vegetation the Isthmus, with an area equal to the State of Indiana, has natural wealth enough for the subsistence of a continent. But it is tropical natural wealth, much of which exists under conditions unfavorable for development. Timber exploitation may one day open the longitudinal path eastward from the Canal Zone through the health-destroying jungles to the Gulf of Darien. Mahogany and others of the precious hardwoods offer the temptation. But the trail will be blazed slowly, a score or so of miles each decade. The mineral deposits also lie to the east. They will aid in the conquering of this hitherto unconquered region, yet gradually.

The territory which will be developed most rapidly is that lying principally west of the Canal Zone and extending to the limits of Costa Rica. Tropical agriculture in the hands of natives of the temperate countries is entirely practicable in this region, much of which has a climate markedly superior to the belt lying between Colon and Panama in the valleys of the Chagres and the Grand Rivers. The fruit industry, and in particular banana culture, has made rapid strides, but its possibilities are only in their beginning. Coffee cultivation was becoming a profitable business until the political disturbances ruined it. The revival may be expected within the five years necessary to bring the trees to the point of commercial production. Ivory nuts, rubber, and the infinite variety of minor tropical products will be stimulated by the market that will be opened. In the extreme west along the Pacific slope, where grazing has been enough of an agricultural industry to create the flourishing town of David, an enduring basis will be given to the live-stock industry.

But none of this agricultural growth can precede the building of roads. These are totally lacking in the interior. The Panama government made sensible provision out of its first revenues for this form of internal improvement, and the policy may be looked upon as a continuous one. The railroad line of development will be from Bocas del Toro on the Atlantic slope to David on the Pacific coast. Bocas del Toro will reach the Canal Zone by a railway through the banana-producing lands, and David in time may be connected with Panama.

In the general sense the prosperity of the Isthmus for many years depends more on the excavation work and on the international commerce than on its internal resources. It is this which will swell the trade of $2,000,000 or $2,500,000 annually to greater figures. Yet the waterway is the sure harbinger of the exploitation of the productive founts. The Canal community and the Canal construction are the potent economic factors.

When all is said, the Zone is the thing. The laws administered may not in their entirety be American laws, but they are such in spirit. Actually, the Canal Zone is a semi-military camp. It must continue such for purposes of sanitation and law and order during the

4

entire period of Canal construction.   What follows is
the establishment of a colony within the Republic of
Panama, yet not of it.   This colony, which includes
laborers, civilian officials, occasional detachments of
marines, and a police force, is not apt at any time
greatly to exceed 25,000 persons.   The early estimates of the very large number of laborers who
would be required were reduced when the engineers
began to make closer study of the degree to which
improved machinery could be used in the excavation
and other work.   It will be a conglomerate mass, —
Jamaican and other West Indian negroes, Chinese coolies, Mexican and Central American peons, possibly a
few American blacks, Italian railway workers, and similar elements.   In spite of all scepticism and detraction,
the Jamaica and Barbadoes negroes will do the bulk of
the work on the Canal.   They did the most of what
was accomplished by the French company.   They
built the railroads along the unhealthy coast of Costa
Rica.   They have shown the greatest adaptability to
the climate and the best capacity for hard labor.   The
Panama Canal will be the monumental contribution of
the despised black race to civilization.

Aside from determining the engineering conditions
of the Canal, which I have no purpose of discussing in
this volume, the most important functions of the United
States on the Isthmus are in regulating sanitation
and hygiene.   This regulation could not be restricted
merely to the inhabitants of the Canal Zone, for to
guard them against epidemics Colon and Panama had
to be protected.

I never shared the enthusiasm over the rose-colored
comparisons of the region lying between Colon and

PANAMA NATIVES FROM THE SWAMP COUNTRY

PANAMA NATIVES FROM THE MOUNTAINS

Panama with Havana and Cuba. Measures of hygiene, public sanitation, and even individual cleanliness will be secured on the Canal Zone and in the seaport cities. This will be valuable in decreasing the danger from yellow fever, bubonic plague, or other epidemics. And it also may be assumed that the strict supervision given by the medical officers will in a measure serve as a preventive against dysentery and enteric diseases, which are common to the tropics and especially so to the moist lands. But the Canal Zone topographically is vastly different from the island of Cuba. The Atlantic Ocean sweeps across Cuba. Every day of the year a healthful breeze is felt in the great central belt of that island. This not only purifies the northern coast, but it also invigorates the interior region, and its effect is felt even on the south coast. But in the Canal belt are the dead calms of the Pacific on one side and the limited area of the Caribbean winds on the other side. The Atlantic breezes are lost in the marshes before they reach the ridge of the Cordillera, while the zephyr which sometimes springs up in the Bay of Panama rarely extends as far as the Culebra Cut. When the Canal is completed, it will not serve as a tube through which the breezes of one ocean will whistle to the other ocean.

I write these opinions without the purpose of opening a controversy with enthusiastic scientists, medical officers, or meteorologists, but merely as a statement of climatic conditions which cannot be changed by the agency of man. There is the peculiar configuration of the Cordillera that causes the moist blankets to hang over the Isthmus and precipitates the enormous quantities of rain. Cuba has its wet season during certain months, but these rains are normal phenomena and are not supercharged with disease.

Miasma must result from the excavation of the decayed vegetation of a thousand years which constitutes the waterway line with the exception of the Culebra Cut, and yet the central belt of the Isthmus has enough of pernicious malaria even with the earth undisturbed. Experiences at Havana and elsewhere will be utilized, and the mosquito, if not exterminated, will have its harmfulness curbed. Whatever can be accomplished by artificial means to combat disease-breeding Nature will be accomplished, and no doubt need be felt regarding the efficiency of the sanitary corps as organized under the Canal Commission. But when all is not simply said but done, it comes to this: the inherent unhealthy conditions of the Canal Zone will be reduced to a minimum. The climate will not be conquered. What may happen will be to reconcile it to the presence of a larger number of inhabitants than the region heretofore has had.

For those who will dwell and work on the Isthmus the suggestions of the sanitary corps are so complete that I can add nothing except to advise to follow these instructions and to take a vacation either to the healthful mountains of Costa Rica or down the Pacific coast or back home as often as possible. The population which will be living in the Canal Zone for the next twenty years in relation to health is to be taken in the mass, and the experiences of a few individuals who have been able to regulate their own occupations with a special view to conserving their strength are not to be accepted as applying to thousands of other individuals. Nor is the result of a few months' life on the

Isthmus in its effect on the human energies to be accepted as the index of what may be expected after several years, during which the mental and the physical faculties are concentrated on one task.

The lessons of the first year's experience are easily learned. In the beginning was the buoyant, hopeful American temperament which goes straight forward to the task and, once determined that it shall be done, takes no note of obstacles. The Canal never would be built if the spirit of pessimism obtained at the outset. Optimism is always better in a great national undertaking. A large number of cheerful and confident Americans flocked to the Isthmus to fill positions in the engineering, the clerical, the sanitary departments and on the railroad. That there were confusion and cross-purposes in administration and complaint of red tape was not important. Actually the Washington authorities cut far more of the red tape than ordinarily can be done safely in government enterprises. But within a few months loud complaints were heard about low wages, the high cost of living, the long hours of labor, and the lack of recreation and amusement. Then the discouraged employees began to come home. They were of two classes. Many of the early home-comers were the adventurous fellows who had gone to Panama wanting a new experience and having had it more rapidly than they had anticipated, returned to spread the discontent. There was the other, and perhaps the more numerous, class who had gone in good faith, expecting to find conditions as to health and personal comfort similar to the United States, and intending to stay. It is likely, too, that both classes, working as they were for the government, expected easier conditions than would obtain in private employment.

The unvarying tendency of the returning employees was to discredit the glowing official and semi-official reports which had been made, and the promises held out of immunity from even the common ailments, including lassitude and homesickness. Then came the yellow fever epidemic of the Summer of 1905 and the long period during which the health authorities were baffled in locating the focus of infection. There was also the disagreeable evidence that pernicious malaria had had time to work havoc in many strong constitutions. The picture of the panic-stricken groups struggling to get away from Colon with every vessel may have been a little overdrawn, but that the feeling throughout the Isthmus was one of illy suppressed and contagious terror was undeniable. Yet to those experienced in tropical diseases the mortality was not an excessive one, nor were the general health conditions bad, allowance being made for surroundings. The permanent hospital records and vital statistics unquestionably will show that wonders were really worked under a scientific and systematic sanitation and provisions for conserving the health of employees. But the medical officials in their spirit of hopefulness had predicted freedom from the inevitable diseases of the Isthmus of Panama, and the failure of their prophecies caused the disappointing results to be exaggerated.

Generally, during the first year the United States suffered from too much expert opinion and advice regarding engineering and administrative work of the Canal and too little practical application to the task in

RUINS AT PANAMA

hand. This was not true of the sanitary authorities, who worked harmoniously and effectively. If only they had been more conservative in their original statements, it would have been better for their reputations as prophets of health. It always is to be remembered that ditch-digging in the most humid and rainiest section of the tropics cannot be made an entirely healthful occupation, and as fast as the subsoil is turned up by the steam-shovel the earth's resentment at being disturbed will make itself felt. The procurement of the permanent class of employees and laborers with the physical stamina and the moral fibre which the work of Canal construction requires, is necessarily an evolution and not the creation of a single year. But that class will be evolved, and the undertaking will go forward.

My own point of view is twofold. The Canal insures the industrial development of the Isthmus of Panama along the lines of tropical agriculture. It creates an international commerce and it adds to the domestic trade. It will secure an increased permanent population to replace the army of construction when the work of excavation shall be completed. This is the certainty in relation to the resources and the people. It will be good for Panama. But there is a wider good which is not local. For ten or twenty years the Canal will be a training-school in which to test and strengthen the constructive energy of the American character. Nowhere will the initiative faculty make greater demands on the individual. For those "who die victorious" the tribute of Time will be the completed Canal. For those who live the task will be from year to year out of their abundant experience to help on the industrial development of adjacent lands, among them the West Coast countries. And that is the civilization which will sweep from the Atlantic through the Canal and down the Pacific.

CHAPTER IV

A GLIMPSE OF ECUADOR

Tranquil Ship Life — Dissolving View of Panama Bay — The Comforting Antarctic Current — Seeking Cotopaxi and Chimborazo — Up the Guayas River — Activity in Guayaquil Harbor — Old and New Town — Shipping via The Isthmus and Cape Horn — Chocolate and Rubber Exports — Railway toward Quito — A Charming Capital — Cuenca's Industries — Cereals in the Inter-Andine Region — Forest District — Minerals in the South — Population — Galapagos Islands — Political Equilibrium — National Finances.

SHIP life along coast from Panama south is dreamful, placid, nerve-soothing.

"This South Sea," wrote the Augustine Friar Calancha, in his chronicle of the early Spanish voyagers, "is called the Pacific because, in comparison with the Atlantic and the Mediterranean, its storms are less violent and fewer and its calm is more tranquil. It is also called the sea of drunkards because a drunken man might navigate in it. Both oceans and ships are ruled over by five beautiful stars in the form of a cross, in a happy prognostic of holy domination over sea and land — at the sight of which the devil even when most enraged retreats and leaves all in tranquillity." This is surely a happy description of the quiet ocean and a devout poet's image of the Southern Cross.

The steamers are commodious floating Summer homes. The smooth waters of the Pacific make it possible to have a type of vessel that would be impracticable for transatlantic voyages. Deck cabins, a dining-saloon on the upper deck, and ample room are properties of them all. Some of the steamers are twin screw, though such enterprise hardly was demanded by the traffic and this type is not so comfortable as the single screw. From Panama to Valparaiso, 3,100 miles by the stops, there is rarely enough of a ripple to send the most sensitive traveller below with symptoms of sea-sickness.

The voyage is a marine trip along a great winding Continental street, with stops at many corners and turns up many lanes. Up and down the coast means putting into innumerable wayports. This makes them more or less acquainted with one another, and one coast community feels an interest in what is happening in a neighbor port a thousand miles away. The vessels bring the gossip, — usually of trade, of the value of the last cargo, of quarantine, of troubles with the native longshoremen, of disputes with the minor officials, and of political events or the latest revolution. The through freight is not yet sufficient for the big steamers to omit the minor landings and make quick time, which could be done if Guayaquil, Callao, and Valparaiso were the only ports touched. This should be a matter of eight or ten days from Panama to Valparaiso, whereas now it takes from twenty-one to twenty-three days. The time will be shorter when the through traffic developed by the Panama Canal has had a chance to grow.

As the steamer threads its way out into the ocean through Panama Bay, the vista is of cone-shaped, vivid green-clad volcanic mountains rising sheer out of the water.   On a disappearing view they look like gopher mounds on the prairies.   At sunset the sky is of indigo-blue and the waters are a maroon expanse, but the next night the great copper disk in the west burnishes the liquid plain, which seethes at its embrace.

For two days the voyage is apt to be disagreeably hot, though the air rarely becomes so stifling that the deck cabins have to be abandoned.   The weather is decently comfortable in the daytime.   The nights may be choking, but this does not last long.   The third day the equatorial line is crossed, not very far out at sea yet out of sight of land.   The Humboldt, or Antarctic, current is met as it sweeps up from Cape Horn, and its refreshing coolness is enjoyed for the remainder of the voyage.   The only unpleasant feature is that during the season from April to August the fogs which hang over the mainland charge the atmosphere with too much moisture, and there is no relief by their precipitation into rain; yet the discomfort from this cause is not serious.

Only the small coasting-vessels put into the minor Colombian and Ecuadorian ports.   On the Pacific side Colombia has but one shipping-point of consequence — Buenaventura, where the bay bends in a deep inlet. It is the gateway to the immensely rich country of the Cauca and of the overland route by Cali and the mountain passes through the Cordilleras to Bogota.

"It is a strange thing," says my Lord Francis Bacon, "that in sea voyages where there is nothing to be seen but sky and sea, men should make diaries." But down the West Coast, after crossing the equatorial line, much more than sky and sea is to be seen and the diary-maker need not be furtive in his occupation.

On the larger steamers one is always straining the eyes for Ecuador's famous volcanoes, Cotopaxi and Chimborazo. They are not often visible from the sea, though Cotopaxi is sometimes to be discerned. One evening I thought I caught a glimpse of one of these giant summits. It was towards sunset. Off shore was a seeming range of peaked clouds, then through a pink mist a sloping green and brown profile disclosed itself; after that bolder conical elevations, a dim fringe of them, and finally an unmistakable crown. "It is Monte Cristo," the ship's mate told me. "We are in the Bay of Caracas." The chalk-like surface was of sheer cliffs sliced as by a knife and with a fleece spreading alongside half-way up to the summit. "Snow?" "Oh, no; only the surf."

We are not more than ten miles off shore, but Monte Cristo dominates as though it were one of the colossal volcanoes. The vapors close in, the ribbons of gold in the western sky unroll themselves and are lost. It is night, and our last chance of seeing Cotopaxi is gone.

The voyage up the Gulf of Guayaquil and the Guayas River gives a vista of conical and pinnacled hills of living green, sparkling in their verdure like raindrops on the leaves when the sun comes out after a thunder shower. The gulf narrows, and the point is rounded at the island of Puna, which is the Ecuadorian customs and quarantine port. There are bathing-houses and pretty Summer or Winter homes,—we do not know which, for we realize that under the Equator there are no seasons. Beyond Puna the river is hardly more than half a mile across from one low bank to the opposite low bank. These are bordered

THE WATERFRONT AT GUAYAQUIL

THE WHARF AT DURAN

with *algaroba* trees and cocoanut palms. There are
open pastures and some neat houses, with ridges of
mountains in the background, brown and green. The
borders of the river are pleasant, but the miasma seems
to hang over the land like a steaming blanket, and one
gets the impression of malaria, — which impression is
a correct one.

Lower Guayaquil is first seen, then the sloping part
of the city proper. The big rectangular building in
the saddle of the hills, the most prominent of all the
structures, is the famous hospital, — a comforting re-
flection for strangers who have heard of Guayaquil's
yellow fever record and are told grewsome tales of the
epidemics. Fewer than eight cases in the hospital
count as a cipher, and ships get a clean bill of health.
The profile of peaks back of the town apparently is
not very high, and the valleys open gently between
them. A closer view of the city from the ship's deck
shows that it is not such a bad sort of tropical port.
Church spires and domes are many, and some very
handsome buildings are discernible.

The harbor is full of maritime life. Pointed shoe-
like canoes and sail-boats are constantly shooting
around, while farther down the river are the *balsas*, or
house rafts, with their tenants, including men and
women, children, poultry, pigs, and other accessories.
The timbers of these house rafts are from a native
wood of the cork variety, said to be unsinkable.
Apparently the living occupants of the rafts also are
of cork, tumbling off into the water and bobbing about
just as easily. I did not hear of any of them, even
the smallest, being drowned. I noted the old American river-boat patterns, and could imagine myself on

the Mississippi or the Ohio, except that this craft is even more blunt as to outline and more tub-like than anything that ever floated down from Pittsburg or St. Paul.

The crooked old part of the city is attractive in its picturesqueness, and is inviting at a distance. The newer section is so regular as to be uninteresting. The Guayaquil climate is trying to foreigners, though many of them manage to acclimate themselves. The mean temperature is 81° Fahrenheit. The extremes in the shade are 90° and 65°. During two or three days in the harbor it seemed to me that there was but one extreme and that the maximum.

The city, in addition to its commerce, has a number of local industries which include sugar-mills, breweries and distilleries, tanneries, foundries, saw-mills, and shipbuilding and repair shops. Besides the *balsas* small vessels built of the native timber are constructed in Guayaquil.

Guayaquil is a city of 60,000 inhabitants, the most populous port south of San Francisco, with the exception of Valparaiso. About 300 foreign vessels, with a tonnage varying from 360,000 to 375,000, enter and clear the port every year. The coasting commerce employs a considerable number of small vessels, — 2,000, whose tonnage aggregates from 22,000 to 23,000. The relation of the port to a waterway across the Isthmus appears very clearly from the statement of the distances, which may be repeated. From Guayaquil to New York around Cape Horn is 11,470 miles, and the time required for the steam cargo vessels varies from 60 to 74 days. From Guayaquil to Panama is 835 miles, and to New York by this route it will be 2,864 miles, or to New Orleans 2,263 miles. The time now required, allowing for transshipment by the railway and the consequent unloading and reloading of the freight, varies from 14 to 20 days. With through water communication and the advantages which will justify supplying coal for faster trips, the time need not exceed eight or nine days. From Guayaquil to Liverpool via Cape Horn is 10,795 miles; to Havre, 10,577 miles; to Hamburg, 11,203 miles. The difference in maritime advantage is exhibited by the subtraction of the distance from Panama or Colon to those ports.

In years when no long-continued quarantine interrupts the commercial movement, the imports vary from $7,000,000 to $7,500,000, and the exports are $9,000,000 to $9,300,000. In 1904 the imports were $7,670,000, and the exports $11,642,000. Relatively, 90 per cent of the foreign commerce of Ecuador passes through Guayaquil. It is the *entrepôt* for the interior region and also for much of the coast. Esmeraldas in the north has a little foreign trade, and also Machala in the south. But their imports and exports hardly affect the volume of commerce that is concentrated in Guayaquil.

One-third of the world's supply of cacao, or chocolate, is had from Ecuador, and this is measured by shipments through Guayaquil of 450,000 to 550,000 quintals, or 45,450,000 pounds to 55,550,000 pounds. In one year, of a total crop of 499,000 quintals, 456,000 were exported through this port. In a later year the value of the cacao exported was $7,624,000. A large section of the cacao-producing region is directly tributary to the city. The exportations of vegetable

ivory — the tagua or ivory nut of commerce — vary
from 39,000,000 pounds to 44,000,000 pounds annually, valued at from $600,000 to $750,000, according to the market price.   In one very successful year
the value was $1,100,000.   For the last year given the
exports of crude rubber reached 1,100,000 pounds,
valued at $600,000.   The United States takes 75
per cent and upwards of the rubber product.   The
coffee shipments were worth $500,000.   There is also
a considerable export trade in the various kinds of
straw and felt hats which are manufactured in the
interior.   Hides are also an article of export.

The statistics of production and of the foreign trade
are compiled by the Guayaquil Chamber of Commerce,
a very progressive institution in a country that is
not excessively enterprising in exhibiting the natural
resources.   From the figures supplied me by the
Chamber, I found that the United States enjoyed a
fair proportion of the Ecuador commerce.   France
takes the larger portion of the chocolate and coffee,
but the United States furnishes Ecuador a market
to the amount of $2,250,000 to $2,600,000 annually,
and ships goods in about the same proportion.
Germany received in one year about $2,150,000;
Great Britain, $2,000,000.   In the imports England
has the advantage over all others in cottons and
woollens.   The heaviest item in the exports from the
United States to Ecuador is provisions, which amount
to $500,000 yearly.   Petroleum, lumber, machinery,
and hardware also find a market.

This United States trade and all the foreign commerce of Guayaquil are so essentially a Panama Canal
traffic that their details do not call for analysis.   In the

WEED-KILLER PLANT, GUAYAQUIL AND QUITO RAILWAY

RAILWAY SPRAYING CART

increase of the future the largest proportion belongs to the United States.

The ambitious project of a railway to connect Guayaquil with Quito, the capital, was many years in assuming form, but the narrow-gauge line is creeping to Quito. The railway starts at Duran, on the bay across from Guayaquil, and runs eastward through a very rich agricultural plateau to Alausi, 80 miles distant, where it bends to the north. The tropical vegetation of foliage and weeds along the road-bed is so very luxuriant that the railway company has found it necessary to erect a plant midway in the hothouse belt for preparing and distributing, by a process of spraying, a solution composed of arsenic and nitre. By means of vats and steam-pipes the ingredients are boiled and dissolved into a strong solution, which is drawn off into a large tank, similar in construction to a regular railway water-tank, from which the spraying-car is filled. When the rainy season opens, the weed-killing plant begins its operations, spraying the roadbed at regular intervals. This is a very interesting feature of tropical railway operation.

The road surmounted the greatest engineering difficulties when it reached Guamote, 115 miles from Guayaquil; and the mountain section was completed so that trains could be hoisted from the coast level to the Andine plateau, a sheer vertical distance of almost two miles. The railway will cheapen the traffic both for imported merchandise and for exports.

The corporation had an up-and-down financial history. The railway construction was begun, or rather a local line was continued, by Americans who secured the concession from the government of Ecuador, the money being furnished mainly by Glasgow and London capitalists. The Americans who held the concession had frequent difficulties, not only with the bondholders but with the contractors and the laborers. The work of excavation and grading was done by Jamaica negroes. The nation guaranteed the bonds of the railway, and by a somewhat subtle process the government debt was funded into these railway bonds which are a second mortgage on the customs duties. The obligations were issued as the respective sections of the railway were completed. Notwithstanding the frequent financial difficulties of the contractors and of the English bondholders, the government paid the interest, 6 per cent, regularly.

Quito is accounted by all travellers, in what relates to climate and picturesqueness, one of the most charming capitals in South America. It lies in the central plateau, at an elevation of 9,371 feet. Though an ancient and historic capital, it has been modernized by electricity. The city has a population of 80,000, and supports a variety of local industries, including flour-mills, woollen mills, potteries, sugar refineries, and small manufactories of Indian felt hats; yet it is chiefly interesting as the seat of government. Forty years ago a German-American, Frederick Hassaurek, who had represented the United States as Minister and Consul-General, wrote his impressions of Quito and its people,[1] and there has been little to add since then.

One leaf from the Quito municipal records may be worth extracting. The *Cabildo*, or Council, under date of August 16, 1538, adopted this resolution:

[1] *Four Years among the South Americans*, by F. Hassaurek, Cincinnati, 1865.

" Since the arrival at Quito of a certain attorney, Bachiler
Guevara, many suits have been stirred up whereby, as there
was no other attorney in the town, many persons might lose
their legal rights; and therefore the said Bachiler Guevara is
forbidden to exercise his profession, or to give advice or his
opinion on any controversy or matter of litigation, under penalty of 100 pesos for the first offence and one year's banish-
ment for the second offence."

Cuenca, in southern Ecuador, is an important industrial and commercial centre.   It has between 25,000
and 30,000 inhabitants, and is surrounded by a rich
agricultural and stock-raising district.   It is seeking
a railway outlet to Machala on the coast; but in the
course of years it will have railway communication
with Quito, for the route is a natural one for commerce along the central plateau.   This location is a
link in the ultimate Pan-American Railway trunk line.
From Cuenca to a junction with the railway already
built from Duran beyond Guamote is less than 100
miles.

Misunderstanding of the topography of Ecuador
causes the country's resources to be underestimated.
By many persons no account is taken of any section
except the humid and productive coast lands.   But
there is the vastly productive inter-Andine region
between the two chains of the Cordilleras.   The transverse ranges between these two Cordilleras have the
appearance of knots, and are generally described as
the *nudos*.   They do not offer insuperable obstacles
to railway construction and other interior development, though ordinary roads are lacking.

All the cereals are grown in this central plateau lying under the torrid zone at an altitude of 10,000 feet.

It is the growing of corn, wheat, and other grains at these heights which causes the Spanish writers, with their warm imaginations, to write so enthusiastically of cultivation in the clouds. The region offers great opportunities for stock-raising, and generally it may be said to be the field for future immigration and colonization. Public officials of Ecuador glow with enthusiasm over this section of their country. A cabinet minister, in his official report, thus poetically and prophetically voiced the national aspiration:

"Not much time will have passed when the inter-Andine railway, vanquishing all the obstacles which have halted our progressive march, will salute the wall of the Andes and come with the whistle of the locomotive to awaken the spirit, almost dead, of our mountain populations to the civilizing influence of industry and commerce, giving easy outlet to the richness of our fertile zones, and assuring us a broader life by placing us in immediate contact with the coast and bringing us nearer to the exterior at will, multiply the relations of common interest, break the yoke of preoccupations and routine custom to which we have submitted blindly, and will stimulate us for work, and supply the deficiencies of our education.

"The line of iron and steel will traverse our climates and will go collecting in its train diverse productions, to bear them to our ports and deliver them to the commerce of the world. The struggle for subsistence will then be borne among the peoples of the interior, and from province to province will be established reciprocally the interchange beneficial to their respective provinces."

The Montaña, or forest region lying on the eastern slope of the Andes and with its network of river basins stretching to the Amazon, is less exploited in the Ecuadorian than in the Peruvian territory. The rubber in these tropical forests will be secured in the process of time. The development of this region on the part of Ecuador is not remote. But there must be means of communication. The government, realizing this, decided to build a railway from Ambato, on the Guayaquil and Quito Railroad, 100 miles to the Curarey River, a branch of the Amazon with headwaters near Iquitos in Peru. This line will enable that district to export its rubber through Guayaquil instead of out through the Atlantic Ocean. The railway route lies east of the Andes.

Tobacco is grown in the north near the coast for home consumption. Sugar-cane is cultivated successfully on the nearer border of the Montaña and also nearer the coast, but it will be a long time before Ecuador exports sugar in appreciable quantities. This may be less true of cotton, which is becoming a national industry. A fine quality is grown in the northern districts, of which Ibarra is the centre, and the cotton tree thrives in other sections. The mills, which employ the cheap labor of the native Indian women, have proven successful, and they find a profitable home market, though it will be many years before Manchester is seriously hurt by their output.

The minerals of the country are principally in the southern zone, though there are rich placers in the rivers of the north. The southern province, of which Zaruma is the centre, in the last century was famous for its gold-mines, and it is still known as El Oro, or the gold country. In late years little has been done, though the quartz veins have been worked intermittently and in some of the streams gold-washing has been carried on. Minerals are abundant farther south in the district of which Loja is the centre. Some copper is found, and there are deposits of iron and anthracite coal, silver, and lead. The engineers who made the Intercontinental Railway survey were impressed with the richness of this district, but its development awaits the building of the links in the Pan-American railroad, for the lack of transport facilities under present conditions renders exploitation of the mines too costly to be attempted except with large capital.

In proportion to its size Ecuador, though sparsely populated, is as well inhabited as other South American countries. The population is very largely Indian, with the usual Spanish intermixture. The total number of inhabitants is 1,275,000. The whites and the *mestizos*, or mixed bloods, comprise about 25 per cent of the population. The central plateau easily could sustain an agricultural population of twice that number.

The volcanic Galapagos Islands, lying 600 to 700 miles west of the mainland, on the equatorial line, usually are considered an Ecuadorian asset. They are not, however, a source of revenue, and the 300 or 400 people who inhabit them are not likely to increase to a larger number. At different times the government has been willing to dispose of the islands under the form of a perpetual lease for coaling or naval stations. Tentative offers have been made in Europe, but European governments hardly would seek to lease them for naval purposes without ascertaining the wishes of the United States. Since the Monroe Doctrine as interpreted under President Roosevelt's administration forbids military establishments of foreign Powers to be set up in the Southern Hemisphere, no European country is likely to come into their

CACAO TREES

possession. Naval officers on various occasions have urged the purchase of the Galapagos group by the United States, but the high price at which they are held by Ecuador, or opposition in Washington, prevented a bargain. The last negotiation was by Secretary Blaine during the Harrison administration. With the authority of the United States established on the Canal Zone and with the Pearl Islands in Panama Bay under the same authority, the necessary naval base in the Pacific is secured, and no further suggestions for purchasing the Galapagos group are likely to be favored by public sentiment. The only ground would be that, through the control by the United States, European intrigues and, possibly, complications would be avoided.

Chile at different times has been credited with wanting to control the Galapagos Islands and establish a naval base at the Equator. Since the Chilean national policy is no longer one of unlimited naval expansion, it may be doubted whether that country now would care to undertake the expense of establishing and maintaining a station off Ecuador. But should Chile take this course, probably there would be no objection on the part of the United States, which, in the broad sense, as related to Europe, is a party in interest with Ecuador.

Of recent years Ecuador has maintained political equilibrium, if not absolute political stability. President Alfaro during his term was compelled to combat the reactionaries and the Church party, but his programme of Liberal measures was sustained. The greatest progress that has been made is toward financial stability. The money of the country was put on the gold basis, and that having been maintained for several years, the promise of its continuance is encouraging. The standard of coinage is the gold *condor*, equal to the English sovereign in weight and fineness. The common circulating medium is the silver *sucre*, ten of which constitute the *condor*, or the pound sterling. The *sucre* is equal to 48.66 cents. Paper money is circulated, but the outstanding issue is not very large. There are two banks of emission, each of which has a capital of 3,000,000 *sucres*. By the last report the total amount of bills emitted was 6,356,000 *sucres*.

The Ecuador banks do a profitable business in international exchange. The Guayaquil institutions regularly pay 14 and 15 per cent dividends. Their deposits in the period from 1898 to 1904 rose from 20,688,000 to 31,492,000 *sucres*.

CHAPTER V

PERUVIAN SHORE TOWNS

WE steamed out of the Guayas River and into the Zambelli Channel for Tumbez by moonlight one evening. A hazy ridge lay directly in front of us, " Isla de Plata," or little Silver Island, where the Spanish pirates buried their plunder. The gold and silver have not yet been found. So many treasure islands with the buried booty of the buccaneers lie off the Pacific coast that one does not have time to stop and exploit them all.

I always take a long look at Tumbez. There is not much to see, — a low crest of mountains somewhere inland; a long line of sandy beach bordered by mangroves and *algaroba* trees; a slit in the fringe of foliage, which is the mouth of the river; and a monotonous stretch of watery greenness. Back among the bushes, hidden, is the port. A few small sail-launches are hovering around, and after a time

the port official comes out to the ship in one of them.

Tumbez is historic. Somewhere among these mangrove trees Pizarro and his hardy followers penetrated with their boat one day and began that wonderful march known as the Conquest of Peru. And Tumbez lies just over the line from Ecuador in what is still Peru and what was then the Empire of the Incas. Pizarro stretched his iron claws not only south to Cuzco but north to Quito. But I shall not recount history. Tumbez may be viewed to revive historic memories, but also it should claim a lingering look in order to keep alive a sense of the freshness of Nature. After it there is no green on the coast, — only rugged mountain masses, sand-hills, and towering snow-peaks. After Tumbez the coast chains of the Andes and the sublimity of Nature at rest, frowning but always majestic. Sometimes the brown cliffs with cavernous mouths rising sheer from the water, and then the plateau between this wall and the Coast Range. Oftener the sandy plain stretching from the shore to the lower flanks of the Cordilleras; beyond, the table-land; and then the lofty profiles of everlasting hills made loftier to the sight by the one range having another for its background.

The view of Paita after entering the expansive bay is a vision ranged by sand-hills. To the left are a hazy mountain, and a long reach of earth platforms, rocks, sand, and clay, rising longitudinally. To the right the land mounts to one level with torn sides like gravel viscera. The whole forms the rim of a bowl. The town hangs over the water's edge like a drooping willow tree. The buildings are cream-colored.

The harbor is full of life. There are many small schooners and floats for loading cattle sail rafts, and bobbing canoes with keg-like anchors. A cloud of whirling sea-gulls hangs over the bay seeking the spoils of the kitchen refuse. The captain of the port in brilliant uniform comes out with his crew in their white caps, blue blouses, and red trousers, as though they were manning a Roman emperor's barge. The steamer is received, and then twoscore rowboats make for the vessel. The pirates board it. They are the *fleteros*, or boatmen, who must be braved and pacified at every port on the Pacific, for there is no other means of getting ashore. "*A tierra, a tierra, Señor,* — To land, to land, Sir," they cry. One of them has you before you know it, and you are in the town.

Meantime the women pirates have swarmed over the ship. They have all kinds of wares for sale; clay drinking-vessels, knick-knacks, limes and other fruits, and the Panama hats, for the manufacture of which this district is celebrated. But we may leave them while we go ashore. There are a custom-house and government warehouse, good piers and wharves, and a passable hotel. A group of stocky soldiers, in part police and in part army, are in blue uniforms with heavy cartridge belts. All their faces are of the Indian type.

The life of Paita is seen in the market-place among the chattering women venders and their customers. All is animated, good-natured, obliging, but it is chiefly Indian with very little of the Spanish trace. The houses are of mortar, adobe, wild cane, or bamboo laths, some having mud roofs, and they are not bad dwellings. We go on a trip of exploration and find

a really clean town — that is, as clean as a town can be that is swept by constant sand-storms — and evidences of good local administration. A hum like all the bees of the universe proves to be merely the murmur from the open school-room. There are two churches, one of cathedral architecture and a more modern one with a wooden steeple like a Congregational meeting-house in New England. In the plaza a forlorn but determined effort is made to coax Nature. Some palm blades are enclosed, and around the borders are scraggy carnations and scrub roses, while in the centre are Kansas sunflowers. Many of the dwellings also have climbing vines, dusty yet still green.

Paita is historic in the annals of the West Coast on account of the legends that have been grouped around it. Most of them relate to its dryness. The rain is said never to fall. This is not quite correct, but difficulty is experienced in finding when a shower may be expected. On my first visit after returning to the ship I casually mentioned at the dinner-table the information given me by an old inhabitant that it rained every seven years. The polite German merchant from Lima corrected me with an apology. "You did n't quite understand the gentleman," he said. "He told you that it had n't rained for seven years and they did n't look for rain for another seven years." After a while the Swiss drummer came aboard just in time for coffee. "Think of it," he remarked, "it only rains in this place once in twenty-one years." From later and reliable sources of information I learned that rainfall can be looked for with a reasonable degree of expectation about every fourteen years

in the Piura desert, though the moisture sometimes dries before it reaches Paita and the coast. The mean annual temperature is 77° Fahrenheit.

One of the legendary libels which has clustered around Paita is that of the endless flock of goats. The basis of this legend is that the goats are driven down to the port to water, and by the time they get back in the foothills they are so thirsty they have to return, and thus the procession is continuous. Seeing a long flock of them filing through one of the town streets and waiting in vain for the rear-guard to pass, the legend does seem to have a basis in truth, but it is a perversion or exaggeration of facts.

Another libel is that the little dwarf palm which is seen at the top of the highest hill is not a palm at all, but only a slab of boards painted in imitation, so that the inhabitants may believe that a tree can grow in that soil. Actually it is a palm and not a painted post. Moreover, there are real trees. I found a group of the hardy pepper trees just back of the town, where the foothills branch off, and also some acacias, or thorn bushes.

But while it is libelled, Paita also accepts some of the stories which are circulated concerning it. One is that of the English consul or commercial agent who had lived there forty years. When his pension and retirement came, he went to his old home in England, announcing that he would spend his remaining days in the grassy downs where his boyhood had been passed and would be laid away in the green cemetery of his native village. In six months he was back in Paita, declaring that it was the only place in the world in which to live and die. In the course of nature the old gentleman passed away at a very advanced age, and was given the largest funeral that Paita ever had known.

Passing from these legends, Paita, which is now a town of 5,000 or 6,000 inhabitants, has a future as the emporium of northern Peru. It will be the Pacific gateway to the Panama Canal for the Amazon country. Its splendid sheltered bay, with all the facilities for docks and wharves and sea-room for the commercial fleets of a dozen nations, assures its future greatness. It once was the rendezvous of the Yankee whaling-fleets. The railroad runs 60 miles back to Piura, the largest interior city of northern Peru, which has a population of 15,000. Piura is the centre of the cotton-growing district, and with the extension of the irrigating systems the cotton product alone will give Paita a considerable commerce. The total of its imports and exports is between $1,400,000 and $1,500,000 annually. The certainty of the railway being extended as far as the Pongo, or Falls of Manserriche on the Marañon River 400 miles distant, is to be viewed as one means of diverting the rubber and other commerce of the Amazon from the Atlantic to the Pacific. The railway may be built before the Canal is completed.

Paita is the petroleum port. The oil fields lie between it and Tumbez at Talara. The Pennsylvania oil-drillers whom I met on two visits were graphically frank. They thought the petroleum possibilities were great, but they had a poor opinion of the English and French companies. The sulphur beds are near the Bay of Sechura, and are connected with the port of Bayovar by a railway thirty miles long.

A night out from Paita and the morning discloses a sandy shore with round bluffs. After traversing what seems a causeway, there are rocks with a salt crystalline surface. "Guano," briefly says the experienced traveller, "the Lobos Islands." "But where is the port of Eten?" "Eten is over there," pointing to a shell-like side of the hill. A smashing surf is beating, and nothing can be seen but the outline of a pier. Finally heavy surf-boats with strong-armed crews to handle the long oars make their appearance. The passengers are disembarked by means of crane and basket and are hauled up to the pier by the same agency. Eten is the outlet for the sugar and rice of the Lambayeque region, and a railroad spur runs a few miles back in the interior to Ferrenafe. Its yearly commerce is $1,300,000. The Yuncas Indian dialect is spoken in this region. It antedates the Quichua, which was the language of the Inca tribes.

From Eten to Pacasmayo there is a low beach or no beach at all, with the mountains humped up at the foot of conical jagged peaks, beyond which are more peaks in regular order, the Coast Range of the Andes. Pacasmayo bathed in the sunlight and lying at the foot of a high mountain, presents a very pretty picture. The surf is heavy, but the *caballitos*, or grass canoes, of the natives, are at home in the tumbling waves, and the going ashore is not an unpleasant experience barring the ever present possibility of an upset. The jetty which aids commerce was built by an American company. Pacasmayo ships large quantities of sugar from the valleys beyond and also some rice and fruits. Its oranges are famous. I never saw so many sea-birds as are in this vicinity. The pelicans hang like clouds, and often they dash for the water like an inverted whirling pyramid. Porpoises are numerous, while some seals and whales are found in these waters.

Pacasmayo was the seaport for the transcontinental trail or route to the Amazon which was followed both by the natives and the early Spaniards. The road led over the Cordilleras to Yurimaguas on the Huallaga River. Various projects have been attempted for the purpose of securing through steam and river navigation. An American company has received liberal land grants and other concessions from the Peruvian government. The traffic is large enough to justify building a railway line from Cajamarca to connect with one of the existing coast spurs.

Cajamarca lies across the Continental Divide in the valley of the Marañon River. It is a town of 12,000 or 15,000 inhabitants, and is the centre of a large commerce. Freight rates by burros to the coast, the only present means of transportation, amount to $7 per ton. Historically Cajamarca has an attractiveness all its own. It was here that the usurping Inca emperor Atahualpa, who seized his brother Huascar's birthright, hospitably received Pizarro, and, simple savage that he was, propounded the question which puzzled other untutored minds in other parts of the world during that epoch of discovery and conquest: By what right could the great man called the Pope give to the other great man called the King of Spain power and jurisdiction over land where he himself held no control?

Beyond Pacasmayo is the little sugar-loading port of Huanchaco. When the vessel puts in there, it is worth while going ashore and taking the diligencia (stage) or a horse across to Trujillo, for the road leads through a *huaca,* or ancient burial and treasure ground of the Incas. There is not much to see except the mud walls, but the short journey is a good introduction to the old civilization. Trujillo is a very pretty and active little place on a small river. The railroad runs down to Salaverry on the jutting slope of the mountain, the summit of which is marked by a cross. It is the fourth port of Peru in point of trade, the commerce being about $2,500,000 each twelvemonth. There is a cemetery which tourists seek in order to read the inscription, " *Se prohibe pasar la muralla los botes* — boats are forbidden to pass over the wall." From this it may be understood that this graveyard sometimes is under water. From the sea Salaverry is an open roadstead nestling by a little cub of a mountain which crouches at the feet of a big mother mountain. All the time the towering peaks of the Andes are growing in grandeur.

Chimbote, the next port, as yet has little commercial importance, because the coal and other mineral wealth of the country back of it have not been developed. It has great prospects in the future, possibly as an American naval station, for the Peruvian government, it is understood, is anxious to grant the United States certain privileges there. It lies nearly midway between Panama and Valparaiso. The Bay of Ferrol, of which Chimbote is the port, is protected by a large number of islets. Its waters are always tranquil and seem more those of a lake in the interior than of the sea. The bay measures seven miles by five, and at all points offers anchorage of the first order. It is deep and a very large number of vessels of the heaviest tonnage could at all times find a shelter. Quays and wharves could easily be erected. The railway extends to Suchiman, a distance of thirty-two miles. It is to be prolonged to Recuay, and some day may form an important link in transcontinental communication to the affluents of the Amazon. The ruins of the Inca aqueduct at Chimbote possess an interest alike for tourists and for engineers.

Farther down the coast is the landing-place of Supe. I know Supe well. Five days were passed there once, not, the officials said, in quarantine, but simply under observation for the bubonic plague. The hamlet has artesian wells and a lighthouse, due to the public spirit of the planters. It ships cotton, sugar, cane rum, and rice. It also has a *huaca*. Several of my fellow-voyagers went ashore and dug in the graveyard. They came back with their finds, — pottery vessels looking suspiciously new and some of which, as they afterwards admitted, they bought from the natives. The visitor is allowed to dig up the pottery himself. The villagers are hospitable. They made no objection when the ship's doctor unearthed a skeleton and left them a gratification, or hush money, for the privilege of carrying it off. His bribery was fruitless, for the captain of the *Tucapel*, complaining already of ill-luck and sailors' superstitions, gave him the choice of dropping the skeleton overboard or of being dropped overboard himself.

Ancon is one of the minor ports sometimes utilized for commerce when Callao is under quarantine. When the fog rises, a perspective is disclosed of sandy mountains and of palm trees along the shore. The bay is a fine one. Seals and whales frequent it without disturbing the bathers, for Ancon is a resort to which all Lima comes by taking the railroad for thirty miles through the winding paths that penetrate and surmount the overlapping white sand-hills. Ancon is famous historically as the place in which the treaty of peace with Chile was signed when that victorious nation was exacting terms, and it is the Treaty of Ancon to which reference is so often made in the discussion of the still unsettled Tacna-Arica question.

To enter the port of Callao, the vessels follow a semicircular course around the rocks to get within the shelter of the island of San Lorenzo and the long sandy tongue of land. It is sometimes stated that the island of San Lorenzo was split off from the mainland by an earthquake, but geology gives no support to this assumption. Of recent years the government has initiated many improvements in the bay. One of the best is a fine new navy mole, and as the warships of all nations make Callao their frequent station, this improvement is appreciated. There are also the *darsena*, or system of wharves and piers, controlled by the government, and the floating iron dock which was constructed by a French company. This dock has a capacity of 5,000 tons. A new contract between the government and the company in 1905 relieved commerce of many burdens. Callao is a fine port. The plaza in the centre, with its blending of tropical trees and statuary, forms a refreshing picture. The custom house is the most pretentious building, but there are other tasteful structures. The population of Callao is 30,000, but in the daytime it seems to be larger, as many of the people doing business at the port live at

Lima, which is only nine miles inland and is connected by an electric trolley and two steam railways. The foreign commercial colony is a large one. Much of its social life centres in the English Club.

All the commerce of central Peru passes through Callao. The shipping is extensive. Enterprising Chinese merchants have established a direct line to Hongkong via Panama, but the ships flying the English flag exceed all the other nations. Callao is visited annually by more than 1,000 coasting-vessels, steamers, and sailing-ships, with a cargo tonnage of 175,000 to 200,000 for discharge. England is first in the shipping, Chile next, and Germany third. The maritime movement is more active than at any port south of Panama except Valparaiso. With the completion of the Canal its commercial importance will be prodigiously enhanced. At present nearly half the trade of Peru pays tribute to its shipping, and the bulk of the revenues of the country are collected in its custom house. For the last year for which statistics are given, its foreign commerce amounted to $16,908,000 out of a total for the whole Republic of $37,058,000. The imports were about $13,000,000 and the exports $4,350,000. The coastwise traffic, in which foreign vessels are permitted to engage, centres in this port.

From Callao south are a large number of open roadsteads which hardly deserve to be called vessel landings, for they are entirely without harbor facilities. By means of lighters and small craft, freight and passengers are loaded and unloaded through the surf. Cerro de Azul means "blue hills," but the place is not very blue except for ship-captains. It is a shipping-port for sugar and cattle which are driven in from the interior. Lomas is another wretched little place. Chala is an attractive coast village, chiefly a cattle-loading port. The region is noted for the production of the granadilla fruit. The granadilla is similar to the mandrake, or May apple.

Pisco is a thriving port, with an open bay sheltered by rocky islets. Among these are the Chinchas, or guano islands, which are yet capable of exploitation. The beach, with smooth rounded hills in the background, bends like a scythe. There is green vegetation, which is always grateful, and palm, olive, pine, and other trees. The beach is possible for bathing, but the sharks are too numerous to make it enjoyable.

The town lies about a mile back from the port, with which it is connected by a mule tramway. The commerce exceeds $1,100,000 yearly. A railroad runs from Pisco to Ica, forty miles. It follows a rich valley in which there are many fine haciendas, or plantations. The products are both tropical and temperate. They include cotton, sugar-cane, alfalfa, and corn. A big cotton field on the edge of the port looks like a small section of North Carolina. Pisco is noted especially for the vineyards, which extend to Ica and beyond. From these grapes is made the wine called Italia. It is enclosed in queer-looking oval-shaped earthen jars, some of them of enormous size. The best brandy that is to be had anywhere in South America takes its name from Pisco. It is a grape brandy. The pure article is superior to French cognac, but, alas! the art of adulteration has been learned, and the real distillation of the grape juice is not often procured.

The district around Pisco is famous for its variety of tropical fruits, including bananas and *paltas*, or

alligator pears. The Pisco watermelons also are noted.
In the markets of Lima they are what the Georgia
watermelons are in the markets of New York. I
never tasted finer ones. The whole of the surround-
ing country, when it can be watered, is of enormous
fertility. A vast irrigation scheme has been projected
for the region which extends south. There is a high
range of blue-veiled, cloud-shrouded mountains, and
then the plain of Noco, which spreads down to the
gentle bluffs that overlap the sea. This plain parallels
the coast as far as Tambo de Mora, and all of it is
capable of irrigation. Tambo de Mora has some
ancient tombs or burial-grounds and high mounds
marked with crosses right on the edge of the village.
Its shipments are cotton in bales, and liquors in casks
and barrels.

Mollendo, which is the railway outlet of southern
Peru and of northern and central Bolivia, is one of the
three worst ports on the West Coast. Iquique and
Antofagasta farther down dispute the claims, but it is
impossible to see on what grounds. They are positive
and comparative while Mollendo is simply superlatively
worst. Seen from the sea, the town looks well enough,
spreading on the flat slope of the hill, with its party-
colored houses glistening in the sunlight. On a feast
day or national holiday the many foreign flags flying
indicate the presence of numerous consuls, which is a
sure indication of commercial importance. It is the
getting into the port through the open roadstead that
is terrifying. There is a causeway, and in order to
land it is necessary to pass through this rocky opening.
Sometimes the vessels have to wait several days before
they can transfer their cargo to the lighters.

View of Mollendo Harbor and Railway Yards

For voyagers there is only one way, and that is to risk life and the hope of further voyaging to the care of the strong-armed native rowers. Long practice has enabled them deftly to grab the passenger from the ship's ladder and stow him or her in their craft. The manœuvres are repeated until all who are courageous enough are in the boat. Then it is a question of breasting the breakers. The first time I went ashore there were three Peruvian women aboard. One was an old lady who made the trip to Lima twice a year; the others were wives of local merchants. The dame began her "Ave Marias." The younger women were less devout. Every moment they exclaimed, "*Jesu Maria*" and "*Madre de Dios*," but in the tone of a man swearing. A huge breaker swept over the boat and gave us all a bath. Then the craft danced on the crest of the next one like a cork. The aged lady became more calm, though she continued to pray. Later, when we were safely ashore, she confided to me that she always was terrified till the first ducking, and after that she felt that the shore would be reached.

The sea is not always quite so bad, but it cannot be counted on two hours in succession to be what the natives call "*consolodora*." By that they mean, not tranquil or consoling, but comparatively calm. "Comparatively" is the difference between a raging sea and a roaring surf.

Around the point from Mollendo is the Bay of Islay, calm, sheltered, and deep. It was once a place of importance. Now its population consists of a few fishermen. Everyone inquires why it was not made the port, to which one answer is that when the railroad was built the landowners became exorbitant in their demands, and there was no way for the line to secure terminal facilities except by paying more than the road was worth. Another explanation is that the property-owners of Mollendo, by liberal subsidies and other inducements, persuaded the railway to stop at the causeway. Whatever the reason, Mollendo now has vested rights as a port, and the change could not be made to Islay without encountering the most strenuous opposition. Consequently it will not be made. Recognizing this, the government in 1905 undertook harbor improvements for Mollendo at an initial expense of $500,000.

Mollendo has a kind of double-jointed custom house, the first for imports into Peru, and the second for imports which are to be carried through Peruvian territory up to Bolivia. The exports which come from the interior are chiefly alpaca and other wool. The last year for which figures are given, these amounted to 71,000 Spanish quintals, or approximately 7,200,000 pounds. A considerable quantity of borax and minerals are exported and a small amount of coffee. The shipments of crude rubber amount to 500,000 pounds. Mollendo is second only to Callao in its exports and imports, the total commerce averaging $5,000,000 annually according to the figures of the Peruvian officials. When the Panama Canal is opened, the major portion of the shipments from this district, which are light freight, will have the benefit of competitive ocean rates through the waterway with the tolls added, or around Cape Horn without tolls but with heavier coal bills and longer time in transport. The traffic will tend toward Panama.

CHAPTER VI

LIMA AND THE CORDILLERAS

Pleasing Historic Memories — Moorish Churches and Andalusian Art — Pizarro's Remains in the Cathedral — Transmitted Incidents of the Earthquake — The Palace, or Government Building — General Castilla's Humor — Decay of the Bull-Fight — Cultured Society of the Capital — Foreign Element — San Francisco Monastery — Municipal Progress — Chamber of Commerce — A Trip up the Famous Oroya Railway — Masterwork of Henry Meiggs — Heights and Distances — Little Hell — The Great Galera Tunnel — Around Oroya — Railroad to Cerro de Pasco Mines — American Enterprise in the Heart of the Andes.

PLEASANT Lima! Fairest of transplanted capitals! The Moorish memories of Andalusia linger over the City of the Kings which Pizarro founded. The stern monuments of the Inquisition are yet with her. Seek them in the Senate Chamber, where the inquisitors sat in judgment; search for them just over the bridge, where the doomed victims after condemnation awaited their fate; or in the Plaza Mayor, where the *autos de fe* were celebrated and the condemned were burned or hanged. Reflect, the last victim of the stake was a woman, Madame Castro. She was burned, in 1736, "for being a Jewess." She would talk heterodoxy !

Historic Lima! Seat of the viceroyalty; throbbing heart and scourging soul of the Spanish colonial empire; home of the Royal Audiencia, centre of law-giving and delegated authority, whence the Ordenazas — the minute code of government and administration alike for subjugated savage and freebooting colonist — were promulgated for all the vast territory from Panama to the Straits of Magellan and from the Pacific far beyond the Andes to the Amazon and La Plata!

But the glory of rulers perishes. Few can name their quota of those forty-four viceroys of Spain who held the sceptre on the Pacific coast. After Pizarro, the Conquistador, of the iron fist and will of steel, and as his superior, came — who? Blasco Nuñez Vela was the first of the viceroys, — a harsh, haughty, obstinate servant of the Crown, whose blundering nearly overwhelmed Spain with the sunset of the splendid colonial empire at its very dawn. Who came between and who was the last?

The sentimental antiquarian grieves over the de-struction of the viceregal residence of this last delegated ruler. It lay in a grove of palms and orange trees under the shadow of Mt. San Cristobal, with the ancient garden of the Descalzos, or Barefoot Friars, neighbor-ing it. The mansion was mediæval and tropical. But the big brewery encroached on it. The horses and mules of the big brewery had to be stabled; the beer wagons had to have room. Mr. Champion Jones, the English manager of the industry, gave a breakfast to foreign and resident society one Sunday morning. We revived the memories of the viceroys over an exquisite French menu, and some of us carried away a few mementos. The next day the vandal destroyer pulled down the walls. The mules are stabled there now.

Yet there is cheer for the sentimentalist who mourns over departed glories. The mansion never really was the residence of the viceroy. It was only the bower of his favorite mistress, who dispensed hospitality and received the recognition that the stern society of the times gave to power and place without questioning the private morals of the high and mighty. Besides, it was long after the Inquisition, for the viceroyalty lasted till the young years of the nineteenth century.

But the fourscore churches, with their minarets and towers, their tessellated mosaics and blending of bright colors, — they are Andalusian adaptations of Moorish art. Very shabby are most of them and not kept in good repair. There are too many mosque-like worship-places, and too few devout and open-pursed worshippers. From the roof of the American Legation I counted thirty of these churches. The artist might preserve all the charm of antiquity and yet satisfy the craving for the picturesque if the means were provided and the disposition to do it existed. These edifices are of Spain in the colonial epoch, and Spain never repaired church or castle or dwelling. Let them rust and fall apart, for have not crumbling stone and fading colors a graphicness of their own? Yet with these decaying and neglected Moorish churches in Lima the ruin discloses too much that is tawdry, too much veneer.

The Cathedral is modern, not moth-eaten or weather-rusted within or without. It took the place of the old structure, which was destroyed by earthquake. The interior is tile-paved and clean; there are antique mural paintings, fine examples of wood-carving in the pulpit, solid silver altar fixings, the money value of which the guide recites with swelling pride; and, greatest of all memorials, the bones of Francisco Pizarro.

On my first visit to Lima, in the hurry of business matters and social engagements, I indulged in no sightseeing. The hotel runner who was piloting me about was puzzled. The Cathedral was only a block distant. "Won't you go to the Cathedral," he said, "and see the bones of *Mister* Pizarro?" The lingering and respectful emphasis on the "Mister" was almost too much for my gravity. The Pizarros, as my recollection runs, were swineherds, and the appellation Don never was theirs. But if respect were lacking for their family tree in their lifetime, no descendant could complain of irreverence or want of courtesy in this volunteer guide who sorrowed because of my apparent indifference regarding the late Mr. Pizarro.

On a subsequent visit I went to view the remains. The caretaker irreverently draws the curtains from the niche in the little chapel of the Virgin. I am sure the hotel runner would not do so. But habit in satisfying tourist curiosity has made the Cathedral guide a showman. The remains are in a marble casket. The skeleton is well preserved. The frame is that of a big man; the brains are kept apart in a jar. Rolled in a metal case is the parchment certificate of authenticity. This is what was the mighty conqueror, the most heroic of the Conquistadores, the peer of the indomitable Cortez. Shall we muse curiously, or shall we give way to the physical sensation of being in the anatomical museum of a medical school? It depends on the temperament.

The Cathedral has more than Pizarro's remains. It

INTERIOR OF CATHEDRAL, LIMA

possesses the manuscript records of the Municipality of Lima. They are bound in modern calf, though the original parchments are sear and rusty and yellow. There is also a modern library which is open to the public. I found among its attractions, in one of the stairway vestibules, a unique painting on the wall typifying life in Lima in the sixteenth century. It represents a scene in the plaza. It pictures the gay cavalier of Spain in his fancy habiliments; the sedate matron demurely wearing the historic mantilla; the maid in the same headdress, but coquettish and answering the sly glances of the cavalier; the native Indian race in groups of individuals; women market-venders; the Indians from the country with the llamas and burros, — all as we may guess it was in the sixteenth century and much of it as it is to-day with the native race.

Lima's earthquake record is a continuous one from 1683, when the great trembling was experienced, until the present day. One of the most memorable of these seismic disturbances was that of October, 1746. The memoirs of the viceroy, Count Superunda, tell a curious story of those days of wonder and terror and the scenes enacted, — how debtors sought for their creditors in order to pay them; how enemies became reconciled and embraced one another in fraternal forgiveness; how slanderers on their knees besought the pardon of those whom they had slandered; and how courteous cavaliers, seeking injured husbands who until then had been ignorant of their wives' transgressions, asked forgiveness, which the injured husband, in spite of his surprise, would grant with an effusive embrace. A strange picture of morals — ten years

after the Inquisition had burned Madame Castro for
being a Jewess!

The balconies and arcades of Lima, the *façades* and
graceful arches, are Andalusian, yet there is a trace of
Greece in the adaptations of Doric and Ionic columns.
The *paseos*, or walks and drives, the parks and
gardens, in their grace and symmetry are Moorish
again; so are the kiosks.

The Palace, or Government Building, which is to be
supplemented by a new structure, is neither archaic nor
modern. It is somewhere midway between two epochs.
The tree which Pizarro planted, a fig, is in one of the
inner courts. I saw the tree, but was more interested
in the pictures in the anteroom of the Foreign Office,
— old prints of American subjects. One of them was
of Washington crossing the Delaware.

In the Palace is a portrait of Joaquin Castilla, one
of the sturdy characters in Peruvian history. He
was a Spanish soldier without education but of great
natural ability who joined the patriots in the struggle
for independence and afterwards became President.
He had the humor of Sancho Panza. Once a delegation of women waited on him. The request they
had to make related to some matter of administration
to which an answer would be embarrassing. The
old warrior, though he was of low birth, had all the
courtesy of a Castilian hidalgo. "Why, ladies," he
said, "you chatter like birds, all trying to talk at
once. Now let's have silence and let one of you
speak for all." A pause. "Let the oldest lady
speak." The tradition is that the delegation at once
filed out and bothered the grim soldier no more.

I have encountered many evidences of poverty in

CHURCH OF SAN FRANCISCO, LIMA

CHURCH OF SAN AUGUSTIN, LIMA

Lima, but the poorer classes seem to be contented. When the nights are chilly, they gather their blankets or shawls around them, according to the sex, and huddle in the Plaza. When the day is bright, they bask in the sunshine. The beggars are a nuisance in their obtrusiveness, but they are tolerated.

On a down voyage a party of young foreigners persuaded the captain to hurry the ship into Callao Saturday night, so that they could get ashore and go over to Lima to attend the Sunday bull-fight. The spectacle did not meet their expectations, which had been whetted by what they had seen in Spain. Once the bull-fight in Lima was a recognized social institution and was very brilliant, but its glory has faded. Humane impulses have found place in the municipal regulations, and the horrible spectacle of the bull goring a few poor old horses is not permitted. This takes away much of the excitement. The bull-fight has to be tolerated, and the President of the Republic attends the function given in his honor, but I noticed in the newspaper accounts that it was an indifferent affair. In time the bull-fight will entirely disappear. The races, which are popular, will take its place.

The lottery will stay longer. The drawings are held on the public square every week. The lottery is legalized, and a portion of the proceeds goes to the charitable institutions. That is why it is so difficult to grapple with this evil which demoralizes all classes.

Lima always has been noted for its cultured society. The Spanish spoken is the purest heard in South America. It is as pure as that of Andalusia or Madrid. Music, art, and literature, — these always have had their place. At the hospitable board of Dr.

Isaac Alzamora, the former Vice-President, the wittiest host in Peru, I met many persons whose talents and accomplishments hardly could be equalled. The life of the rich families is refined, and notwithstanding its seclusion comes nearer to the American ideal of home than anywhere else in Spanish America.

Lima has two leading clubs. The National is the more conservative, and is where all that is solid in business, politics, and professional life is met. The Union Club is composed of the younger element, and one of its attractions is that more liberty is permitted in gambling.

The foreign society of Lima I found to be more in sympathy with the native society than almost any other place. Its dean, and the most popular foreigner, is Mr. Richard Neill, for twenty years the Secretary of the American Legation, affectionately called Don Ricardo by his Peruvian friends. French, Germans, Italians, even the English, find something in common with the Peruvians. The British colony is numerous enough to be split into factions. The Scotch element, very masterful in business, predominates.

Among the Europeans the Italians are by far the most numerous. They have very largely the retail trade and they are property-holders in an unusual degree. A Little Italy lies across the Rimac River.

A very large Chinese population exists in Lima. Much of it is the second and third generation. Originally the Chinese were brought to Peru as contract coolie laborers, but of late years the immigration has been of a normal kind. The Chinese of this period have discarded the queue and have adopted the conventional dress. Some wealthy Chinese merchants have

an appreciable influence in the commerce of the country. These rich merchants are antagonized by another
faction which objects to their assumptions of superior-
ity. This element also is getting rich. China keeps
a Consul-General in Peru with semi-diplomatic functions, and usually he has enough to do.

I went one day in company with Minister Dudley
to call on one of the notable figures in the cultured
life of Lima. This was Dr. Ricardo Palma, Director
of the National Library, the learned author of an instructive History of the Inquisition and of many other
books, both historical and literary. Dr. Palma, during
the war with Chile, lost his own library and had the
anguish of seeing the accumulated historic treasures
of the National Library sacked by the victorious in-
vaders, but he set to work at once to form a new collection. He has gathered together 400 manuscripts,
and the Library itself is the best arranged and most
easily accessible that can be consulted on the West
Coast.

The University of San Marcos also has played a
notable part in the intellectual life of Peru.

Of the many churches, convents, and monasteries,
the most interesting is that of San Francisco. I went
there one afternoon with Mr. Alejandro Garland, the
best-informed man in Peru, to learn in a scant half-
day something of the ancient institution, though a
week would not have been long enough to wander
through the cloisters.

The monastery covers several squares. The con-
templative, meditative life of the Middle Ages no
longer exists. The friars are engaged chiefly in charitable work. The jovial priest who was assigned to

be our guide enjoyed having visitors. He explained that the incandescent electric lights had been adopted because they were cheaper than candles, and the Order, being poor, had to economize. But the monks in their cells are still restricted to the tallow dips. He courteously asked us to take afternoon tea with him. Here certainly was an innovation. We hesitated, but he pressed us so heartily that there was no escape. When the bell sounded, we passed into the refectory, were seated on a wooden bench alongside the board table, and were served with coffee and a slice of bread. The friars filed in, bowed politely, and took their places. Some of them looked with evident surprise at our host and his guests, but none with reproof. To ourselves our presence seemed incongruous, yet as a variation of the monotonous routine of their daily life it did not appear unwelcome to the Franciscans. We chatted in an undertone for a while, and on our departing the monks all rose and bowed. My companion, though a *persona grata* to the monastery and well acquainted with the priests, was as much surprised at our novel experience as myself. He never had heard of a layman or a visitor taking afternoon tea or coffee with the friars.

The patron saint of Lima was Father Francis Solano, the founder of the Franciscan Order in Peru, and the missionary who went through toils unutterable in seeking to Christianize the Indians. I was shown the cell in which he died, and then (a somewhat rare privilege) was permitted to see his skull. Newspapers are received within the walls of the monastery, because, as the good father explained to me, in these stirring days it is necessary to be *en rapport* with what

SCENE ON THE OROYA RAILWAY, CHICLA STATION

is going on in the outside world in order to do good works. Some of the friars read English.

Until recently Lima was not a progressive municipality. It preserved the old Spanish traditions of dirt and indifference. But it had an awakening. Public works, such as befit a city of its political and commercial importance, were initiated. A loan for municipal improvements was taken by the local banks. This was gratifying, but the improvements themselves were more gratifying. The town is becoming an industrial centre, with many small factories as the basis.

A very important factor in the progress is the Lima Chamber of Commerce, whose members include all the leading merchants, both native and foreign. The Chamber has exercised a marked influence on the fiscal policy of Peru, and the Government with its coöperation has been able to strengthen the credit of the country abroad and to carry through the measures which are the basis of the commercial and industrial revival that has been enjoyed. Without the aggressive support of this body the establishment of the gold standard scarcely would have been secured. Its advice with regard to the negotiation of commercial treaties to which Peru aspires is valuable, and its suggestions concerning administrative reforms in the customs usually receive respectful attention. I do not know any nation where the business man in public affairs — not in partisan politics — fulfils his proper functions so well as in Peru, and this is done through the concentration in the Chamber of Commerce.

In the public works municipal sanitation is a leading feature. That is good. The death rate of Lima, in spite of a healthful climate, is disproportionately high. The returns show a birth rate of 28.37 as compared with a death rate of 37.43. The ignorance of the poorer classes of the proper means of living is not the only cause of this high death proportion, but they have to be taught hygiene, and the municipality has to lead the way.

The climate of Lima merits the praises given it, yet the Winter season from June to September is raw and disagreeable and especially bad for rheumatism. Tuberculosis claims many victims. The legend is that rain never falls, that the dews and the moisture from the clouds, which is not precipitated, and the fogs on the coast, take the place of rain. This is not quite true. Sometimes there is actual rain and sometimes a drizzle. Minister Dudley and I had the proof two successive evenings, when we were out to dinner and had our high hats spoiled through our failure to carry umbrellas.

Peru, as far as the main Cordillera of the Andes, is bisected by the Central Railway, which runs from the seaport of Callao to Oroya, following the course of the Rimac River. The distance is 138 miles. In these later days of mechanical triumphs it is still possible to declare that this railroad is the engineering marvel of the world. It is an often told story, but one that bears re-telling.

The name of Henry Meiggs in the Yankee mind is vaguely identified with something big in South America and with something wrong in the United States. Meiggs was a fugitive financier from California. He had been the treasurer of San Francisco County, had loaned the public funds to his friends, and when they failed to pay up had been forced to flee as a defaulter. He afterwards made good the defalcation. He first went to Chile, but in a few years settled in Peru. He built the Southern Railway from Mollendo to Lake Titicaca, which is itself a marvellous work. But his fame as a captain of industry and his reputation as a benefactor to Peru rest on the Central Railway. Meiggs was not an engineer. He was a financial genius with a bold imagination and daring mind. He had the capacity to get other men of genius, among them the Polish engineer Malinowski, to carry out his ideas on the side of construction. He could win the confidence of the money-bags of London and float South American bonds at good prices, when the countries issuing those bonds could not give them away.

In 1869 Henry Meiggs signed the contract with the Peruvian government to build the Oroya Railway for $29,000,000 in bonds, which he took and floated at 79, thus making the actual price $22,000,000. He carried the railroad construction as far as Chicla, 88 miles, and built the great Galera tunnel ready for the rails, though they were not laid through it till years after his death, when the extension of the road from Chicla was carried to the terminus at Oroya by the Peruvian Corporation. The road climbs to its greatest elevation in a distance of 88 miles without a single down grade. The ascent is from the tropical ocean border to everlasting snow, through the sublimest scenery that the eyes of man ever dwelt on. There are curves, tunnels, bridges, viaducts, switchbacks, almost without number.

What the railway is as a marvel of engineering

construction can be exhibited in no better way than by a simple table giving the distances and heights above sea-level and the " V's " and " V V's," or switchbacks and double switchbacks.

DISTANCES AND ELEVATION ABOVE SEA-LEVEL OF THE CENTRAL RAILWAY OF PERU

Name of station	Distance in miles	Elevation in feet
Callao	0.0	8.7
Lima	7.7	499.9
Santa Clara	18.3	311.7
Chosica	33.6	2,800.6
Cocachacra	45.0	4,622.6
San Bartolomew, station and switchback	47.1	4,959.4
Agua de Verrugas, bridge	51.9	5,839.4
Cuesta Blanca, tunnel	52.8	6,001.1
Surco	56.5	6,660.9
Challapa, bridge	61.8	7,504.1
Matucana	63.9	7.788.8
Quebrada Negra, bridge	65.5	8,054.1
Tambo de Viso, bridge	68.8	8,706.5
Chaupichaca, bridge	73.0	9,472.6
Tamboraque, switchback	74.9	9,826.9
Aruri, switchback	76.3	10,094.5
San Mateo	78.7	10,534.1
Infiernillo, bridge, and tunnels	80.4	10,919.9
Cacray, double switchback	81.6	11,033.1
Anchi, bridge	83.9	11,306.4
Copa, bridge	84.8	11,638.8
Chicla, lower switchback	88.0	12,215.5
Chicla, upper switchback	90.0	12,697.1
Casapalca	95.5	13,606.2
Galera, tunnel	106.4	15,665.0
Yauli	120.5	13,420.8
Oroya	138.0	12,178.7

I travelled up the road tourist fashion in the regular passenger train, but that gives only a faint idea of the

Scene on the Oroya Railway, San Bartolomew Switchback and Grade.

wonders of the railway or the splendor of the scenery.
The down trip is the best for observation. This can
be taken on an open flat car which is used for the
bags of ore. Sometimes the railway officials transport
favored guests part of the way down in hand cars, but
while the experience is thrilling enough to satisfy the
craving of the most exacting nature, the pace is too
swift to give a chance for observation. I repeat, the
proper way is on an open freight car.

The tunnel and bridge, or viaduct it might be called,
like a cobweb reaching from the gorge up to the sky,
which generally is most sought after for experiences, is
Infiernillo, or Little Hell, also called the Devil's
Bridge. The elevation here is 10,920 feet. The
road plunges out of one tunnel and across the great
cobweb of steel and iron into another tunnel.

The principal station is Casapalca. It is here that
the biggest smelting-works are located. Both silver
and copper are treated. Black Mountain Peak is the
dominating spur in this neighborhood. Its height
is 17,600 feet. San Bartolomew and Verrugas are the
places that have a sad fame for the peculiar malady
known as *verrugas*, or bleeding warts. It is a deadly
and malignant disease of the blood, is of native origin
and confined to a limited area. Its ravages were
frightful among the laborers who built the road, but
it rarely is heard of now.

The most glorious views of the valleys shut in by
the colossal precipices are at San Mateo and Yauli.
On the up trip, until Chosica is reached, the valley of
the Rimac is broad and regular, a panorama of green
and yellow and white, — alfalfa, corn, sugar-cane, and
cotton. Here, too, the ruined terraces on the steep

mountain sides, vestiges of the Inca system of aqueducts and irrigation, are numerous.

Mt. Meiggs, 17,575 feet high, is the marker for the Galera tunnel. The mountain is snow-clad. Ordinarily the flagstaff on the peak is visible. The tunnel is three-quarters of a mile long. On the down trip I noticed that we were four minutes in passing through it. The time, it might be supposed, would seem longer than it is, yet my guess was three minutes, and I was surprised when the watch showed a minute more. The cold air draughts were invigorating, like tempered blasts from an ice furnace, and there were to me no disagreeable sensations. I merely wondered when and how we would get out.

Many persons who take this journey complain of the *siroche*, or mountain sickness, the nausea and headache destroying their pleasure. For those who suffer from this distemper a good plan is to allow two days for the trip and stop over night at one of the stations half-way up, Matucana being the most convenient.

Night trains never have been run on the line, but this innovation may be made. Practical railroad men say that there is no more danger in the night than in the day, for in the daytime, with so many abrupt curves and tunnels, it never is possible to see very far ahead, and the locomotive headlight might really be an advantage. The chief trouble of the railway management is in preventing landslides, but the greatest damage has been wrought by cloudbursts.

The Central Railway was built in order to cheapen the transportation of the ores and the minerals to the seaboard. The bulk of the traffic always will be in one direction, though with the development of the Andine region a considerable increase in agricultural products and general merchandise in both directions may be expected. The management has not always been alive to its own opportunities as a freight carrier. Various companies formed to exploit the coal deposits were discouraged by the railway officials on the ground that the railroad would be put to too much trouble in hauling the output if the mines proved successful!

Oroya is snuggled in among four *cañons*, which branch off almost at the points of the compass. There are gigantic granite and limestone wedges which split the town into triangles and have resulted in two distinct villages on the bends of the river. The elevation of Oroya is 12,179 feet, but the peaks around are easily a thousand feet higher, and a climb up one of them gives the most splendid view of mountain grandeur that I have seen in any quarter of the world. I have pleasing memories of several days spent in this neighborhood in amateur explorations.

Oroya is a good place in which to observe the native life, both that of the *cholos*, or mixed race, and the pure Indians. All that is characteristic of civilization or partial civilization in the heart of the Andes may be seen here. The Quichua, or aboriginal Indian race, seems to have preserved its identity side by side with the tincture of Spanish or Caucasian blood which has produced the *cholo*. They appeared to me a reasonably industrious people, especially the women.

Oroya is the mining-centre for all this district and is the outlet for Cerro de Pasco. It used to be a vastly interesting trip by the highway from Oroya to Cerro de Pasco, and the interest is not greatly lessened

now that the American syndicate which controls the
copper and silver mines has built a railway 87 miles
long. The railroad follows the *cañon* for 15 miles,
and then strikes across the great level plain, or pampa,
of Junin, which it leaves at the foothills in order to
climb up to Cerro de Pasco. The elevation of this
mining-town is 14,200 feet.

A pyramid on this plain catches the eye, and the
inquiry is made as to its significance. It is the historic monument marking the last battle between the
Spanish forces and the patriots in the war for Independence. The town of Junin near the lake of the same
name, while it is one of mud huts and grass-thatched
dwellings, is clean and pleasing in appearance.

I never met quite so many weather changes as were
encountered in riding across this pampa of Junin.
We were in the midst of clouds so thick that they
wet us through. Just ahead was a broad level of
sunlight, and beyond that a driving snow-storm, and
we found the sunlight and the snow exactly as they
had appeared. There was a hail-storm which we also
saw ahead of us. When it was pelting us, we could
look back and through the snow see the sunlit plain
and then the violet mantle of the clouds.

Cerro de Pasco is a cold place, but the Montana
people who are engaged in developing the mines say
that they like the climate, and they compare it ap-
provingly to that of their own State. Heretofore the
silver output has been the great source of the wealth
of this region. It is a story of the romance of always
romantic mining history. It was in 1630 that an
Indian shepherd, having made a fire to cook his
humble meal and warm his hands, found the stones

PYRAMID OF JUNIN

INDEPENDENCE MONUMENT, LIMA

covered with silver threads. That was the beginning
of the silver mining, and since then 450,000,000
ounces are known to have been taken out. The
quantity was probably much larger, because the Spanish tax of one-fifth was so heavy that it put a premium
on evading it. The American capitalists who invested
in the Cerro de Pasco region did so chiefly with
the purpose of developing the copper deposits. By
the burros and other pack animals the freight for the
copper ore down to the railway at Oroya amounted to
$40 per ton. That is why the first move of the
Americans was to build the railway to connect Cerro
de Pasco with Oroya. The coal outcroppings also
gave encouragement that the smelters which were
erected could secure cheap fuel. The money actually
paid out in buying the mining properties and in building the railway was understood to be $8,000,000.
The probability is that at the present time the cash
investment is not less than $10,000,000, and the capi-
talists are considering another outlay to the amount
of $15,000,000, to build a railway paralleling the
Oroya road down to the coast, unless the London
directors of the Peruvian Corporation make satisfactory traffic arrangements for freighting the copper and
the bullion turned over to their line.

Should the yet untouched mineral wealth of the
Cerro de Pasco district prove a fraction of what the
mining-experts have declared it to be, the output of
ore will be only in its initial stages when the interoceanic canal is opened and the advantages of this
route are set off against the long course around Cape
Horn to Liverpool or New York. American private enterprise in the heart of the Andes will respond

to American national enterprise on the Isthmus of Panama, and the pleasing historic memories of Lima will be blended with the more pleasing prospect of the Cordilleras' contribution to the material progress of Peru and her people.

CHAPTER VII

AREQUIPA AND LAKE TITICACA

Capital of Southern Peru — Through the Desert to the Coast — Crescent Sand-hills — A Mirage — Down the Cañon — Quilca as a Haven of Unrest — Arequipa Again — Religious Institutions — Prevalence of Indian Race — Wool and Other Industries — Harvard Observatory — Railroading over Volcanic Ranges — Mountain Sickness at High Crossing — Branch Line toward Cuzco — Inambari Rubber Regions — Puno on the Lake Shore.

AREQUIPA is the commercial, ecclesiastical, and political capital of southern Peru. It has a university, several colleges, an Institute of Agriculture, and a School of Arts. A fairer city never bloomed in volcanic desert. The valley of the river Chili is so vividly green that it seems alive. The snow cap of the extinct crater of El Misti is ever in sight, while the fleecy dome of Coropuna and the glistening pinnacle of Chachani stand out like sentinels in white robes, all of them above 19,000 feet. Their icy breath is seldom felt, for Arequipa enjoys the balmiest climate that mortal could long for. It banishes pulmonary diseases. Life is gentle in this soft atmosphere, yet some persons complain that the night air chills the marrow. The mean temperature is 57° Fahrenheit, but water freezes in June and July.

Arequipa, which is in south latitude 16° 24′, is 7,500 feet above sea-level, about the altitude of the

City of Mexico. The railway from Mollendo winds
along the shore and through the volcanic soil for 106
miles to reach the city, climbing almost spirally. This
road was the first experience of Henry Meiggs as
a railway builder in Peru. He took it as a sub-
contractor, and spent $500,000 in supplying fresh
water to the laborers and the animals during the
eighteen months which its construction required. The
length of the entire main trunk from Mollendo to
Lake Titicaca is 330 miles.

A better idea of the region which lies between Arequipa and the coast is had by the slower mode of
travel with horse or mule. I made this journey in
company with two others during one of those periods
when the port of Mollendo was closed on account of
the bubonic plague, and when in order to get out of
the country it was necessary to reach the little port
of Quilca forty miles north of Mollendo. Leaving
the railway at Vitor, an hour's run from Arequipa, we
took the animals and started across the sand-hills to
the ranch of Santa Rosa. It is the only habitation
in fifteen miles, for there is no possibility of human
dwelling amid those dunes. Stone heaps have been
placed at various points to mark the route which is
followed by the llamas and the burros and the occasional wayfarer, but the frequent wind-storms cover
the mounds and they are not always to be discerned.

It is the region of the famous moving sands and
travelling hills. An experienced desert traveller, if he
should be without a pocket compass, might " sense "
the direction for the first half of the distance from the
contour of the mountain range on the horizon. After
that his danger of losing himself would not be so

great, for there is an ascent to the top of a ridge of hills, and the landmarks here are more stable. The descent is down the flank of the *barranca*, or ravine, into the river valley. This is diversified by several pretty *fincas*, or farms. The dwellings are of adobe or bamboo. Alfalfa is raised and is the common fodder. There are also vineyards, some of them quite extensive.

We put up for the night at the *finca* of the former prefect of the Department. The owner of the estate was away, but the Indian tenants in charge gave us the hospitality of their dwellings, — the privilege of spreading our blankets in one of the cabins while they prepared for us the always appetizing broth, or *chupé*.

We were up with the stars in the morning, for fifty miles had to be covered in order to reach the ocean, and there was no intervening shelter, no camping-place, — only billowy sand-plain, rugged ravine, and sombre *cañon*. One of the Indian lads acted as our guide till we had wound our way up through the steep ravine and again out on the open. Then he gave us some hints to keep from losing our way and bade us " *adios*."

The pampa was spotted with many curious formations of white sand in half-moon and crescent form, geometrical figures, as the whims of the winds had willed it. Some of these had gaps or circular passes; others could be passed by circling around the foot-hills, while still others could be surmounted only by a straight-away ride ahead to the crest and down the slope. The sand was packed so tight that it withstood the animal's heels as readily as a paved road.

This vista of crystal crescent sand-hills impressed me as of a gigantic Turkish scymitar beginning in the limitless desert and stretching to the unbounded horizon.

There was no vegetation, not even a blade of tuft grass or of the common cactus, nothing for the sight except the half horns of sand and the unbroken level of the pampa stretching ahead to the sloping mountain wall which seemed to lie straight across the path. But though the plain was absolutely barren, experiments have shown that this sterile soil is capable of producing in infinite variety, if only it is given water. The rain, if it could fall, would bring the oasis in a single season. Provide artesian wells, bring the snow rivulets down from Coropuna by the methods of modern irrigation, and this desert becomes carpeted with the verdure of growing green grain and yellow ripening fruit.

In bargaining at Arequipa for the animals, we had been fortunate enough to secure cargo mules for our baggage and good horses for ourselves. At every level stretch the horses took the bridle and cantered off, racing for miles until checked by the riders. Then, after a few minutes of slower pace, again the canter and the exhilaration of the Arab on his Sahara steed. In this manner the snow-peaks of Coropuna and the crystal apex of Chachani were lost to sight before the mid-day rest, and the sheet of glistening water ahead ceased to fret us or puzzle us to determine how a lake came there. It was the mirage, the quavering effect of the hot and dry atmosphere on the white sands.

When the base of the mountain spur was reached, we found it an easy climb to the ridge, and then

plunged down a long ravine and up again to another
plain partly shut in by the hills. The woman member
of our party claimed the privilege of her sex to question and doubt. She was sure we were getting lost.
The glint of the sea far off did not reassure her. She
insisted that we were going in the wrong direction.
We should be headed southwest in order to reach the
coast, and she had satisfied herself that we were going northeast. I took out my pocket compass to
convince her. Our actual direction was north. We
had made one turn, and the gorge through which we
had to descend in order to reach the sea required
another turn, but she maintained to the end that we
might have got there by some other route.

The *cañon* had many crevasses, clefts, and gashes,
but none of these was wide enough to turn us aside,
and after a time we reached the willow marshes and
forded the Vitor River. Then a very steep climb to
the hill, which was crowned by the church, and we
were in Quilca. The *caleta*, or cove, which constitutes
the port, lies below, and it took a half-hour's winding
ride to get there.

The vessel for Callao which we had hoped would
be waiting had put in and out four hours earlier.
When another ship would be along, no one could tell.
The last passengers who had come overland had
waited for two weeks. Every day we climbed the
outjutting cliff and scanned the sea, watched some
vessels go by without heeding our signals, and said
harsh things of them. Then we dug into some of
the aboriginal huts. The work was hot and not interesting enough to be pursued. The villagers had some
relics, but the most valuable ones and those which

indicated the highest lost civilization had come from the interior. Mica deposits abounded in the vicinity, and a passing American miner had posted up the legal denunciation, or claim, to them. The copper and gold mines were a hundred miles back somewhere in the red volcanic hills.

The people were a kindly folk, and a vacant house was put at our disposal. They loaned us chairs, and our own sleeping-bags and blankets were all the rest of the furniture that was necessary. But the fleas! Neither Texas, Havana, nor San Francisco ever bred fleas equal to those in the sands of Quilca. Fortunately for us a big shipment of cattle was coming down from the interior, and the owner had more influence with the steamship company than we had. I had spent a small fortune in cables. Mr. Meier, our consul at Mollendo, had reënforced me, and our minister in Lima was enlisting the full influence of the government. But all this would have been without avail if the steamship managers had not decided to put in and take the cattle away and the waiting passengers with them. Consequently instead of a fortnight our stay was less than a week.

But back to Arequipa. It is a blending of old and new towns, a grouping of sandstone houses and eucalyptus or camphor trees surrounded by greenish-white hills. The streets are fairly wide, and have open drainage, which is facilitated by the slope. They are not kept too clean. Blue is the dominant color of the dwellings and other buildings. Ambitious and somewhat gaudy decoration is attempted in the way of painting the outside walls. The subject and the execution generally are more novel than artistic. The

View of Arequipa and the Crater of El Misti

place has a peculiarity that I did not note elsewhere. The *tiendas*, or stores, the dwellings of the poorer classes and of some of the fairly well-to-do, are tent-shaped with whitewashed mortar roofs. These give to the section of the town lying along the river the look of a permanent camp. The public institutions, the Carmen Monastery, the hospitals, are shut in by mortar walls. The thermal springs of iron and sulphur are a few miles distant at Yura.

Arequipa is a city of churches. One side of the plaza of San Francisco is taken up by the Cathedral. It is a new structure, rebuilt after the earthquake of 1868, and was consecrated in 1893. It is roomy, but not notable as an example of ecclesiastical architecture. There are twin spires, and an arch at either end, the front being of smooth white lava rock. The Cathedral is not meant to be an earthquake tempter ; that is the reason for its simplicity of construction. Other churches are much more mediæval and therefore much more picturesque. One of them has been partly wrecked by a seismic disturbance.

Arequipa has been noted for its religious intolerance. This has entered into political affairs and has made it the centre of reactionary influences. Sometimes this reactionism has been the basis of revolutions or attempted revolutions against governments of liberal tendencies. But this spirit is slowly yielding. Ex-President Edward Romaña, who, notwithstanding his education at a Jesuit college in England, antagonized the reactionary clerical influence, has an estate near Arequipa and makes it his home. His administration was of immense good in carrying Peru through a critical period.

Despite its inheritance of Spanish blood and customs, Arequipa still illustrates the predominance of the Indian type. Natives with their burros and llamas fill the streets, gossiping and sometimes working. The official and higher classes show their Spanish origin. In the morning the women on their way to church with their black shawls and mantillas wrapped around them are followed by the servants carrying chairs, but in the afternoon and evening the sombre mantillas are changed for Paris hats and smart gowns, and the brightness of Andalusia sparkles in those piercing black eyes.

Like Lima, Arequipa was founded by Pizarro; and, like Lima, it has its earthquake history. The record runs quite evenly.

The population is 35,000. There are a number of local industries, including a cotton factory and flour-mills, and it is the mining-centre for all the region that extends up to Lake Titicaca and beyond. It also is beginning to be a possible centre of the rubber export. The Inca Company, which controls the Santo Domingo gold-mines and which has valuable concessions for opening up the Inambari rubber region, has its head-quarters in Arequipa. But the chief trade comes from the wool industry. All the alpaca and other wools are marketed here. The alpaca wools are divided into two grades, the production of the superior being about two and a half times as large as the inferior. Much of the wool is handled by American firms and is shipped to New York and Boston. The vicuña, or finer grade, is shipped to France, and some of it finds its way back to the United States in the form of expensive rugs.

The foreign colony of Arequipa includes a number of Americans engaged in mining, wool, railroading, and miscellaneous business. The Harvard Astronomical Observatory, half-way up the slope of El Misti, insures the presence of cultured Americans. During my visit Professor Bailey, the director, was off on a trip to the rubber country, and I did not have the privilege of meeting him.

The journey from Arequipa up to Lake Titicaca affords a day of varied mountain scenery. The valley of the Chili is like a green thread looped or knotted somewhere far down amid the volcanic mountains. Conical and domelike snow-peaks, cupolas, apexes, pagodas, and pinnacles are scaled, gorges entered, and cross-chasms passed. These do not have to be bridged. Since there is no rainfall and no snow-slides from the distant peaks, the abysses are filled in and ballasted for the roadbed. Besides the long via-duct at Arequipa and a bridge across the gorge at Sumbay, there are no bridges on this railroad, hardly any culverts, and no long tunnels. The earth's surface is igneous soil, ridges of lava and plains of pumice stone. In some places the lava bowlders stand out in isolated, grotesque forms, the play of the fancy to name them. I amused myself for an hour in this manner. The sulphur deposits ought to have a distinct commercial value. There is brimstone enough for a continent.

The railroad, in the parlance of the South, "coons" the ridges at a maximum grade of 4 per cent. A gentle slope is reached, and we are on the edge of a plain intersected with clear streams over which hover many beautiful species of water-fowl. I have not seen elsewhere so great a variety. The pampa has some coarse grass and mosses, but no fir brush or even cactus. Patches of melting snow diversify it. Droves of llamas, alpacas, sheep, and even the rare vicuñas with their ruddy skins are seen; the latter seem to me more like red deer. The sun is bright, and though the air is sharp the cold is not penetrating; when the train pauses, one can step out on the platform without shivering.

A hill covered with brown bowlders in the background, rounded and sloping mountains a little farther away, an ordinary railway station house, some huts close by with groups of Indian women and children huddled in the doorways, and the sign-post says, "Crucero Alto — 14,660 feet." It is High Crossing, the summit of the Divide. From Vincocaya, at a height of 14,360 feet, to Crucero Alto, the distance is 20 miles, and the approach to the summit is so gentle that it scarcely is perceptible as an upgrade.

Several of the passengers have been complaining for an hour of headache and nausea, the unmistakable *siroche*, or mountain sickness. They tell those of us who are exempt that they always have it at this point. They are relieved when the descent has been begun. The railway follows through many turns and twists along the flanks of volcanic precipices until a chain of lakes lying in the basin breaks on the view, — a fine sight, the placid surfaces soothingly suggestive for irritated nerves and rebellious stomachs. No more *siroche!* These mountain mirrors are Lakes Saracocha and Cachipuscana, 13,600 feet above sea-level, 1,000 feet higher than Lake Titicaca. The smelter for the silver mines is located at Maravillas in this lake region.

At Juliaca the branch road runs off to Sicuani, 87 miles away, whence a cart-road, now traversed by a traction automobile, continues to Cuzco, the historic Inca capital and still the seat of all that is most interesting in Peru, both in ruins and in whatever relates to the descendants of the Incas. Ancient Cuzco's future as a modern city will commence when it becomes a station between Buenos Ayres and Lima on the Intercontinental Trunk Line. An important step in this development was taken in 1905, when the government contracted with the Peruvian Corporation for the extension of the line from Sicuani and the first section, as far as Checcacupe, was finished. The route is along the river Vilcanata through a populous and well-cultivated valley, where the products of the temperate zone abound. There are rich tributary districts which will be benefited by the lowering of freight rates, and encouragement also will be given to immigration through the easier access to Puno and Mollendo.

The station of Tirapata is the starting-point for the Santo Domingo gold-mines in the Province of Carabaya, which have been developed by an American company, the Inca, composed of California miners and Pennsylvania oil-men. Some of the ore runs $4,000 to the ton. The journey to the mines occupies five days. The company, in opening up a through line of communication to the railway, has accomplished some daring engineering work in building cable suspension bridges across the chasms. They are narrow, and the newcomer who knows he is under

observation and wants to show his nerve, rides his
mule along the frail suspended framework and makes
a pretence of looking with unconcern into the gaping
abyss.   But after one demonstration of his physical
bravery he usually develops moral courage enough
to get off and lead the animal.

The mining company has extended its operations
and has acquired privileges of rubber exploitation
from the Peruvian government.   Under the contract
it opens roads and mule trails into the forest region,
and receives land grants and rubber concessions in
compensation.   Ultimately a route will be opened to
the head-waters of the Inambari River, and this district
will add to the output of crude rubber through the
port of Mollendo.

The opening of the river basins of the Inambari
and the Madre de Dios is essential to the future
traffic of the Southern Railway.   In a message to
Congress in 1905 the President of Peru stated that
the bridle-paths and cart-roads under construction,
or contracted for, aggregated 1,300 miles.   A grant
of 2,000,000 acres of land was authorized with the
chief purpose of securing 200 miles of wagon-road.
Besides the American syndicate a Peruvian company
has extensive rubber interests along the left bank of
the San Gaban.   There are extensive gold washings
in Carabaya and Sandia.   Heretofore the rubber product of this region has followed the river courses till
the Amazon was reached and it could be exported to
Europe by way of Para, the time occupied in getting
it to market being from six to eight months.   By
the cart-roads to Tirapata, ten to twelve days are
required, and three days more by railway to Mollendo,

Ruins of an Inca Fortress at Cuzco

whence the transit to Europe after the completion of the Panama Canal may be made in thirty days or less.

From Juliaca, a distinctively Quichua Indian collection of adobe cabins, to Puno, the railway line is again straight up and down over the mountains, cooning the ridge once more, till the road begins to follow the more crooked courses of the waterways. It winds through a rich agricultural district, plain and valley where there are many pretty farms. The live-stock industry seems to be a flourishing one, for there are great herds of sheep, alpacas, llamas, and some cattle.

Puno, on the shore of Lake Titicaca, is 12,540 feet above sea-level. It is a town of blue buildings lying in the concave side of the mountain. It is the head of the Department, has a population of 5,000, and is the customs port and the commercial centre. The vigilance of both Peruvian and Bolivian customs officials is constantly exercised to prevent contraband trade in alcohol, of which the people are inordinately fond. Indian life is seen in many phases, especially on Lake Titicaca, where the natives with their balsas, straw boats with square grass sails and grass hoods that open and shut like an umbrella, lead a half-shore, half-sea life, fishing and trading. They did not seem to me an idle class, but rather good-naturedly willing to work if the labor were not too strenuous.

Lake navigation begins at Puno, and since the place is the terminus of the railroad the shipping causes an unusual degree of activity for an inter-Andine town. Bolivian commerce comes up the Desaguadero into Lake Titicaca or directly across from the terminus of the Bolivian Railway line at Guaqui. The lake is

interesting because it is the highest large body of
fresh water on the globe that has steam navigation,
but I saw no evidences of the peculiar properties
attributed to its waters. The captains of these little
steam-vessels are either Scotchmen or Scandinavians.
I learned to my discomfort that when the winds were
blowing Titicaca could become as unruly as Lake
Michigan and could cause sea-sickness. A daring conception of engineering genius is to tap the waters of
Lake Titicaca for the purpose of securing electric
power and utilize them to supply motive force for the
railways.

Puno formerly had a considerable trade in the highly
prized vicuña rugs which are brought there by the
Indians, but the industry has lagged in recent years
due to the scarcity of the skins. A Chilean established a factory at Arica, and most of the pelts are
carried across the Cordilleras to his market. The
mineral deposits of the district include silver, mercury,
copper, lead, and bituminous coal. The latter is lignite, but the existence of coal-oil or petroleum appears
to be well established. The Americans who control
the Santo Domingo mines had arranged to sink wells,
but the failure to secure satisfactory transportation
rates from the railroad company caused them to give
up their project.

CHAPTER VIII

THE REGIONS AND THEIR RESOURCES

*Topography a Key to Economic Resources — Coast, Sierra, and
Montaña — Cotton in the Coast Zone — Piura's High Quality — Lima and Pisco Product — Prices — Increase Probable
— Sugar-Cane as a Staple — Probability of Growth — Rice as
an Export and an Import — Irrigation Prospects — Mines in
the Sierra — Geographical Distribution of the Deposits — Live-
Stock on the High Plains — Rubber in the Forest Region —
Iquitos on the Amazon a Smart Port — Government Regulations for the Gum Industry.*

TO know the topography of Peru is to understand
her economic outlook. The key to her industrial growth and to the mastering motives of her national policy is found in the knowledge of the three
zones into which the country naturally divides itself.
A lesson in physical geography is a study of the Peruvian aspect of the Panama Canal.

The zones are the Coast Region, relatively 1,500
miles in length, varying in width from 20 to 80 miles,
and extending from the foot of the Coast Range to
the Pacific; the Sierra, or Cordilleras of the Andes,
including the vast table-lands, averaging 300 miles in
breadth; and the misnamed Montaña, or mountain
region, actually the land of tropical forest, and plains
extending from the eastern slope of the Andes to the
Amazon basins. The settlement of the boundary
disputes with Ecuador, Colombia, Brazil, and Bolivia
may reduce the 500,000 square miles of territory

which Peru claims as her area, yet when the limits finally are fixed this trans-Andine region will still comprise more than one-half the total extent. Its wealth is in rubber and the varied products of tropical agriculture. The Sierra, in the future as in the past, is for the minerals, with alpaca wools and live-stock as an agricultural addition.

The Coast Zone is for tropical and temperate products. The principal ones are the vegetable family, — beans, potatoes; the cereals, — wheat, corn, oats; grapes and the generality of fruits; rice, tobacco, sugar, and cotton. Except in reference to two great world staples, they may be viewed almost solely in the light of domestic consumption. Sugar and cotton are on a different plane.

Peruvian cotton production cannot become large enough to affect the world's markets, yet it may be a gain to the national wealth in the quantity which can be raised for export and also for the domestic spindles. The sands of Piura which stretch from the coast at Paita back to the Cordilleras have in them possibilities that are yet barely dreamed. The cotton tree of Piura amazes the beholder when he sees it in all stages of production, — in bud, in fleecy blossom, and in seed. The quality surprises the expert. It is finer than the finest Egyptian and is equal to certain grades of wool. It is known variously as vegetable wool and as wool cotton. Irrigation is employed to a limited extent. One ambitious scheme which was to bring 60,000 acres under cultivation was stopped for lack of capital. In the Chira valley between 90,000 and 100,000 acres will be utilized for production when a canal 56 miles long is completed, and the crop will be increased by

50,000 bales. An American company experimented on a project of watering the Piura lands by means of pumps to be driven by electric power from the river Quiros. The native field-labor in this region is reliable, and probably is as efficient as that of the negroes on a Mississippi plantation.

Cotton of good quality is raised in the central district of Lima and in the southern region of Pisco and Ica. While rains are not common in these districts, the fogs at certain seasons are heavy enough to be accounted rainfall, and the moisture in the air is precipitated in quantities sufficient for the product, taken with the somewhat restricted means of irrigating employed on the plantations. The cotton plant, no longer the cotton tree as in Piura, is met with for fifty miles north of Lima, and especially in the neighborhood of Ancon. The plantations lie under and between the overlapping sand-hills, side by side with fields of sugar-cane. Cotton is also grown from the north along the river Rimac to the lower slope of the Cordilleras.

Farther south from Pisco the region extends as far as the little port of Cerro de Azul, where an excellent quality is obtained. This is sent north to Panama for transport across the Isthmus and then to Liverpool instead of through the Straits of Magellan or around Cape Horn; but the cargoes will be larger when the Canal is opened and the expense of transshipment by railway across the Isthmus can be avoided. The cotton possibilities of the Pisco region are as yet in their infancy. They will begin to unfold when the projects for irrigating the great plain of Noco are put into effect.

Taken as a whole, the advantages of Peru as a cotton-producing country are a suitable climate, the alluvial soil of the valleys, the facilities for irrigating the sandy plains, and a sufficiency of fairly cheap labor. The price of the land is a fraction of the value of similar soil in Egypt. An official publication of the government places the yield per acre at 630 pounds, of which 250 pounds is lint cotton.

The Peruvian cotton is free from boll weevil. When that pest was ravaging the Texas plantations, a thorough inquiry was made by Minister Dudley under instructions from Washington, and the universal experience of the cotton-growers established that their fields never were visited by it.

Gins for baling the product are imported both from England and the United States. Encouragement has been given the manufacturing industry in Peru by the cotton production. Some of the factories have paid fair returns, though, as in the case of Mexico, capital went into mills somewhat heedlessly and in advance of the demand which could be created for the manufactured goods. Factories, making chiefly the cheaper calicoes, are in operation at Lima, Ica, and Arequipa, where the natives prove satisfactory mill-hands. Part of the manufactures find a market in Bolivia. The total exports of the manufactured goods for a given year were $110,000, while the imports for the same period reached $2,240,000. The exports of raw cotton in the present state of production are approximately $1,500,000 to $1,600,000 annually.

What is known as the hard cotton, rough, is produced in the Piura region, and in the dry years varies from 20,000 to 30,000 bales of 200 pounds. The moderate rough, chiefly from the Ica district, amounts to 40,000 bales. The hard cotton with some of the moderate rough goes to the United States, but the greater portion of the latter is shipped to Havre and Liverpool. The production of the Egyptian, or soft cotton, is about 80,000 bales per year. It is governed by the American price, usually with a premium of 1 to 2 cents per pound over New Orleans middling. The home factories consume 25,000 bales, the bulk of the balance going to Liverpool, though Barcelona obtains 6,000 bales and Genoa 2,000.

From these figures it will be seen that the Peruvian production is about 150,000 bales, or 30,000,000 pounds. An estimate by a leading authority of the increased production when idle lands are brought under cultivation by means of irrigation is 375,000 Peruvian bales (160,000 American), or 75,000,000 pounds. Other authorities double this estimate.

Peru has produced sugar for many years, and the industry has had the usual ups and downs, but it has capabilities of increase. About 125,000 acres were under cultivation in 1905, and 25,000 persons found employment on the plantations and in the mills. Both natives and Chinese coolies form the field hands. The production for export in recent years has varied from 100,000 to 125,000 tons, and it is gradually advancing to 200,000, reflecting the decrease of the beet-sugar crop in Europe and some enhancement of the price, though that is subject to the customary fluctuations. The average production may be placed at 140,000 tons, of which between 20,000 and 25,000 tons are consumed at home.

The raw sugar exported in the period from 1900 to 1905 inclusive ranged in value from $5,000,000 to $7,000,000 annually. The by-products, particularly the *aguardiente*, or cane rum, add substantially to the value of the staple. The alcohol, in addition to the local consumption, finds a profitable market in Bolivia.

The production of sugar-cane per acre in Peru is in the proportion of 56 quintals of sugar from 700 quintals of cane. The plantations are in the valleys of the streams which flow from the foot of the Coast Cordilleras to the ocean. Though the sugar industry is an old one and though partial irrigation is employed, it is doubtful if Peru's present product is more than a fraction of what the soil can yield under universal irrigation. The cane-producing area is not confined to the coast. In the valley of Chanchamayo in the inter-Andine region are productive regions, and also in the valley of the Apurimac River in southern Peru. It may reasonably be said that within the next quarter of a century, provided the material development of the country goes forward without interruption, Peru will be producing 400,000 tons of sugar-cane, the major portion of which will be freighted through the Panama Canal to New Orleans or Brooklyn refineries at lower rates than can be had by shipments through the Straits of Magellan. Of the output some goes down the coast to Chile and some up the coast to San Francisco, a relatively small quantity around Cape Horn to Liverpool, and a large quantity across the Isthmus for transshipment to New York. The freight via the Straits is about 23 shillings per ton. The Canal is a positive factor in Peruvian sugar production.

Peru imports rice for her own consumption and exports it for foreign consumption. The great rice fields are in the north, in the Lambayeque valley, and from this district in one year 4,100 tons were exported. But much larger imports came from China. The industry is capable of development, yet chiefly with a view to local consumption. The normal expansion of this agricultural industry would appear to be in fully supplying the home demand and then in cultivation for the export trade.

Cotton, sugar, rice, — all call for an artificially watered soil. Irrigation is ancient in Peru. No new system for intensive cultivation and for ordinary crops can be expected to surpass the marvels secured by the Incas. Whether the ruins of the artificial waterworks be those still observed at Cuzco, the ancient seat of empire, or in the great passes of the Central Cordillera now traversed by the railway, or the old aqueduct at Chimbote, the wonder does not lessen. Can the moderns do as well as the ancients? They must do better. While they may not excel the Inca system of aqueducts and of packing water up the perpendicular slopes of the mountains, they may surpass them in inducing production in the arid plains. The topography and hydrography favor artesian wells in some sections and in others complete systems of irrigating ditches. The artesian wells may tap those lost rivers which, starting from the Cordilleras, dry up and reach the sea through subterranean channels. The arid tracts are fertile, probably due to the damp which is retained for a certain depth underground.

Peru has a very excellent irrigation law, the practical

workings of which are satisfactory and from which good results have been obtained. The government has given wise attention to this subject.

The future growth of the Coast Region in wealth and population may be said to be largely one of irrigating ditches and artesian wells.[1]

The treasure beds of the Andes, as they have been exploited for centuries, are in the Sierra, though the output of the precious metals in the Coast Region has been great. The Department of Ancachs, which comes down to the sea, has enormous mineral wealth. The district lies within the two Andean chains which parallel the Pacific, and which are known as the White Cordillera and the Black Cordillera, the latter being nearer the coast. Raimondi, whose studies and

---

[1] On this general subject United States Consul Gottschalk quotes C. Reginald Enock, an English engineer, as follows :

"Peru possesses a valuable element in the yet undeveloped hydraulic power which exists on both the eastern and western slope of the Cordillera of the Andes. The source of this water supply is the ice cap above the line of perpetual snow which crowns the summit of the range and the continual and exceedingly heavy snow and rain storms of the high plateaus. All along this vast chain, from Ecuador to Chile, there exists a series of lakes, practically astride the summit of the Andes, at altitudes varying from 12,000 to 17,000 feet above sea-level, and these, together with the streams to which they give rise, form the source of enormous hydraulic energy. The volumes of water which descend upon the Pacific side are not necessarily very great, but they are numerous and constant, and their fall is exceedingly rapid.

"As an example, the river Rimac, which rises in the ice cap of the Cordillera, at an elevation of more than 17,000 feet, debouches on the coast at Callao, with a course not more than 80 miles long. This river is already used as motive power for generating electricity for the railway between Lima and Callao, and could furnish constant and unlimited power over any portion of its course. Similar conditions exist, more or less, with the numerous other rivers and streams all along the 1,500 miles of Pacific littoral belonging to Peru."

A Farmhouse in the Forest Region

surveys were the basis of much subsequent exploitation, estimated that this Department could supply for export 700,000 tons of minerals annually for an indefinite number of years. Silver, gold, and copper are the chief sources of mineral wealth. In the Cerro de Pasco district, since control was secured by the American syndicate, the copper output is more important than the silver production. Yet it is doubtful whether, notwithstanding the possibilities of the nobler metals, Peru has not more to hope from coal as a new industry during the next few years and especially during and after the Panama Canal construction period, than from gold and silver.

The petroleum deposits are in the north between Tumbez and Paita, around Tolara, Zorritos, and Cape Blanco. Several of the English companies were not very successful, owing to bad management. The French company seemed to have the promise of better results. No contention is made that the oil is not there. In 1905 the output of the districts of Amotope and Tumbez was placed at 12,000,000 gallons. The supply which is now obtained is utilized as fuel on the railways and in many of the smelters. The value of the annual production is approximately $750,000.

Government data regarding mining often are tinctured with the enthusiasm of the private prospector, yet for guidance the distribution of the minerals as they are given in official publications may be quoted. I have not undertaken to present the complete statistics of production, not only because they are confusing and unsatisfactory, but also because local and temporary conditions destroyed their value as an

index of the normal output.[1]   An example of this
was afforded by the practical suspension of silver
and copper mining in the Cerro de Pasco properties
of the American syndicate until the new railroad
could be completed and the smelters built and put
in operation.   But for the prospector and the capitalist the preliminary information that is desired may
be accepted in the form adopted by the government,
that is, the geographical distribution of the minerals :

Gold — Paucartambo, La Mar, Union, Angaraes,
Cajamarca, Otuzco, Luya, Huamachuco, Arequipa,
Aymaraes, Huamalies, Carabaya, Sandia, Tayacaja,
Ica, Huanuco.

Gold Washings — Marañon, Inambari, and nearly all
the rivers that flow from the eastern side of the Andes.

Silver — Hualgayoc, Recuay, Yauli, Huancavelica,
Pallasca, Pataz, Cailloma, Castrovirreyna, Cerro de
Pasco.

Copper — Huaylas, Huaraz, Camana, Yauli, Cerro
de Pasco, Ica.

[1] The mineral output for a recent year when there was little activity
was placed at the following figures:

	Kilograms	Value in pounds sterling
Gold	1,078	145,205
Silver	170,804	580,000
Copper	9,496,583	477,000
Lead, chiefly in argentiferous minerals	1,302,365	5,141

The production of borax was 2,466 tons ; crude petroleum, 25,440
tons, and its by-products 11,639 tons.

Mercury-Cinnabar — Huancavelica, Chonta, Dos de Mayo, Puno.

Iron — Piura, Larez, Calca, Huaraz.

Sulphur — Tumbez, Paita, Chancay, Huaraz, Huarochiri, Cangallo, Arequipa, Camana, Moquegua, Tarata.

Coal — Huamalies, Dos de Mayo, Yauyos, Huarochiri, Canta, Tarma, Huaylas, Cerro de Pasco, Caylloma, Puno, Recuay.

Petroleum — Tumbez, Lambayeque, Piura, Puno.

Lead — Yauli, Huarochiri, Pallasca, Huari, Chilete (Ancachs).

The Peruvian mining-code and the corps of engineers which is maintained under it are of very great value. The annual tax on *pertenencias*, or mine claims, is 15 *soles* ($7.50), but in the administration of the law frequent complaint is made of the encouragement given to claim-jumpers. Unlike most other countries of South America, Peru lays no export tax on minerals except gold. The future of the mining industry depends so largely on cheapening and increasing the facilities of transportation, that it will be better understood in connection with the explanation of the Peruvian railway system and the plans of the government for further railroad development.

Live-stock or grazing may be said to be one of the industries of the Sierra, but in relation to the foreign commerce of the country it does not promise to be an appreciable source of national gain. Sheep-raising — alpacas, vicuñas — is of the high plains. With the increase in the population at these altitudes through mining settlements, the flocks are not likely to grow extensively. The vicuña, not being domesticated, is more apt to recede before the advance of civilization.   Such growth as the live-stock industry may have in the Cordillera region may be looked upon chiefly as a means of supplying local consumption.   The exports of hides and wool, while not necessarily stationary, do not indicate a heavy increase.   The exports of hides are $750,000 per annum, and of wools, chiefly alpacas, $2,000,000.

The world does not yet fully grasp the possibilities and limitations of the Amazon rubber production, but the Peruvian government has a proper conception of it and has enacted legislation both to secure the development of the gum forests and to preserve them from heedless destruction.   The rubber region within Peruvian territory has its main extension in the Department of Loreto and in the provinces of that interior country, but the area reaches almost to Cuzco and Lake Titicaca.   All of it is within the Montaña, or forest region.   In the Loreto district the population does not exceed 100,000 inhabitants, if it reaches that number.   The productive forests lie along the banks of the rivers.   The crude rubber that is of the best quality is known as *jebe*.   The coarser article is called *caucho*.   The *jebe* is obtained from the incisions made in the tree, while the *caucho* is the sap that is had from cutting down the tree which produces it and then extracting the milk.   It is claimed also that the rubber tree can be sown and cultivated, but for many years, or until the supply grows scarcer, this effort is not likely to be made.

It is the aim of the authorities to prevent wanton waste and to preserve the trees.   These are not allowed to be cut down.   Two forms of contract are adopted.   Under the first form the government leases to the grantees a certain number of acres for the term of ten years on condition of receiving a royalty approximately of 1 cent per pound in addition to the export duty. Under the second form it leases the rubber walks (*estradas*) of groups of 150 trees at an annual rate of about 10 cents plus another 10 cents for each 2½ acres (1 *hectare*) on which they are situated. A decree was issued in 1900, in pursuance of the law passed two years previously, fixing the manner in which the *estradas*, or rubber groves, could be located. Land in the forest region can be bought outright, can be located under rental, or acquired under contract of colonization.

Iquitos is the centre of the rubber trade for Peru, and substantially all the product now goes out from it to the Atlantic coast under the name of Para rubber; but with the completion of the central highway or transcontinental railway much of the product unquestionably will come to the Pacific coast and pass through the Panama Canal. In 1858 Iquitos was founded by the Peruvian government as a strategic outpost. In 1885, the year in which the rubber exploitation began, it was an obscure settlement. In 1905 its population was 20,000, and it was agitating municipal sanitation, electric lighting, and inviting bids for sewers. It is the third port of Peru in point of its foreign commerce, which amounts to $3,575,000 to $4,000,000. The exports of rubber from Peru for the year 1904 were $2,142,000, and they passed almost entirely through Iquitos. Since a contraband commerce is carried on in order to escape the export tax, the full production in a stated year is not obtainable. The quantity exported ranges from 1,200 to 1,500 tons each year. The exports are divided about equally between Havre and Liverpool.

When Bolivia settled her controversy with Brazil over the Acre territory, she transferred a boundary dispute with Peru. The latter country and Brazil, after some threatening passages of diplomatic arms, agreed on a *modus vivendi*, and that the extent of rubber territory belonging to each Republic should be fixed by arbitration. This dispute did not relate so much to the territory contiguous to Iquitos as to the Yavari River frontier. This basin has an annual known production of 1,500 tons and a large contraband output. The southern districts as yet are in the initial stages of exploitation. The Inambari River basin, including the Marcapata valley, is an almost virgin field.

The Peruvian government, having adopted effective measures for the protection of the rubber forests from prodigal destruction, also has sought to aid the various private enterprises by supervising the supply of labor. This is a much more difficult problem. The native Indians and the *cholos* are hardly numerous enough to meet the needs of the industry in its present state, and both persuasion and compulsion are exerted in order to force them to work. Its ultimate solution and the full exploitation of the rubber wealth of Peru must rest on the colonization of the trans-Andine region, and a gradual transformation into tropical agriculture of the districts which are not rendered unfit for habitation and cultivation by the annual high-water overflows of the Amazon's affluents. But for this river region, as for the other regions of Peru, there is no artificial aid which can compare with the Panama Canal.

CHAPTER IX

WATERWAYS AND RAILWAYS

Importance of River System — Existing Lines of Railroads — Pan-American Links — Lease of State Roads to Peruvian Corporation of London — Unfulfilled Stipulations — Law for Guaranty of Capital Invested in New Enterprises — Routes from Amazon to the Pacific — National Policy for their Construction — Central Highway, Callao to Iquitos — The Pichis — Railroad and Navigation — Surveys in Northern Peru — Comparative Distances — Experiences with First Projects — Future Building Contemporaneous with Panama Canal.

NEITHER the economic future of Peru nor the prospect of realizing the national aspirations can be understood without turning to the map and studying the waterways and the railways. The Marañon, having its source in Lake Lauricocha within the inner slope of the Central Cordilleras, flows in a northwesterly direction till about south latitude 40°, when it turns abruptly northeast. The Ucayali, receiving its initial waters farther south and east of the eastern range of the great Cordilleras, flows north until it joins the Marañon below Iquitos and the two form the mighty Amazon. Between them flows the Huallaga, smaller than either, yet a great river. It empties into the Marañon. The general parallelism of the Marañon, the Huallaga, and the Ucayali afford alternative routes from the Amazon basin to the

Pacific coast. The Huallaga was on the transcontinental trail of the early Spaniards, who crossed the mountains from Pacasmayo to Cajamarca and then continued to Yurimaguas on its banks.

The existing railroad lines of Peru extend from the coast toward the Andes, the only practicable system in the first stages of national development. The second stage is to secure a spine for these disjointed ribs by means of a main trunk line north and south — the Intercontinental or Pan-American idea — and to fill in the lacking links in rail and water transport from the Amazon or trans-Andine region to the Pacific. The intercontinental project contemplates rail connection to the shores of Lake Titicaca, so that ultimately there will be through communication with Buenos Ayres, and also the gradual and necessarily slower plan of joining railroad and water links north to the boundary of Ecuador. All of this will make for mineral development.

The rubber industry of the Iquitos and tributary territory is to Peru what the fur trade of Oregon was to the United States in the period between 1830 and 1850. The populating of the vast inlying country, the trans-Andine slopes and the river basins, means to Peru what the settlement of the Rocky Mountain region extending to the Pacific meant to the people of the United States. If the hardy pioneer class is lacking, and it is, the Peruvian national instinct is not wanting. Enlightened public men are seeking to find expression for it. Immigration, colonization, are the only means. Access, transportation facilities, ways of getting in and out, must precede colonization. Therefore the railway policy. But imperative reasons of state polity require that the development shall converge from the Amazon toward the Pacific instead of from the Continental Divide toward the Atlantic. Hence the inestimable value of the Panama Canal as an incentive, a stimulating cause, an influencing factor in the national advancement. It fixes the Pacific coast as the unchanging goal toward which all Peruvian industrial growth must tend.

It is desirable to have an intelligent grasp of the present railway systems of Peru, their management, and their bases of extension. The total length is about 1,400 miles. Most of them are of the standard gauge of 4 feet $8\frac{1}{2}$ inches, and with few exceptions they are the property of the State. However, substantially all of them are operated by the Peruvian Corporation of London under the sixty-five years' lease executed by the government in 1891, when the English bondholders assumed the foreign debt and took over the railways in compensation. This was the substance of the contract that relieved Peru from a crushing burden, though it also entailed heavy responsibilities which were viewed with misgivings that afterwards were justified. The contract included huge land grants, a practical monopoly of the guano deposits for a long period, exclusive rights of navigation on Lake Titicaca, and freedom from burdensome taxation.

Some of the provisions in this agreement were very evil for Peru, and some were bad for the bondholders. Always it will be a subject of controversy whether the government or the Peruvian Corporation has been most at fault in the non-fulfilment of the conditions. The disinterested observer must admit that both have been to blame. Both entered on obligations which they could not meet, — the Peruvian government to pay annually £80,000, or approximately $400,000, to the corporation; and the corporation to make important extensions of the railways, particularly toward the Amazon, and to plant colonies. For the latter purpose it received a grant of 1,100,000 *hectares*, 2,750,000 acres of land, in the fertile Chanchamayo valley.

The corporation taunted the government that but for its lease of the railways they would have been abandoned and have become nothing more than trails over the mountains. On its part the company was as monumental an exhibition of English incompetence and mismanagement as can be found in foreign lands, where there are so many monuments of incompetence made possible by confiding English investors and dull-witted London directors. When the disagreements with the government got acute, its officers exerted themselves principally to blacken Peruvian credit in London and to keep other capital out. Their success for several years was satisfying to the resentful sentiment of the managers and stockholders, if not profitable to their pocketbooks.

The Peruvian Corporation, not on account of progressiveness of its own, but through the enterprise of the American capitalists who acquired the Cerro de Pasco mines and built the railroad to connect with the line to the coast, and whose industries are furnishing it with traffic, began to earn money. Nominally it represents a capital of $100,000,000. While this capital is inflated, in the new and improving conditions of Peru there is a prospect for earning a reasonable return on the actual value of the leased railways. The corporation and the government have reconciled some of their differences, and the remaining ones may be compromised and the coöperation which is so essential be secured.

I have noted that the physical feature of the Peruvian railway lines is their general direction from the coast straight to the Andes, and that the policy of the government is to supply them with a backbone by filling in links along the intercontinental location and to extend the transcontinental outshoots so as to secure the through rail and water outlet from the Amazon to the Pacific. Definite measures of legislation have been adopted in furtherance of these plans. The law passed in 1904 with the purpose of encouraging foreign capital, set aside the proceeds of the tobacco tax to the amount of $1,000,000 annually after 1905 as a guaranty for capital invested in railway building. The returns do not indicate that the income from tobacco will reach this amount for some years, yet the value of the legislation in establishing a fixed railway fund is very great.

The government took energetic measures, and the extension of the existing line from Oroya to Huancayo was assured, as also the one from Sicuani to Cuzco. That leaves between 300 and 400 miles to be built across savagely broken country from Huancayo to Cuzco, in which the engineering difficulties are serious. But while it is ultimate rather than immediate, the closing up of this section is inevitable, and though the local traffic will not pay the government can afford to aid the enterprise just as the United States government helped the transcontinental lines by subsidies and bonds. The impetus given to railway building in Bolivia which insures through connection from

Lake Titicaca to the border of Argentina makes it imperative that Peru, for strategic reasons of the greatest significance, shall reach Titicaca in time to become linked with the general system.

The extension of the line from Oroya south to Huancayo, the first dozen miles of which was coincident with the other railway construction, insures the progress of a very rich section. Well-populated valleys rich in agricultural products are traversed, while mineral veins, especially copper and coal, are tapped. The famous quicksilver mines of Huancavelica are in this zone. The region as a whole, from the variety of its climate, offers encouraging prospects for immigration. The valley of Jauja is one of the most inviting fields for irrigation that is to be found within the limits of Peru.

Routes from the Amazon to the Pacific are many. The one which promises the earliest realization is that known as the Pichis, or the central highway. When the contract was made with the Peruvian Corporation, this was one of the proposed extensions in which the greatest faith was felt, and the enormous land grant was chiefly to insure its construction. Disappointment at the failure to carry forward this line was one of the causes of the resentment of the government toward the corporation and of the friction that followed. The surveys and explorations of Arana, Werthemann, Tucker, Wolfe, Barandiaran, Father Sala, Carlos Perez, and others, showed the feasibility of navigation from Iquitos to the Pichis, a total distance of 900 to 1,000 miles according to the river courses followed. Navigation was established. Then came the greater problem of climbing the clinging eyebrow

VIEW OF OROYA, THE INTER-ANDINE CROSSROADS

of the Eastern Cordilleras through untried passes and scaling mountain walls to the *puna*, or table-land.

Plans formed during the term of President Prado in 1879 were inaugurated by President Caceres, and under the administration of General Pierola in 1896 the government undertook to open communication from the terminus of the present road at Oroya to the Pichis. The central highway was laid out and made passable for man and beast. "The mule path grows to a trodden road" — but not in the Andes. For much of the distance the highway meant only a trail, yet a way was opened chiefly through the genius of the Peruvian engineer, Joaquin Capelo. It was enormously expensive, especially since, on account of the controversies with the Peruvian Corporation, the government made a detour to avoid crossing the lands granted to that company, and by pushing straight up the steepest mountain-sides ignored the engineering basis of road-making.

The history of the central highway has been written by Señor Capelo and other Peruvians. It is a brilliant chapter in hardy enterprise. Like so many State projects, the full benefits were not reaped immediately, and much costly engineering work was allowed to fall into disuse. But in spite of misuse and disuse the achievement stands out that the Pichis road was opened and communication with the Amazon established. This helped to preserve and strengthen the national spirit when the territorial integrity was threatened by the abortive movements for the separation of Iquitos and the Department of Loreto.

The methods of locomotion employed and the means

of following the central highway from Lima to Iquitos are given below:

ITINERARY FROM LIMA TO IQUITOS

Method of travel	Place of transit	Days	Total distance from Lima in kilometres
By railroad .	Lima to Oroya	1	206
" horse . .	Oroya to Tarma	1	236
" mule . .	Tarma to Huacapistana	1	280
" " . . .	Huacapistana to La Merced . . .	1	314
" " . . .	La Merced to Vista Alegre	1	348
" " . . .	Vista Alegre to Tambo Enenas . .	1	390
" " . . .	Enenas to Tambo kilometro 93 . .	1	432
" " . . .	Tambo kilometro 93 to Azupizu . .	1	482
" " . . .	Azupizu to Puerto Yessup	1	524
" canoe . .	Puerto Yessup to Puerto Bermudez .	1	544
" steamer .	Puerto Bermudez to Iquitos	7	1,500
	Total	17	2,044

In English terms the distance is 1,265 miles. The return journey requires five days more, as it is upstream from Iquitos to Port Bermudez. Variations of this route are possible. With a through railway from Lima to Port Bermudez, Victoria, or other navigable point, and the improved navigation which will follow, the time will be ten days. A telegraph line extends from Lima to Bermudez, and an irregular postal service is carried on with Iquitos. Under present conditions the traveller who makes the entire trip is rare, and there is no through traffic. Officials who may be ordered from Lima to the Department of Loreto prefer to make the trip by steamer from Callao to Panama, 1,570 miles, by rail and steamer to New York, 2,030 miles, by steamer from New York to Para at the mouth of the Amazon, 3,000 miles, and up the Amazon, 2,300 miles, to Iquitos. A journey of 8,900 miles in order to cover a distance of less than 1,300 miles is the most graphic illustration that can be given of the compelling force of through rail and water communication on the part of Peru with its Amazonian territory. It also is an example of the prospective advantage of traffic by the Panama Canal route, since the productive and undeveloped region of the Ucayali basin rivers is nearer to the Pacific than to the sources of the Amazon.

The route traversed by the central highway with some modifications is feasible for a railway. The government recognized this, and under the authority conferred by the law of 1904 put surveyors in the field to determine which is the most practicable and cheapest in the engineering sense of several alternative routes. The reasonable belief is that the distance to be covered need not exceed 250 miles, at a maximum cost of $10,000,000. The calculation made by Monsieur A. Plane, the representative of French commercial societies who studied the region with a view to determining the prospective capacity of the rubber production, was $13,000,000.[1] But this was a general estimate and not an engineering reconnaissance. While it would not pay at once as a commercial proposition, he believed that the government would be justified in undertaking it. Some of the estimates have been as low as $7,500,000. Unquestionably the Peruvian government can afford, though not in a short period, to spend $10,000,000 or $11,000,000 to secure this connection to the forest

---

[1] Le Perou, par Auguste Plane, Paris, 1903.

regions and the development of the rubber and other resources which lie there. The rich Chanchamayo valley is within the zone of productive tropical agriculture and offers an incentive to colonization. The settlement of the boundary dispute with Brazil regarding the frontier territory is a further motive for securing transportation facilities for that portion of the region which may be conceded to Peru, and for improving the unsatisfactory navigation of the Ucayali and its tributaries.

When the government took measures for bringing the Pichis line within the sphere of early realization, representatives of the northern Departments sought to secure similar advantages for their localities which had been reconnoitred by Von Hassel and other explorers. Various surveys were ordered, and concessions in force were amplified.

A project related to the central highway is that which contemplates prolonging the short spur of railway which runs from Chimbote so that it will reach Recuay, 137 miles from the coast, and then some point on the Cerro de Pasco line. The mineral deposits which exist along this proposed route include anthracite coal, and are exceedingly rich, but heretofore they have not been alluring enough to draw the full amount of the capital needed for the railroad construction. When the central highway is converted into a railroad, the connection of Cerro de Pasco with Recuay will be more easily secured, and the Amazon region and the Ucayali basin may obtain an outlet to the seaboard through Chimbote as well as through Callao. Another route which has received official sanction is from Cerro de Pasco to Huanuco and beyond, following the course of the river Huallaga along the Pan-American location.

An American company, the Pacific, which had valuable mining and railway concessions in the North, and which among alternative routes had made engineering reconnaissances for a line from Pacasmayo through to the affluents of the Amazon, secured additional exclusive privileges of navigation and exploitation of the rivers.[1] However, the selection of Paita as the seaport is more probable, and the government authorized a liberal law for this location, though the terms did not carry a financial guaranty. The project of a railway from Paita to the Falls, or Pongo of Manserriche, has captivated the imagination of the explorers and engineers who have reconnoitred this route to the Amazon, and who have foreseen the certainty of an outlet to the Pacific as one result of the Panama Canal. Large vessels navigate the Marañon 425 miles above Iquitos.

The railroad necessary to connect the Pongo de Manserriche or Borja with Piura and Paita would be less than 400 miles. The extension of cotton cultivation in Piura might prove of more utility in securing the railroad than the iron ore deposits, the commercial value of which capitalists may distrust. An advantage of this route is that the engineering difficulties are not serious, and the highest pass to be surmounted is not more than 7,200 feet. By one survey the Marañon

---

[1] Under the terms of the concession the Pacific Company was given the right to construct branch lines north to Ecuador and south to latitude 10°, along with trading and water rights on the Amazon and its tributaries. Construction of the railroad lines was to begin in 1907 and to be completed within ten years.

is 310 miles from Paita, though this is at a point above the Falls of Manserriche, the power from which it is proposed to utilize for electric traction. The railroad now covers the distance from Paita to Piura, and leaves the following distances along the proposed location :

	MILES
Piura to Vinces	30.0
Vinces to Chalaco	30.0
Chalaco to Cumbicus	19.5
Cumbicus to Huancabamba	27.0
Huancabamba to Tabaconas	30.0
Tabaconas to Tambo-botija	25.5
Tambo-botija to Perico	34.0
Perico to Jaen	42.0
Jaen to Bellanista	12.0
Total	250.0

Whenever this rail connection from Paita to the navigable waters of the Marañon shall be made, Iquitos will be at least 1,000 miles nearer to New York by way of the Pacific and the Panama Canal than by the Amazon and the Atlantic.

Other tentative locations are one from the port of Eten through Jaen to Bellanista on the Marañon, about 240 miles, and from Salaverry via Cajamarca to Balzas on the Marañon, 200 miles. From through Suchiman to the Huallaga River are several trails which make the distance about 185 miles. From Pacasmayo several engineering reconnaissances have been made. One of these through Cajamarca reaches the Marañon at Balzas over a route which is asserted to be only 138 miles in length. Other routes vary from 140 to 150 miles. But it is to be remembered that Balzas is farther than Bellanista above the Falls of Manserriche, that is to say, above the waters of the Marañon open to steam navigation.

It may be that the waiting for the full fruition of the Peruvian waterway and railway projects will be a long one. The public men who are guiding the policy of the nation in the present progressive channels will have their spells of dejection, and the checks, and discouragements will cause periods of doubt. That is the history of most countries in their measures for material development, but it more especially is the history of Spanish-American republics. The Southern Railway, which was to cross the volcanic Cordilleras and reach Lake Titicaca, was long a dream. Then the enterprise took form, was abandoned, reinaugurated, halted, and finally the government pushed a line of rails through the desert to the town of Arequipa. After Arequipa was reached came the longer and more formidable extension to Titicaca. But in time the work was done.

The Central Railway, the Oroya, was a huger task. Henry Meiggs carried it forward, with reckless confidence and superb courage, half-way up the gigantic Cordilleras, and died. Destructive war came. Peru was prostrate amid industrial ruins and political chaos, yet the forces of recuperation were not dead. After years they were vitalized. The Oroya line was pushed through to the mining-region for which it was meant to be the outlet, and there only remains the extension, in the face of lesser engineering and commercial obstacles, to the navigable waters which reach the Amazon. The Southern and the Oroya roads were contracted for in the times of riotous national wealth, the era of the guanos and the nitrates, when the saying " As rich as a Peruvian " was the common way of describing the opulence of the country and its favored classes. They were built extravagantly, as national luxuries.

Future railways can have none of this profuseness. They can be had only by husbanding the revenues; by strict retrenchment, even parsimony; by outrunning at hardly more than a hare's pace the industrial and commercial development of the country in order that greater growth may follow. But they can be built for sound economic conditions, and patriotic reasons are their basis. If not simultaneous, their construction at least may be contemporaneous with the Panama Canal.

CHAPTER X

THE PEOPLE AND THEIR INCREASE

Density of Population in Time of the Incas — Three Million Inhabitants Now Probable — Census of 1876 — Interior Country Not Sparsely Populated — Aboriginal Indian Race and Mixed Blood — Fascinating History of the Quichuas — Tribal Customs — Superstition — Negroes and Chinese Coolies — Immigration Movements of the Future — Wages — European Colonization — Cause of Chanchamayo Valley Failure — Climatic and Other Conditions Favorable — An Enthusiast's Faith.

IN the times of the Incas the territory which is now Peru supported a dense population. The vestiges which remain of the intensive cultivation of the land show that it must have sustained a very large number of inhabitants. This population extended from the Sierra and its sides to the coast, and took little account of the forest region stretching to the Amazon. The enumeration made by the Spanish colonial officials in 1793 has little value as a basis of estimating the increase, because it was not limited to the present Peru. It is interesting only as showing that out of a total of 1,077,000 inhabitants there were 618,000 Indians, 241,000 *mestizos*, 136,000 Spaniards, and 82,000 negroes and mulattoes. Another estimate made at that period was of 1,250,000 persons.

It is difficult to figure out that the population of Peru at the end of 1905 exceeded 3,000,000 to 3,250,000, though an estimate of 4,000,000 was

attributed to the Geographical Society of Lima a few
years ago. The last census was taken in 1876. It
gave a total of 2,673,000 persons. The enumeration
admittedly was deficient, and an open question was
whether the semi-civilized tribes in the trans-Andine
region had been underestimated or overestimated. In
subsequent years the Province of Tarapacá was ceded
to Chile, and Peru suffered not only the losses caused
by the war with that country, but also from the complete industrial prostration which supervened and from
the intestine struggles of the revolutionary factions.

Only within the last decade a basis of normal growth
of population may be said to exist, and, with reference
to the natural increase, the high rate of infant mortality both in the cities and in the Sierra has to be kept
in mind. A long period of comfortable existence and
of hygienic education must elapse before this mortality
will be sensibly diminished. In many communities the
birth rate and the death rate are evenly balanced,
while there are districts in which the grave claims
more than the rude cradle.

By the national census of 1876 Lima had 101,000
inhabitants. In November, 1903, a municipal count
fixed the population at 131,000. Lima has received
the cream of the immigration in recent years, and has
drawn to itself all the floating elements. The smaller
coast cities have shown no such growth, while in
the interior the towns appear almost stationary as to
their inhabitants. If the rate of increase were 30
per cent for the whole country, as with Lima, and if
the census of 1876 could be accepted as a safe basis
of calculation, the total population to-day would be
approximately 3,500,000. The notable increase of

Peru's foreign trade in recent years is evidence of improved consumptive capacity, due to industrial prosperity, rather than of an increased number of consumers. It came too swiftly to be accounted for by the growth in population, and therefore does not support the theory of upward of 3,500,000 inhabitants.

I have taken into account the statement of travellers in the interior, who have found the people more thickly distributed than they had thought. Two young Americans, Messrs. Whitehead and Peachy, who in 1902 travelled through northern Peru to the Amazon, encountered a relatively dense population. The engineers who in 1895 made the Intercontinental Railway Survey from the border of Ecuador to Cuzco, calculated the number of inhabitants along the route to be 482,000, substantially in agreement with the national census and with no signs of a marked increase. The location was through the Sierra and directly on the line of many of the most populous Andine towns. Engineers for private companies who made a reconnaissance of a route along the left bank of the Marañon, were surprised to find every little stretch of plain or valley between the glaciers occupied and cultivated by an Indian family, yet when they came to estimate the aggregate of the inhabitants the total was not a large one. This inter-Andine population may be numerous enough to justify the belief that the census of thirty years ago was not wide of the mark, but it is impossible to find grounds for the assumption of an increase of 30 per cent since then. The population of Peru at the beginning of the Panama Canal epoch reasonably may be placed at 3,250,000.

In the enumeration of 1876 the estimate was that of the inhabitants 57 per cent were pure Indian, 23 per cent *mestizos*, and, except for a fraction of negroes, the remaining 20 per cent was Caucasian, chiefly Spanish. The aboriginal proportion is now smaller than it was thirty years ago, since European immigration has added to the white population, and the mixed blood also has been augmented.

There is no more fascinating history than that of the Quichuas, the aboriginal population of Peru which still survives. The distinctions are yet marked between this basic race and the races which were subjected, such as the Yuncas, who dwelt in the northern part and along the coast and whose language is still spoken by their descendants. Some of the tribes around the shores of Lake Titicaca are not of pure Quichua descent, being sprung from the rival race of the Aymarás, while in the forest region the Chunchos and others of the uncivilized tribes have little of the Quichua traditions or customs and speak dialects of their own. But the great mass of the population of Peru to-day is Quichua. The Spanish and other intermixtures which have produced the *cholos*, or half-breeds, have had four centuries to work out the blood mingling, and the *cholo* in every community is very easily distinguishable from the pure Quichua.

The Quichua is of the soil. Under the Incas the communal system of land cultivation prevailed, and the natives, even in the loftiest recesses of the mountains, were agriculturists. They found means to irrigate the most barren spots. On the plains and valleys they cultivated the land. The fondness for

GROUP OF PERUVIAN *CHOLOS*

the freedom of the country still survives, and many of them prefer this life to being grouped in villages.

On some of the great haciendas the crops are apportioned on shares almost as in the times of the Incas. The natives are born shepherds, and the pastoral life suits them. In the Cordilleras, wherever there is a pass or a valley, the cabins of the Indians are scattered about as thickly as the producing qualities of the land will permit.

Much of the work in the mines is done by the *cholos* or *mestizos*. These also are the freighters who handle the droves of llamas, burros, and mules that bring the ore from the mines and take back the supplies. On the coast the population might be called chiefly *cholo*, for here the intercourse with other races has made the conditions different from those in the Sierra.

In the forest region the tribal customs are observed almost as before the Spaniards came. Many of the tribes are still restricted to bows and arrows, and as they are hostile to the government and accept its rule unwillingly, the authorities take pains to see that they are not encouraged in procuring fire-arms and learning the use of modern weapons. The marriage relation is primitive, but the traditions are rigidly maintained. An Englishman who had spent some years in the basin of the Ucayali told me that in one tribe polyandry was practised. An epidemic of smallpox had left many more men than women.

The owner of an hacienda on the edge of the forest region gave me an account of the marriage customs which had prevailed almost immemorially. One instance which had come to his attention was of a girl of nine who was married to a boy of eleven. When the child-wife was eleven years old, she was a mother. The gentleman had verified this incident himself and had no question of the age of the husband and wife.

The native is deeply attached to his surroundings and does not take readily to labor elsewhere. The climate has something to do with this unwillingness to move. It has been found by experience that the inhabitants on the *punas*, or table-lands 5,000 feet above the sea-level, do not work well when taken up another 5,000 feet. They are not only homesick; they suffer from real physical illness. It is the same with those who are brought down to the lower plains. Alcohol is the worst drawback to their physical well-being and moral advancement. The coca leaf, the essential principle of cocaine, which they use as a food, is far less responsible for their lack of physical stamina than cane rum.

In many of the villages of Peru which I visited I formed an impression that the natives were further advanced than in similar villages in Bolivia and Chile. There was more cleanliness, more evidence of good order and of wise local administration. They are a brooding, solitude-loving race, though not altogether spiritless. How far they still preserve the traditions and sorrow over the Incas I do not profess to know, but their gentle resistance makes it more difficult to impose civilization on them than would be sullen opposition.

While the army is distasteful to the Indian population, and while they evade the conscription wherever possible, it is one of the strongest civilizing forces.

The discipline is good, and the change of environment also is advantageous. Obedience has been so fixed a habit of the natives since the Spanish conquest that they never think of questioning authority. As to the degree of superstition which is mingled with the nominal adhesion given by the Indian populations to the Church, I do not profess to judge.

The Peruvian government seeks to enforce a good school system, and in the larger towns and villages with some success. But on the part of the mass of the Quichuas there is still inextinguishable hostility to learning Spanish, not the less effective because it is passive. The suggestion has been made that the authorities provide a system of primary schools where Quichua shall be the language and shall be taught systematically. It is the *lingua general*, or common speech, of a large majority of the inhabitants.

At Huanuco, where a German agricultural colony was established forty or fifty years ago, the sons of the early colonists still speak German, and many of the Quichuas in the neighborhood have acquired a smattering of that language. Apparently they distinguished between the tongue of the conqueror and another strange tongue.

Under good industrial and administrative conditions a natural increase on the basis of the present Quichua and *cholo* population may be expected. More comforts of life, a little rudimentary knowledge and practice of hygienic conveniences, will help to alter the disproportion between the birth rate and the death rate. Somewhere in their nature a spark of ambition may be kindled.

The negro element in the population in Peru is

sometimes remarked by strangers. They are told that it has become thoroughly intermixed with the native race. In the early days of the viceroys, when African slavery was exploited by the two great Christian powers, England and Spain, many Africans were brought to Peru. It is thence that the name Zambo or Sambo came. They are yet called Sambos. Though the Spanish and Indian intermixture is said to be thorough, there seems to be much of the African racial identity still preserved. One day in Lima I watched the religious procession in honor of Our Señor of America. Nearly all the processionists were negroes, unmistakably so.

The Chinese coolies were brought to Peru in the fifties. They still work in the sugar plantations and the rice fields and a few of them also in the cotton fields. The coolie in the second generation, however, becomes a storekeeper and a property-owner. On some of the sugar estates the Chinese steward in the course of a few years leases the plantation and later becomes the owner. There are many wealthy Chinamen in Peru, and not all of them made their money as merchants at Lima. The policy of the government is not to encourage coolie immigration.

For the industrial and political future of which Peru dreams there must be immigration as well as the natural increase of the present native population. The potter's clay is not all at hand. Some of it must be brought in. This immigration will be along three lines, which may be called topographical or geographical, — first, on the coast; second, in the Sierra; third, in the trans-Andine country and the vast basin of the rivers that feed the Amazon. A phenomenal growth in the population of the latter region during the present generation is not probable, though it has enormous colonization possibilities which gradually will be utilized, especially with the opening up of the means of communication.   Some of them, too, are European or Caucasian possibilities, for the explorations of numerous scientists and their studies have shown that the European can live and thrive in these regions.   These climatic and similar observations may be had from a score of books giving the experiences of individuals.

In the development of its mines Peru necessarily must add to the population of the Sierra.   Mining labor now is hardly sufficient, and the preference of the natives for agriculture and for service as freighters makes the problem one of increasing difficulty.   The wages in the mines are good, varying according to locality.   In the Sierra day labor can be had for about half a *sol*, which is equivalent to 25 cents gold. The American syndicate, in building the Cerro de Pasco Railway, paid the natives a *sol*, or 50 cents, and got satisfactory returns.   But for the mining development of the future miners from Spain and Italy should supply the deficiency that will exist so long as sole reliance is placed on the natives.   They may come in considerable numbers.

Irrigation of the region between the Sierra and the coast is assured, and this is going to furnish the basis for the largest and earliest increase in population.   A portion of this increase should also come from Italy and Spain and perhaps also from Germany, for the Germans are highly successful in semi-tropical agriculture.   The Italians have been very successful in Peru in retail trade and in some of the mechanical employments, but the conditions also are favorable for them in the agricultural pursuits. The vineyards in the region around Pisco and Ica seem to afford an especially inviting field for them. By the time the Panama Canal is open the big transatlantic liners from Genoa and Naples which now come to Colon should be bringing a full quota of Italian immigrants through the waterway to the Peruvian ports.

The government has enacted liberal legislation providing for immigration and colonization, but it does not follow the theory of government-aided colonies. Its course is sound. It grants lands to private enterprises for colonization, and in the industrial plans which are now a part of its political policy there is a certainty of an increased population to be drawn from abroad. An old law authorizes an annual appropriation of $50,000 for encouraging immigration, and the passage of immigrants may be paid, but this is the limit of state aid.

Colonization plans by private enterprise received a check a few years ago, when the Peruvian Corporation abandoned its efforts. Of the total grant of 2,750,000 acres in the region of the rivers Perene and Ene and the Chanchamayo valley, more than a million acres were set aside for immediate peopling. The corporation began to attract settlers to the lands, but the movement was feeble and was not sustained. The complaint made was that instead of inviting fresh and virile European immigration it drew the dregs from neighboring countries, taking colonists who had proven their own worthlessness in the places where they first settled. The experiment was still another instance of ignorant London directors and incompetent management.

Many of the earlier colonists in this district went into coffee-growing with fair success. The climate, the soil, the slopes of the Cordilleras, all were favorable. Good crops were raised and found a profitable market. But this market was obtained at the period when Brazil was changing from the Empire to the Republic, and when through that and subsequent disturbances the supply to meet the world's demand was interrupted. When the Brazilian crop became abnormal in its productiveness, weighting the price down below the level of profitable production, coffee-raising no longer was business for the colonists in Peru. They themselves did not clearly perceive the cause of their distress. Many of them, instead of turning to other products, got discouraged and went away. But merely because of this failure there is no ground to believe that in the future colonizing movements in this region, intelligently directed by the Peruvian Corporation or by any private company, will not succeed. The climatic and soil conditions are inviting, and the only question is the means of utilizing these gifts of Nature. The entire Pichis zone is favorable to European colonization. When it is connected with the Pacific by the extension of the present railroad to Port Bermudez or some other river point, its colonization capabilities will be appreciated; for the lack of access has been the drawback. This rich region lies within 300 miles of the coast.

A similar observation may be made concerning the northern districts. From any one of half a dozen little seaports the valleys of the Marañon and its tributaries are less than 200 miles distant. But the Continental Divide lies between, and this mass of mountain wall must be pierced by the railroad. Once this is done, the immigration possibilities of northern Peru will develop rapidly.

For all this there must be faith, and resolution, and definite measures. It is not a question of settling a new land, for Peru is an old, old country. Nor is it the problem of reconstructing the ancient civilization of the Incas, or the civilization which twentieth-century iconoclastic antiquarians charge the Incas with stealing from other races. In its economic aspect the matter is simply one of getting more people into a country which has plenty of room for them.

During a stay in Lima I spent an afternoon with the Rev. Dr. Wood, a Methodist Episcopal missionary, who had been in South America for thirty years, and who had made the most discriminating study of social conditions of any Yankee living in the Andes. I came away permeated with some of Dr. Wood's enthusiasm and, I hope, with some of his devout faith. The South American continent, he declared, had been held in reserve by Providence for a time when the population of other countries would press for room and for means of subsistence. The present Peru, he thought, was easily capable of supporting 20,000,000 inhabitants in conditions of life and comfort similar to those enjoyed by dwellers in the Alps and the Apennines.

But if, in the years pending the completion of the Panama Canal, Peru by natural increase and by immigration can add 1,000,000 to her population, that modest addition will determine her industrial future. A million more people during the next ten years will mean an extra 2,000,000 in the decade that follows. The horizon does not need to be extended farther.

CHAPTER XI

PERU'S GROWING STABILITY

Seeds of Revolution Running Out — Educated Classes Not the Sole Conservative Force — President Candamo's Peacemaking Administration — Crisis Precipitated by his Death — Triumph of Civil Party in the Choice of his Successor — President Pardo's Liberal and Progressive Policies — Growth in Popular Institutions — Form of Peruvian Constitution and Government — Attitude of the Church — Rights of Foreigners — Sources of Revenue — Stubborn Adherence to Gold Standard — Interoceanic Canal's Aid in the National Development.

WHEN Professor James Bryce wanted an apt illustration of the numerous elections in the United States, he compared them in their frequency to revolutions in Peru. The comparison was not unjust. Civil wars have occurred almost as often. The bloodiest drama was enacted as recently as 1895. In that year the streets of Lima were choked with corpses and ran with the blood of brother shed by brother. No one to-day can give a rational cause for it. A few years earlier, when Peru yet was prostrate at the feet of Chile, there were revolutions and counter-revolutions.

But the seeds of revolution do run out after centuries. The soil grows barren. The soil in this case is the mass of aboriginal population, the Indians and the mixed bloods, who have known only blindly to follow one chief or another. Slowly they learned that in the revolving of rulers they were no better off. An

English monarchist repeated to me the story of an old
Indian at Chosica. He was bent with age and hard
work, was in rags and was a beggar. This was after
the Spanish power had been broken and independence
established. He came one day to the group of political chiefs who were then in control and were controlling for the benefit of themselves. They were
eulogizing Liberty and the glory of having done with
kingships. The old fellow listened and then meekly
remarked : " But, sirs, it is all the same. Under the
viceroy I was a beggar. Under the Republic and
your Honors, I am a beggar. I don't see that Liberty means anything to poor old Juan Martinez."

For the bulk of the inhabitants it has not been quite
so bad, because even the republican semblance of
government has been better training for them than the
monarchical rule. Yet in the uprisings and counter-
uprisings they were like the old beggar. Whatever
dictator was in and was promulgating high-sounding
proclamations of liberty, they were no better off than
under his predecessor. They followed one *cacique*
(chief or boss) or another, killed one another at his
behest, and then settled back in the old way. But of
late years the condition of the mass of the Indian
and mixed population has improved. I take this
statement on the evidence of discriminating foreigners, and not as a conclusion from my own observations, which were made within too short a period
to afford a basis for comparison. It is the testimony
of the Europeans that more than one ambitious
leader has been willing to lead revolt when his faction lost, but he could not get followers or dupes,
and therefore he acquiesced.

It is true also that the educated classes have become more stable and have put forth a stronger influence against political disturbances.   Yet over-credit should not be given them, for the hot Spanish blood in all of them has not been brought down to an even temperature.   This was very forcibly impressed on me during the Spring of 1903, when the presidential election was pending.   Señor Miguel Candamo, for several years president of the Lima Chamber of Commerce, was the only candidate who had a political party back of him. He had been an influential supporter of the liberal administration of President Romaña.   He was the choice of the Constitutionalists and Civilistas.   There was another aspirant whose canvass was entirely personal.   Besides the Civilistas the only important political organization was the Popular Democrats, who were supposed to represent the popular element, or the masses.   They nominated no candidate, but they sought to control the Congress.

One of their leaders, Señor A——, calmly explained to me that they would get control of Congress, would declare the election null and void, and substitute their own man for Señor Candamo.   He looked on this as perfectly legitimate politics.   Señor A—— had been educated in the United States in order to have the benefit of free government, had spent his youth there, and after returning to Peru had held important public offices.   When he was explaining to me the plans of his faction, the future of Peru hinged on the peaceful succession to President Romaña.

After Señor Candamo had been chosen for a faction which had not even proposed an opposing candidate, to seek to prevent his inauguration and put in its own man — who never had made even a pretence of seeking the suffrage of the electors — meant to precipitate, if not actual revolution, a condition fully as bad. It meant to destroy the confidence of foreign capital, and to take from Peru the prestige which she slowly was regaining among South American nations. It was inconceivable how a patriotic Peruvian could harbor a purpose of encouraging such a condition, and yet Señor A—— was intensely patriotic and ready to fight for his country.

The election was held, and some of the hot-heads, among whom was Señor A——, did undertake to question the result, and for a brief period the fate of Peru trembled in the balance. It was settled by the stern displeasure of General Nicolas de Pierola, the former President, himself the chief actor in many revolutions and at that time the leader of the Popular Democratic party. He told his radical followers that insurrection against the government would be treason to the nation, and Señor Candamo was inaugurated with his support.

In this incident I do not mean to lose sight of the real significance, which was that patriotism did triumph, but it was in spite of Señor A—— and a group of highly educated Peruvians, like himself, who would have revolted if they could have been sure of enough followers. It showed that Peru's educated classes were not yet educated to the point where they alone could be trusted with the destinies of their country, but that the bulk of the population, this common clay, was acquiring a conservatism which insured the future. Let hard times come and there may be some discontent among this mass, yet it will not be moulded

to the ambitious purposes of selfish leaders so easily
as formerly. The national policy on which Peru has
entered is one that, by the material development which
it promises and the industrial and agricultural prosperity which its carrying out assures, is a guaranty, so
far as administrative measures can be, against economic
depression, and consequently of conservatism among
the mass of the people.

Another test came when, a few months after President Candamo's inauguration, he was taken ill and
in May, 1904, died. He had been conspicuously and
honorably identified with the history of Peru, had the
confidence of the whole people, and especially of
the commercial classes both foreign and native. His
programme had been purely a civilian one. All the
political parties had been harmonized and were supporters of his administration. His death inevitably
brought on a contest for the succession. In this
struggle there was to be an alignment of political
organizations. Again Peru was approaching a crisis
which would test her stability, and show the world
whether confidence could be placed that the progressive career on which she had entered would be un-
interrupted by domestic dissensions.

Under the Peruvian Constitution a first and a second
vice-president are chosen, but the vice-president has
not exactly similar functions to that official in the
United States. The first vice-president, in the absence of the president or his temporary retirement
from official cares, discharges the responsibilities of
the executive office, and in the absence or disabil-
ity of the first vice-president the second one acts.
But in the event of the death of the Executive, the

vice-president fills the office only until an election can be called and a successor chosen. It happened in 1903 that Señor Acorta, who was chosen first vice-president, died before the inauguration. On the death of President Candamo, Señor Serapio Calderon, the second vice-president, discharged the executive functions and issued the call for the election of a new chief magistrate. If the emergency had been pressing, he could have called the Congress in extra session.

The administration between the death of President Candamo and the inauguration of his elected successor was in essence a provisional one. Judge Alberto Elmore was called from the Supreme Bench to become Minister of Foreign Affairs and president of the Council of State. By Peruvian law the nation can have the services of its jurists in political positions temporarily without the necessity of their leaving the bench permanently. I had known and esteemed Judge Elmore as a colleague in the Pan-American Conference in Mexico, and in common with other friends of Peru was reassured on reading the news that he would be at the head of the cabinet during the period of uncertainty that was to ensue. His firmness and equipoise were a pledge of public order, if not of complete tranquillity. Mr. Manuel Alvarez Calderon, the Peruvian minister in Washington, in announcing that the death of President Candamo would cause no halt in the progress of Peru, had spoken with the voice of authority.

After some delay nominations were made by the opposing political parties. The Civilistas united on Señor José Pardo as their choice, and the Constitutionalists endorsed him, he becoming the candidate of this coalition. The Popular Democrats and a political group known as the Liberals named General Nicolas de Pierola, the former President, as their candidate. His career in the stormy periods of Peruvian history for forty years had made him a leading character and he had strong influence with the masses. On his retirement from the presidency he had become the head of a business enterprise in Lima. His old opponent, General Caceres, one of the Constitutionalists, supported Señor Pardo.

José Pardo is a member of a distinguished family, one of several brothers influential in the business and politics of the country, sons of the President who founded the Civil party in 1872. He was educated for the law, and had been in the diplomatic service in Europe, but had returned to Peru and was occupied as a sugar-planter when Miguel Candamo was chosen President. He was one of Señor Candamo's active supporters, and entered the latter's cabinet as Minister of Foreign Affairs. He was generally recognized as the coming leader of the Civilistas, and was surrounded by a group of young men who were aggressive in their advocacy of civilian policies. His speech in accepting his party's nomination was singularly free from the generalities and the apostrophes to Liberty with which presidential candidates and dictators in the Spanish-American Republics are accustomed to season their discourses. Instead it was a plea for a school system, internal improvements, railways, irrigation, harbor works, fiscal reforms, and economical administration.

General Pierola also made industrial measures the leading feature of his programme.

The campaign caused anxiety, though the tension

Portrait of José Pardo, President of Peru

clearly was less than in the previous year in the period between Señor Candamo's election and his inauguration. Demonstrations by the rival political groups resulted in bad blood, there were collisions with the police in which several persons were killed or injured, and election riots after the manner of some sections of the United States. But these incidents were not numerous enough to show the existence of a revolutionary spirit, and they were dismissed with the euphemistic designation of " electoral effervescences."

Meanwhile the real electoral contest was going on in the newspapers, in meetings, and by manifestoes and addresses to the public. It soon became evident that the Civil party with Señor Pardo as its leader would triumph. The Pierolistas asked the government for a postponement of the election. This was refused on the ground that under the laws and the Constitution no authority existed for such postponement. Then the Pierola ticket was withdrawn by the Popular Democrats and the Liberals, and their followers were advised not to vote. This action was a resort to the minority method practised in Spain and her offshoot countries in America. It is an admission in advance that the other party will win.

After General Pierola's withdrawal the Civilistas and their allies exerted themselves against what in the United States is called apathy. To comply with the law and make the election valid, it was necessary to have one-third of the registered vote cast. The proportion of the ballots was much larger than that. Señor Pardo was elected in August and inaugurated in September. He formed his cabinet with young blood tempered by experience. Señor Leguia, who as his colleague in President Candamo's cabinet had been Secretary of the Treasury and had been the warm advocate of the new industrial policy, was called to the Treasury again and became president of the cabinet. Other members of the cabinet selected also had the confidence of the public. The continuance of civil administration and the dominance of civilian measures were reaffirmed, and it was shown that Peru had taken another stride toward stability by the acquiescence of the defeated party. The opposition made no effort to question the election.

Peru's growth in genuine popular institutions and the recognition of public sentiment has been shown in the caution with which the executive power has been exercised by the presidents during the last twelve or fifteen years. There has been little of the dictator either in disguise or in proper person. Under President Pardo representative government is certain to make further progress.

I have given the substance and the spirit of the government of Peru as it exists to-day, leaving only brief space for an analysis of the form. The Constitution now in force was adopted in 1860 and was modelled after that of the United States. Power is centralized, though there is a reasonable measure of local self-government or local administration. Geographical isolation of the different sections is one cause of the centralized authority. The political division of the Republic is into 21 departments, which are subdivided into 97 provinces, and these into 778 districts. The source of administrative authority in each department is the prefect, who is named by the central government. In many of the departments the prefect is an officer of the regular army. Each of the provinces has a sub-prefect, and the districts have their local rulers or governors, depending from the higher power. In the municipalities the *alcalde* is appointed, but the members of the Council are elected. The Amazon Province of Loreto has a system of administration somewhat different from the other departments. It is more under military administration. The customs administration at Iquitos also requires a close supervision by the national authorities.

The powers of the Executive are defined with clearness. They are complete, though there is something of a limitation in the Council of State and the cabinet. Members of the cabinet occupy a position midway between constitutional advisers and clerks of the Executive. The Council of State, which was created by law in 1896, is in some respects an executive body. When the cabinet is in full sympathy with the President, the Council of State is his instrument. But when this body is made up of warring political elements, the President is not always able to have his way. The system obtains of having the various political groups represented, and when there is a hostile majority in the Congress that is the only means by which the government can be carried on. Frequently it results in an administration of cross purposes. The cabinet members may be also members of the Congress, and may be summoned before either branch of that body to give explanations and may take part in the debates. The Peruvian Congress is peculiar in one respect. This is in the election of *suplentes*, or deputy representatives and deputy senators. When the election is held, it is both for members and for deputy members. Thus it happens that the Congress never need be without a quorum in either branch, and no district or department need be deprived of representation temporarily by the death or absence of the senator or representative. His deputy can be counted on to attend the sessions.

The Church is a part of the state in Peru, and has been usually an unprogressive part. The ecclesiastical organization consists of an archbishop, resident in Lima, and eight suffragan bishops for the various dioceses. The Church as an institution has opposed movements to liberalize Peru, and has instigated revolutions against reforms.

Roman Catholicism is intrenched in the Constitution, not only as the religion of the state, but by the prohibition of other forms of worship. The Protestant congregations are not numerous, and it is still necessary to call their places of worship halls instead of churches. Yet under liberal administrations no real difficulty is experienced by the missionaries who temper good sense with zeal. In remote districts the central government cannot always insure protection against local prejudices, but its authority is exerted to that end. The testimony of the missionaries themselves is that they are meeting fewer and fewer difficulties, and even in the strongholds of intolerance, such as Cuzco and Arequipa, they are able to carry on their proselyting labors without interference.

In the passing of years the Constitution of Peru will be amended so as to welcome Protestantism, though the Roman Catholic Church will remain the state church. This constitutional amendment is somewhat cumbersome, since it requires consecutive action by two Congresses in order to become effective; but the sentiment in favor of it is spreading and propositions already have been presented to Congress. Wise Protestants do not believe in urging it too rapidly. They realize that, with a succession of liberal governments and with the toleration that already is manifest, Protestantism can afford to wait and work.

The provisions of the Peruvian Constitution and the laws with regard to foreigners are liberal. Foreigners may be naturalized after two years' residence. The government at Lima through the prefects extends every possible protection to those who are travelling or who seek to engage in mining or other industries. The trouble which arises generally is with the local authorities, and Europeans or Americans who have a reasonable degree of tact and are willing to adapt themselves to their surroundings usually can make themselves *personas gratas*. Where they start in with the disposition to flaunt their foreign citizenship and to override the natives, not even the central authority can prevent local antagonisms. In four cases out of five the foreigner in Peru who gets into trouble with the local authorities has only himself to blame.

The government in the laws it has promulgated for the mining industry, for the exploitation of the rubber forests, for irrigation, and for the navigation of the waterways has sought especially to protect and encourage foreign capital and individuals. Foreigners may be members of the deputations or delegations which are provided in the mining-code, and they also may serve in the municipal councils. On the aldermanic ticket at Cuzco and other places I found English

and German names, and was told that these candidates had not been naturalized and had no intention
of being. This provision should be of particular
value in colonization movements where communities
may be established without the native Peruvians.

In relation to income and outgo there are three
sources of revenue, — general, municipal, and departmental. The general revenues are had from the customs import and export duties, from the stamp tax,
and from the internal revenues on tobacco, alcohol,
sugar, matches, and similar articles of consumption.
Salt is a natural monopoly. The departmental revenues are from the land tax (which is very light),
from the imposts on property transfers, from the inheritance tax, and from a variety of industrial sources.
The municipal taxes are obtained from local tolls, li-
censes, surveys, and like means. They are not heavy.

Somewhat curiously in this age, the collection of the
internal taxes is farmed out by the national government. A joint-stock company known as the National
Tax Collection Society, *Compania Nacional de Recau-
dacion*, by an agreement with the government collects
all these revenues and turns them in, retaining its percentage and providing loans when needed for current
purposes. The stock of this company was taken
mainly by the Lima Chamber of Commerce. There
is also in Lima a provincial tax collection association,
which takes charge of the local revenues in the same
manner that the national company collects the general
revenues. Contrary to what might be supposed, this
system works very well, and is satisfactory to the tax-
payers, while the government gets a larger return than
if it itself were the collector.

Peru is almost exceptional among the South American Republics for establishing and maintaining the gold standard. This is a brilliant and instructive chapter of financial history. The beginning was made in 1897, following the presidential election in the United States. General Pierola was President and was strongly in favor of the gold basis. Though Peru was a silver-producing country, a law was passed providing that gold should be the sole standard, that the customs duties should be thus paid, that there should be no further silver coinage, and that the ratio should be ten *soles* of silver, equal to the English pound sterling, or the Peruvian pound sterling, which is the exact equivalent in weight and fineness of the English pound and is known as the *inca*. It also was provided that silver should not be legal tender in amounts greater than $100, that no person should be permitted to bring more than ten *soles* into the country, and that the export duties on silver should be repealed.

Subsequent legislation strengthened this law, and the government by an arrangement with the banks called in and melted into bullion the redundant *soles*, itself taking the loss. There was opposition, especially in the Cerro de Pasco mining-region, where the output of silver was greatest. In the interior also the Indians, who had been accustomed to silver, could not be made to understand gold. But as they have few transactions in which a yellow coin is necessary, this was not a serious drawback. Silver enough remains in circulation, and at Arequipa and other interior commercial points gold yet can be had only by paying a slight premium. In the natural processes of commerce a considerable quantity of the minted gold of other countries is imported, the amount having reached $1,900,000 in 1903. No question exists that Peru's gold standard has been immensely beneficial in maintaining the credit of the country abroad and in facilitating commerce at home.

Paper money, either bank emissions or national notes, is prohibited by the law of 1879. The currency which was in circulation in 1881 was converted into the internal debt. This internal debt grew out of the calling in of the paper currency and the liquidation of old accounts. The total is approximately $15,000,000. A small yearly disbursement is required for its service. Part of this so-called internal debt earns 1 per cent yearly interest, and the remainder receives no interest, being provided for out of a redemption fund which amounts to $125,000 annually. The liquidation has been regularly carried on since the bonds were issued under the terms of the law of 1888. The yearly fund appropriated for interest and the sinking fund remain stationary unless increased by Congress.

In the ten years following 1895 the banking capital of Peru increased at the rate of 150 per cent, while the deposit accounts ran up from $4,500,000 to $14,000,000. The banks pay dividends of 14 to 16 per cent. Volumes might be written about the causes which are leading to the commercial and industrial prosperity of the country and contributing to the political stability. The convincing evidence of the fact is the growth in the bank deposits.

In the chapters on Peru I have sought to show something of the country and the people, of the resources and the commerce, of the economic prospects and the political conditions, for all of them must be known if the country's future is to be judged. What the joining of the Amazon to the Pacific means, what the new industrial life promises, what the governmental stability signifies, may find an answer in what has been written, for I believe in the destiny of Peru, but not an iridescent, dazzling destiny to be realized within a twelvemonth or a decade. Instead, a gradual growth to be attained by a plodding policy, sympathetic to the popular aspirations yet rock-rooted in sound principles of national progress. The Panama Canal helps to develop the Amazon section of Peruvian territory, vivifies industries, and strengthens already stable governments by contributing to their commercial prosperity. Its impression on Peru is deep and lasting, for under its beneficent influence the seeds of revolution will cease to germinate.

CHAPTER XII

ALONG COAST TO MAGELLAN STRAITS

THE emerald gem of the West Coast is Arica, a day's voyage from Mollendo. After days and weeks of rocky coast without vegetation and of the long chain of the naked Andes farther inland, the clumps of green trees and the bushy fringe of verdure along the sandy beach are a seeming paradise and a close one too. The huge cliffs which beetle over Arica do not appear so barren as those farther north, and the flat-topped hills do not limit the vision so entirely as to shut out the thread of valley which marks the line of the railway back to Tacna and the desert. On the highest hill is a great cross, but down on the level are ancient and modern windmills. The train is slowly puffing its way across the plain, while the bay is filled with rowboats and small launches. In all it is a charming, reposeful sight. The island fort at the base of the cliffs is rugged and stern, but it does not spoil the picture.

Ashore are a handsome little plaza with an elliptical enclosed plot of shrubbery in the centre, blue morning-glories and purple vine trees. Lieutenant Commander de Faramond, the French naval officer who went ashore with me, stopped to look at the flowers a moment. "Aha!" he remarked, "they have the fever here. This is the purple fever flower of Algiers. Wherever it grows you find sickness." Later I made inquiries and learned that he was correct. Arica, while a most charming spot, is peculiarly subject to malarial influences.

But a walk through the town deepens the pleasing impression. There is a well-built custom house, the sloping cobble-paved streets are clean, and the dwellings are very attractive. The latter are neat one-story structures. Some are blue as to exterior, some subdued green, others brown or orange,—a real prismatic blending. Most of them have arbor-arched entrances, and the passing view of the interior is delightful. The church is the biggest building, and at a distance it is not unattractive, though it does not improve architecturally on near approach. Glimpses of native life are afforded by the Indian women coming in from the country. Some of them are mounted astride their donkeys, while the panniers, or baskets which contain their merchandise, almost smother them. Others trudge along by the sides of their animals. The buildings in Arica are of galvanized or corrugated iron. They are of one story, so that they will not be shaken down by the earthquakes.

Arica's history has been a memorable one. Sir

Francis Drake and his sea-hawks from the *Golden Hind* who touched there in 1579, found a collection of a score of Indian huts. The earthquake record begins in 1605. The most celebrated of these convulsions of Nature was that of 1868, when the United States frigate *Wateree* was carried a mile inland by the tidal wave, and left there to become the dwelling of a number of Indian families, until another earthquake and tidal wave drew it back toward the beach without harm to the inmates. The companion ship, the *Fredonia* was destroyed.

Commerce passes through Arica chiefly for Bolivia. Mules and burros transport the freight from the railway terminus at Tacna into the interior. The imports are mining-supplies and miscellaneous merchandise. The exports are saltpetre, salt, sulphur, and some minerals. There is a shop on shore in which are sold the noted vicuña rugs. These are brought down from Bolivia. The skins of the guanaco, much coarser, are vended to unwary buyers for vicuñas. For several years the annual commerce of the port at the maximum was $1,000,000, but it will grow rapidly.

The railroad from Arica to Tacna is of the standard gauge and 39 miles long. It was among the first constructed in South America, the concession having been granted by the Peruvian government in 1851 and the line completed six years later. The aspiration then was to continue it over the pampas along the route followed by the ancient highway of the Incas and across the igneous Cordillera of Tacora to La Paz in Bolivia. A waiting of half a century was necessary before the project could be considered as tangible, but by the terms of the treaty negotiated

VIEW OF ARICA

between the Bolivian and the Chilean governments in October, 1904, it approached realization. The distance from Tacna to La Paz is about 300 miles, but the Corocoro copper mines, which will furnish much of the traffic, are 60 miles nearer to Tacna. The freight carried over this route by pack animals — mules, burros, and llamas — of recent years has not exceeded 20,000 tons annually, but in the earlier years the quantity was much larger.

When the railway from Tacna to Corocoro and La Paz is completed, the commercial importance of Arica as a West Coast seaport will be greatly enhanced. This railroad will be an artery of commerce which will bring the heart of Bolivia to the Pacific, for it will lead to and from the most populous and most productive regions of that country by the shortest and most direct route. The line will be finished long before the Panama Canal is opened, but the result will be the same. Arica is 2,200 miles from Panama, relatively 4,200 miles from New York, and less than 3,600 miles from New Orleans. To New York around Cape Horn and Pernambuco is approximately 9,500 miles. From Arica to Liverpool via Panama is 6,900 miles; by way of the Straits of Magellan is 10,400 miles. Can a doubt be entertained as to the course of the commerce which will flow without ebb through the future great port of Arica?

The afternoon on which we left Arica we had a rare privilege. It was the sunlit view of the snow-cap of the distant Mt. Tacora in Bolivia. The summit is 19,000 feet above sea-level. Though the other snow-ridges often are seen, Tacora rarely shows her ghostly face. In the late afternoon the azure mist gathered over the plain and lower mountain range; the shadows fell on the shell-like hillsides; the sun glistened on the chalky, beetling bowlders; the brown cliffs became browner; the faintest suggestion of twilight hovered for a moment; the snow-caps disappeared, and it was night and we were steaming out of the bay.

From Arica south the cliffs rise from the sea almost perpendicularly. In the morning Pisagua is sighted. This is a centre of the nitrate industry and of what remains of the guano traffic. Colonel North, the hotel-keeper who became the nitrate king, had his beginnings as a captain of industry here. The mountains come down to the sea in parallel ridges. Pisagua is like a little Pennsylvania mining-town, except that it seems likely to slide into the sea. A fearful visitation of fire and plague depopulated it in 1905.

Double-header engines drawing short trains climb the steep walls as though they were going up a ladder. After a time they wind their way to the nitrate plains and then across the dreary desert to Iquique. There is not much to be seen on the railway route, and travellers prefer to keep the ship along the sheer cliffs till Iquique is sighted through the masts of the sailing-vessels which are clustered in the harbor waiting for their cargo. Sometimes a hundred of these are gathered.

There is really no harbor, and scarcely what can be called docks, for the vessels must anchor outside and the rude breakwater is hardly more than a pretence. To get ashore the reef has to be crossed in a small boat. Upsets are frequent, and fatalities are not unknown.

Iquique is a fragile city of frame and corrugated

iron buildings. In the plaza are a reasonably tasteful monument and a pretty municipal building. There is a brown wooden church with a wooden effigy of the crucified Saviour, which is far from attractive to look at. The town has a population of 40,000. Iquique has a history which surpasses that of the bonanza mountain towns of the West in swiftness, for in the first days of the saltpetre riches nothing was allowed to be slow. It is more staid and sedate now, but the Englishmen — younger sons and some of the earlier generation — do not let life become too dull. They are terrific brandy and whiskey drinkers, showing a nice discrimination in not exhausting the wealth of the nitrate beds by taking too much soda with their brandy. There is a Country Club and a convenient *café* at Camache, just out of the town proper. An American missionary school is maintained by the Methodist Episcopal denomination. When I was in Iquique, besides the school instructors there were only two Americans. One was a mining prospector, and the other was waiting for something to turn up. But North American enterprise was threatening to invade the nitrate industry.

The municipal administration of Iquique under the Chilean authorities is excellent; that is the common testimony of all foreigners. The population which has to be dealt with is a rough and ready one; the nitrate laborers are like the miners in their rude independence, and the longshoremen and harbor workers are as burly and aggressive as the same class in the United States.

In commercial importance Iquique ranks with the leading ports of the Pacific, all due to the nitrate trade. Its saltpetre shipments about equal those of all the other coast towns, and are valued at from $28,000,000 to $30,000,000 annually. In a single year the ships entering the port, many of them sailing-vessels, aggregate from 850 to 1,200, with a tonnage varying from 1,250,000 to 1,800,000. As the nitrate beds are being worked on a more extensive scale, it is safe to assume that almost any given year in the future will disclose the presence of not fewer than 1,200 vessels in the roadstead. Since the industry is largely in British hands, the English flag is by far the most common, though the German ensign is seen with growing frequency.

It is not probable that the Panama Canal will have a marked influence, either beneficial or detrimental, on Iquique. What nitrate freight may exist by the time the waterway is ready for traffic will be governed by the conditions that obtain to-day. The saltpetre fertilizers form a bulky cargo. Part of the profits of the ocean carrying-trade lies in transporting coal from Australia or Newcastle to the Chilean coast and then taking on the nitrates. That brought from England scarcely would find it profitable to pay the Canal tolls. Nor would the distance be shortened sufficiently to secure an advantage for the nitrates as return cargo. Their ocean route, in the future as in the past, is through the Straits of Magellan or around Cape Horn, and Iquique remains an unimpaired port so long as the nitrate beds are unexhausted. Some shipments may be through the waterway direct to Charleston, to mix with the phosphates and thus fertilize the Southern cotton fields.

At various times projects have been agitated for

extending the nitrate railways in a manner to form a through line into Bolivia, but the preference given by the Chilean government to the Arica route seems to end the probability of such an enterprise. In view of the raw materials right at hand, it is surprising that neither native nor foreign capital has established manufactories of explosives.

Twenty-four hundred miles from Panama, geographically on the Tropic of Capricorn, is Antofagasta, a fair sort of town, with regular streets, rectangular warehouses, and a graveyard on the hillside. Its pride is the plaza, which has been coaxed from unwilling Nature and made to bear evidences of grass and trees. It is the starting-point of the two-foot six-inch gauge railway which runs 575 miles up into the interior of Bolivia, and brings the mining products down to the shore. The railway pays a 6 per cent annual dividend, and is said to earn more. The gross receipts are about $9,000,000 per year. Antofagasta is a shipping-point for the nitrates as well as for bullion and ores. The nitrate shipments are increasing rapidly, and promise to rival Iquique. The harbor is a wretched roadstead. To get ashore it is necessary to brave a lashing, dangerous surf. The Chilean government is promising extensive improvements. They are badly needed. When made, they will enhance the commercial importance of Antofagasta. The foreign vessels entering and clearing annually have a tonnage of 1,000,000.

Antofagasta is the centre of the chief copper-producing district of northern Chile, and also it is the outlet of Bolivian tin, silver, and copper. The reduction works built by the Huanchaca Company of Bolivia are located near here, and a large quantity of the ores are transported to these works to be treated.   It always will be their outlet, but in the future Antofagasta will have sharper competition than at present with Arica and Mollendo, as the shipping-port of Bolivian products.   The Canal will be of some benefit in lessening ocean freights, more particularly for the general merchandise imported.

Below Antofagasta is Taltal, a passably well-sheltered nitrate shipping-port.   Then the coast toward Chañaral begins to vary ; the mountains are lower, more broken and jagged, with more cross ranges.   Chañaral has copper-smelting works.

Caldera is a small town, with substantial warehouses, fronting on a big, fine bay.   It has a Panama potency, for it is the beginning of the Copiapo Railway that in time will cross the Andes and make the plains of northwestern Argentina tributary to the Pacific.   This transAndine route was the dream of William Wheelright, the Yankee pioneer railroader of Chile and the Argentine Republic, often called the father of public works in South America.   The passes are low and easily traversed, as compared with those farther south.   The gradual extension of population in the northwestern provinces of Argentina, the increase in the areas under cultivation, are followed — or, better said, are preceded — by railroad extensions.   A few years will bring her lines to the boundary of the Andes.   In the meantime the Chilean government is encouraging the prolongation of the railway from Copiapo to the dividing line of the Cordilleras.   The time cannot be far distant when Tucuman, the railway cross-roads of northern Argentina, will have rail communication with the West Coast at Caldera, and an extensive district

will be weighing the comparative advantages of the
Atlantic transport and the Pacific and Panama transport for its agricultural products and the merchandise
brought to the people who grow those products for
export.

Coquimbo is a port of considerable importance.
From the sea it is attractive. One main street extends
along the water front, while the others branch off up
the hill at right angles. There is the cemetery, somewhat suggestively prominent. A neat frame dwelling
in the seaside, peak-roofed style, hollowed out of the
hillside, and surrounded by needle-pointed pine trees,
secures attention. Coquimbo ships large quantities of
manganese and copper, and formerly a British coaling-
station was maintained.

We arrived in Valparaiso one morning late in May.
The American woman whose home it was, had prom-
ised we should see another Bay of Naples. The fogs
lifted slowly. They showed apparently a city afloat,
for the vessel masts were first visible and then the port
proper, which seemed to lie flat to the sea. Later the
skies were sapphire, yet it was not Naples. That
morning there was a celebration in honor of the arrival of the Brazilian warship *Almirante Barroso*, and the
bay was alive with small craft and stately ships, while
the people swarmed over the heights and along the
shore like ants.

Valparaiso (vale of Paradise) is the largest place on
the Pacific coast, with the exception of San Francisco,
and it is equally as fine a metropolis. Its population
is 140,000. The city lies at the foot of high hills,
which no one climbs because there are ascensors, or
elevators, as in Pittsburg and Quebec. Unhappily it

has not a golden gate and a sheltered harbor. The finest part of the city is the Avenida, or Avenue Brazil, at once shaded boulevard, business thoroughfare, and promenade.

The city has many fine business blocks of modern construction, and the government buildings are unusually tasteful and harmonious. All bear the impress of Italian architecture. The commemorative spirit finds expression in a group celebrating the heroism of Arturo Prat, the young naval commander who gained unfading laurels in the war with Peru. On the Avenue Brazil is a bust of William Wheelright, the son of Massachusetts, who provided steam navigation as well as built railways for Chile. There is also a statue to Lord Cochrane, the Scotchman who took command of the Chilean fleet in the contest for freedom from Spain and helped to bring victory. It cannot be said that Chile is unmindful of the strangers who have served her, whether in arms or in peaceful progress.

The port, as is natural, is cosmopolitan. The German colony is largest, and after that the Italians in numbers, though in influence they are hardly so strong as either the English or the French. The French community is self-contained and is an important factor in commerce. The Britishers, chiefly from Scotland, are in everything except retail trade. Though the English language is common, Valparaiso is the one city in South America in which I heard German spoken oftener.

The shipping of Valparaiso is vast and varied, a floating panorama of many nations, like a miniature Hamburg. The English lines maintain a regular fortnightly service of cargo and passenger vessels, and

Scene in the Harbor of Valparaiso, showing the Arturo Prat Statue

also a special service of cargo vessels to Liverpool.
The steamers are of 5,000 tons and upward. The
distance to Liverpool by way of the Straits is 9,500 to
9,800 miles, and the sailing schedule is 35 days. The
vessels touch alternately at the Falkland Islands,
both for mail and for the cargo of wool. They coal
at Montevideo, Rio Janeiro, and in the Madeiras.
They bring out to Valparaiso general merchandise,
and they take away products of the country.

The Bay of Valparaiso is a discouraging one. It is
surprising that so extensive a commerce can be handled
with such poor facilities. The shipping approximates
1,000,000 tons yearly. The engineering difficulties in
the way of creating a real harbor are well understood,
though not easily overcome. The rains wash the
hills down into the sea, but the detritus, or silt, does
not fill in what seems to be the bottomless bed of
the ocean, so profound is it. There is no breakwater.

At the beginning of every Winter season the question is raised, — what will be the harvest of disaster?
It seems incredible that vessels of 3,000 tons could be
lost in this bay, but that is what has happened. In
May, 1903, voyaging down the coast in the *Tucapel*,
we were told that the *Arequipa* of 3,000 tons burden
was the next ship following us. She arrived two or
three days later, and took on passengers and cargo for
the return trip. One night a savage tempest arose,
many of the smaller vessels were wrecked, and the
Arequipa foundered and went down with the loss of a
hundred lives. Two weeks later from my hotel
window I watched the wild bay and waited three days
for a chance to get off on the *Oropesa*, one of the big
ships which run between Valparaiso and Liverpool.

Smoke from the funnels showed that the large vessels were keeping steam up, and they frequently steamed out into the open to avoid the dangers of the harbor. This storm was a norther which came in a circular path from the south. The immense floating docks tossed about as if they were eggshells; the buoys bobbed like dancing water-sprites; the schooners plunged their noses into the angry breakers until the mastheads dipped; again the masts and yardarms would be as a stripped forest in Winter bending before the blasts. And the wreckage of the hurricane of a fortnight earlier was still visible,— two big schooners driven hard against the rocks, their masts under water.

In July, 1904, another destructive storm swept along the coast. The lower part of the city was completely covered with mud and water, the sea-wall was destroyed, and the railroad badly damaged. The loss of life was not great, but the destruction of property was serious.

In the period from 1823 to 1893 the shipping statistics show the loss of 378 water-craft in the Bay of Valparaiso, of which 100 were rowing and sailing boats. The money value was incalculable.

The Chilean government after many discouragements accepted the plans of Mr. Jacob Kraus, the Holland engineer, for conquering the difficulties which Nature had placed in the way of making Valparaiso Bay hospitable instead of hostile to the ships that bear the commerce of many seas. The estimated cost of the harbor improvement is $15,000,000 gold, though the initial provision was for $11,000,000. The scheme contemplates the construction of a series of sea-walls in the bay. The water is so deep that it is considered impracticable to build a single breakwater across the mouth of the harbor. It is believed that the several sea-walls constructed in the manner proposed will protect the vessels and the merchandise from the terrific seas which drive in during the storms of the Winter months. A dry dock is included in the proposition. The calculation is that the shipping of the port will be benefited annually to the extent of $1,250,000 and upward by the projected improvements. The Chilean Congress approved the Kraus plans at the Autumn session of 1904.

These harbor improvements will lay some additional charges on maritime commerce, but they can be borne in view of the increased security and the better facilities. If the Panama Canal were likely to impair the commercial prestige of Valparaiso, they would serve as a means of retaining it. Not improbably the Congress had this contingency in mind when sanction was given the government projects for making the dangerous bay a safe shelter. The only loss from vessels which will pass through the Canal instead of making the voyage through the Straits or around Cape Horn, touching at Chilean ports, will be in coaling them and providing other supplies. This is not an important factor in Valparaiso's trade. The imports and exports of the port are based on the products and the wants of the country. Its maritime movement, which is estimated at 3,000,000 tons annually, is measured by the facilities provided for this foreign commerce.

Trade with the United States grows regularly, and agricultural implements and mineral oils, which are

13

among the chief imports, will pay the Canal tolls and still have cheaper ocean transport from New York or New Orleans than down the Atlantic and up the Pacific. It is not an unreasonable assumption that for a proportionate share of the merchandise imported from Great Britain 9,500 miles' water carriage from Liverpool through the Straits of Magellan may be offset by 7,800 miles via Panama plus the Canal tolls and other commercial considerations. The same holds true of Hamburg and the trade with Germany.

On two visits to Valparaiso I found that the shipping interests were not worrying over a dimly prospective loss of commerce through the construction of an isthmian waterway. Instead they were looking forward to it as an incentive to making the bay a genuine harbor, and as a stimulus to closer trade relations with the United States. That appears to be a sound interpretation of the economic relation of the Panama Canal to the port of Valparaiso.

After leaving Valparaiso one feels the pertinence of the suggestion that far enough south the Pacific is not always pacific. The sea is not excessively rough, yet it heaves and rolls uncomfortably. The tops of the Cordilleras, covered with snow, are very clear in the bright sunlight. At Lota there are trees and Winter vegetation on the high hills. Lota and Coronel are really twin ports. They both lie alongside the great vein of coal and copper, and are coaling-stations for the vessels. Most of the steamers come down to Lota for the fuel which will be needed in returning to Panama, while those passing through the Straits of Magellan or around Cape Horn take on enough to serve them to Montevideo. It crops out of the hillside and

VIEW OF TALCAHUANO

is mined in primitive and inexpensive manner. The copper mining is also primitive.

Lota has a good bay, but hardly a harbor. The town is not a bad one. Its main street is well paved. It has an attractive plaza, a club, a shabby church, a *fundicion*, or copper-smelting works in which old processes are used, and pottery and brick factories. It is also noted for the coal tunnel under the sea. Until they were turned into a stock company, Lota and Coronel were the property of the Cousiño family, and the company is still controlled by that family. The widow Cousiño at one time was the richest woman in the world. Cousiño Park at Lota is the pride of Chile. It is bizarre, and blends English and French landscape gardening with some original ideas of Nature improved and unimproved. There is a French chateau on the hill, and there are ravines, grottoes, fountains, statuary, artificial lakes, arbors, terraces, flower gardens, and a small zoo. A lighthouse in the corner commanding the sea has a history. It was brought from Paita in Peru as the spoil of war.

Indian faces are numerous in Lota. They are the strongest type I have seen, and are of the unconquerable Araucanian stock. These Indians and half-Indians, besides being engaged in fishing and water traffic, are mingled with Europeans as mine-workers. It is a half-savage mining population, among which strikes, bloodshed, and murder are not unknown.

For those who wish to visit the Chilean Annapolis, the train may be taken from Coronel to Concepcion, and then to Talcahuano, which is the naval port. The journey does not occupy more than an hour. The Chileans have a patriotic pride in this naval school.

Talcahuano is a principal port and has much shipping. It is about the only good harbor on the Chilean coast.

Concepcion, after Santiago and Valparaiso, is the largest city in Chile, and has a decided importance as the outlet for the great central valley. Many passengers come by the railway from Santiago through the central valley to Concepcion, and take the ship at either embarkation. The English and the Germans divide the foreign trade, which is large and profitable.

Continuing down the coast on a voyage on the *Oropesa*, we passed the briefest day of the year, June 21, out of sight of land. The day was clear and cold. The seas were very heavy. At sunset the navigating officer told us we were in south latitude 41°. The Milky Way never seemed so luminous, nor the evening star, set in the dark southern sky, so bright. The following day was alternate rain and shine, with just a sight of the Chiloe Archipelago through the mists. Few of the vessels now take the more picturesque route into the archipelago and through Smythe's Channel. The wrecks have become too common.

Heavier seas were encountered in the afternoon and at night. What a night! The *Oropesa*, a ship of 7,000 tons, was pounded as with an anvil, tossed like a chip, knocked, hammered, slammed and banged about, chased by huge seas astern, struck obliquely by mountain waves, caught horizontally and spun around like a top. First she went at half speed and then at quarter speed, but with plenty of sea-room no one worried.

The next morning at daybreak the lighthouse which marks the Evangelist Islands was sighted. The name,

Islands of Direction, which is sometimes given them, is a better description. They fix the entrance into the Straits of Magellan. They are four rocky heaps, — Matthew, Mark, Luke, and John. After they are sighted the rough seas become gentler, and the ocean is like a rolling, gently swelling prairie. A knob of brown earth is seen. It is Cape Pillar. The gray clouds change into violet and purple, a blinding snow-storm of three hours follows; then the sun lifts a little, and discloses on the right Desolation Islands and the great snow fields. By mid-day the land on either side is quite close. The channel does not appear to be more than a quarter of a mile across. There is some brush, but no trees. The blue glaciers of which we have read are not blue, but are white against the water-green sky. In the afternoon a gauze spreads over the glaciers like a veil of mist, and they are blue.

A look astern shows that we are passing through the narrowing neck of a long channel with snowy crags and slopes on either side. We are in south latitude 54°, no twilight, a black night, not a star visible, the water not to be seen from the lower deck, the ship groping for anchorage like a blind fisherman. "Two hundred sixty fathoms, no; thirty-six fathoms, yes." We have conquered the treacherous currents, have turned the dangerous elbow corners, and learn that we anchor for the rest of this black night off Cape Coventry. I thought of Ferdinand Magellan and his sail-ships threading those unknown channels nearly four centuries ago.

We are under way at four o'clock in the morning, and come out on deck to find the sun hooded and cloaked in the snow clouds. It clears later, showing the straits much broader and the hills on either side lower but still under a white mantle. We round Cape Froward, latitude 53° 54', at times losing sight of Tierra del Fuego. We get a sight of Punta Arenas, the most southerly town on the American Continent or on any continent, 1,600 miles farther south than Cape Town, 900 miles nearer to the South Pole than Christ Church, New Zealand. It is the world's cross-roads for ocean travel.

The first view is of wide streets running back to forest-clad hills which are almost lost in the snow clouds. Everything about the town is brisk and bright. Ashore the snow crunches under our feet, and we have the buoyant feeling of the Hudson's Bay trapper. There is a Chilean cruiser in the bay, and German, English, French, and Spanish ships. Even rarer is one bearing the American flag. There are hotels, *gasthauses, posadas*, and other signs which tell in many languages of sailors' lodging-houses. The mingling of many tongues is also heard, for the sailors are ashore.

Punta Arenas has very good wharves and ware-houses, substantial bank buildings, some private residences that look like Swiss chalets, and a somewhat pretentious plaza in which on this day the fountain has become a beautiful ice crystal. The town also has sailors' bar-rooms. There is a new church, and a few vacant lots are left in the business section. A troop of urchins come chattering from school, leap into the snow-drift, and pelt the passers-by, the universal privilege of boyhood. Though it is Winter the women are bareheaded, or most of them are, and the black alpaca shawls thrown carelessly over their

SCENES AT THE STRAITS OF MAGELLAN
CAPE PILLAR — THE EVANGELIST ISLANDS — CAPE FROWARD

shoulders do not indicate that the cold is penetrating.
The men wear vicuña robes like blankets, or many of
them have the skins made up into overcoats. The
steamer has brought the fortnightly mail, and every
one gathers at the post-office waiting for letters. The
talk is of new sheep companies and gold washings in
Tierra del Fuego.

Punta Arenas has no custom house. It is a free
port, — a very wise policy considering that its trade is
of an international character, selling to the passing ships
and buying from them only such articles as are needed
for local consumption. The commercial movement
reaches $2,250,000 per year, the exports exceeding the
imports by $250,000. The export commerce is of
wool, hides, tallow, ostrich feathers, foxskins, guanaco
and vicuña rugs. The imports are alcohol for the
Patagonian Indians, cereals, and general merchandise.
The best fur store is kept by a Russian woman. The
town is the seat of the territorial government of
Magellans, and is the official residence of the Governor.
There is also an army barracks and a weather bureau
office. It is a station of the Chilean navy, which has
rendered much service to navigation in the hydrographic work of the Straits. Punta Arenas has its daily
newspaper, filled with shipping intelligence and containing cable news which is transmitted by land wire
from Buenos Ayres. Wireless telegraphy finds it a
convenient station.

Punta Arenas thinks it has a cloud on its future.
This is the Panama Canal. It now is an important
coaling-station, the coal being brought both from
Australia and from Newcastle, and it has a good
business in supplying passing vessels. Some of this

trade will be lost when the Hamburg and the New York ships which follow this route to San Francisco are able to take the shorter course through the waterway. But by that time the improvements which the Chilean government is making in the navigation of the Straits, and the natural development of trade in the far southern regions will have more than compensated for the diminution from the diversion of the through ocean traffic to other channels. As the centre of the sheep industry of Tierra del Fuego and of the Chilean mainland, the southernmost town has a stable future.

CHAPTER XIII

LIFE IN THE CHILEAN CAPITAL

Railway along Aconcagua River Valley — Project of Wheelright, the Yankee — Santiago's Craggy Height of Santa Lucia — A Walk along the Alameda — Historic and Other Statues — The Capital a Fanlike City — Public Edifices — Dwellings of the Poor — Impression of the People at the Celebration of Corpus Christi — Some Notes on the Climate — Habits and Customs — " The Morning for Sleep " — Independence of Chilean Women — Sunday for Society — Fondness for Athletic Sports — Newspapers an Institution of the Country.

IN places the river Aconcagua is like the Platte of Nebraska, which is famous for spreading out so that it is all bed and no depth. Yet the stream is more picturesque than the flat top of Mt. Aconcagua, 22,425 feet high, for the monarch of the snow-covered Cordilleras lacks the majesty of the apex peaks, which are 2,000 or 3,000 feet lower. The railroad creeps along the valley from Valparaiso, cuts across the ravines and transverse spurs into a narrow pass, following the watercourse and clinging to the mountainside like the rim of a wheel. The vegetation is both temperate and tropical. In making the journey on a June day I passed from the balminess of perpetual Spring to the chill of Winter, but Nature was not stern and there was no bleakness. A little back from the seacoast were short and stocky palms, fields carpeted with yellow cowslips, milk-white nut trees, green willows, silver poplars, young apple orchards side by side with orange groves, firs, and the taller forest trees.

After the main valley is left and the gorge entered, it is a steady, curved climb to Llai-Llai. The place is an eating-station, and a very good one too. The name is Indian and not Welsh. Though it was midwinter, the breath of the tropics lingered and the dews had freshened the vines and trees. The railway splits at this point, one branch going south to Santiago and another straight on to Los Andes, where the mule-path leads across the *cumbre*, or summit, but where in a few years the big spiral tunnel will complete the through rail connection via the Uspallata Pass between Valparaiso and Buenos Ayres. In this region I had glimpses of vineyards, of pretty farms, and of pasturing cattle and sheep. The valley below is an agricultural Arcadia. Coming out of the gorge in the wildest part, the beauties of the scenery were temporarily lost, for a big, staring coffin sign greeted my eye. Sometimes the Chileans call themselves the English of South America; sometimes the Yankees. The advertiser's art here is both English and Yankee — it stops at nothing.

But the snow-peaks, the overhanging vaporous milky masses on the summit, and the darker purple masses on the mountain-sides, make it possible to forget the coffin man and his wares, though his sign at first jars the æsthetic sensibilities so disagreeably.

Railroad travel is comfortable on the line from Valparaiso to the capital. There are Pullman cars and other conveniences. But though it is midwinter, the cars are not heated. Every one unrolls blankets and robes. The women settle back to a nap or a

SCENE ON THE ACONCAGUA RIVER

little gossip. The men light their cigars, and between the intervals of newspaper reading, talk politics and the weather. Two or three peruse French novels. The five hours consumed in the journey pass quickly.

This railroad was projected by William Wheelright. The opposition the enterprise met in the Chilean Congress reads like a chapter of George Stephenson's struggles with the English Parliament. Wheelright carried the line as far as Llai-Llai. Then came a long wait, till Henry Meiggs arrived in the first flush of his exile, and with his extraordinary mental activities thirsting for a field for their employment. For ten years the government had been deciding to have the remaining sections of the railway completed "to-morrow." It was in 1861 that they made the contract. They had no idea of quick work. Meiggs, shrewd California Yankee, got a clause inserted giving a premium if Section A should be finished within one year instead of three years, and so forth. Then he built the railroad in the shortest period and collected the largest premium. The authorities, wondering, paid, but allowed no rush clauses in subsequent contracts.

Few big cities can boast the possession of a craggy mountain. Santiago has such a treasure in Santa Lucia, an alluvial outcropping, isolated, and apparently not kin to the granite spur of San Cristobal near by. After waiting many years, the municipality converted it from a sterile mass of rugged rock into a park with drives and gardens, serpentine paths, statues, terraces, parapets, bowers, grottoes, basins, cascades, and aquariums. There is a statue to Pedro Valdivia, the first of the Spanish conquerors, whose

conquering career was ended by the unconquerable
Araucanians, and a chapel and monument to the
public-spirited Archbishop Vicuña.   A theatre, a *café*,
and some other structures also have been erected.
Their value in beautifying the mountain is not great,
yet art and advertising have not been allowed altogether to spoil Nature.

Santa Lucia is Santiago's crown jewel, her Kohi-
noor.   Every day during my stay I went to walk
there, often through the clouds, but always with a
freshened sense of enjoyment.   The approach is like
Chapultepec in the City of Mexico, but this isolated
mountain mass, while less extensive, is more dominating than Mexico's pride.   Though it does not
afford the splendid sight of two volcanic snow-clad
peaks, as Chapultepec does in the vista of Popo-
catepetl and Ixtaccihuatl, yet the circular snow profile
of the Andes through the violet mist is an always
pleasing vision.

A morning or an evening stroll along the Alameda
de las Delicias — Delicious Walk, in English — shows
much of Chilean life.   It is a shaded avenue with a
central *paseo*, or walk, a roadway on either side between rows of poplar trees,— the roadway being given
over to the trolley cars, and then the main thorough-
fares which form the street.   There are some handsome residences and many commonplace ones.   The
stores are not fine.   The Alameda is too long (three
miles) and too broad for trade, and the shopping district locates itself elsewhere.

Chilean patriotism is rampant on the Alameda,
though it is not always artistic.   The avenue has
statues to O'Higgins and other national heroes, with

groups commemorative of incidents in the war for independence. A statue has been erected to the international hero, San Martin, the Argentine chieftain who led the allied armies of the patriots to victory against Spain. An unambitious monument to Buenos Ayres typifies the completion of the telegraph line between Chile and the Argentine Republic across the Andes in 1865.

While many of the groups on the Alameda commemorate war heroes and war incidents, peace also is recognized. There is a statue to Benjamin Victor MacKenna, the historian, with the inscription that the heroes thus pay tribute to the chronicler of their prowess. He was defeated for the Presidency by a soldier. I like even better the memorial to Father Molina, the Jesuit naturalist, who rendered distinguished service to science. It is an obscure little statue, yet it shows that the warlike nation has thoughts of the sacrifices and the achievements of science as well as of arms.

Santiago is an ancient capital, for when the Boston tea party was held, its population was larger than that of either Boston or Philadelphia. With its suburbs included, it numbers about 300,000 inhabitants. It was laid out by the old Spanish town-makers with the customary regularity of streets and plazas, but not in the usual checkerboard form. The Alameda and the Mapocho River form a triangle which encloses the most densely populated sections like a fan, so that the east and west streets are not parallel. Santa Lucia is at the vertex or the rivet. The fan opens from the Alameda, and spreads over Cousiño Park, the race-track, and various public institutions.

The principal square is the Plaza of Arms, one corner of which is occupied by the Cathedral. Nothing about the Cathedral is especial, nor are the churches themselves particularly striking, for they are not mediævally ecclesiastical. Some of them are Florentine. Santiago as a whole has less of the typical Spanish architectural appearance than any other large city in South America. The business blocks are substantial structures of two and three stories, with many arcades and portals. The private residences have fronts with many *façades*, and are quite ornate. The *patios*, or courts, within are paved with variegated tiles. The glimpses of the fountains and of green trees and yellow oranges afford a pleasing picture to the stranger. He longs to enter and be at home in these secluded orange groves, set, as they are, in the amphitheatre of the snow-covered Cordilleras.

Some of the public edifices are comparatively new, while many are of the Spanish and colonial epoch. The Moneda, or Government Building, belongs to the latter class. It is rambling and old, with no exterior pretensions, but with many courts, circular balconies, and grilled windows. The President occupies a smaller house for his residence. The Congress building is new, and is of the architecture of the Renaissance. It is on the site of the Jesuit Church that was burned in 1863, — one of the world's holocausts, in which 2,300 persons lost their lives. In front of the Supreme Court building is a statue to Andre Bello, the author of the Chilean Civil Code and an eminent authority on international law.

The National Library is housed in the old Congress hall. It has a very extensive collection of manuscript records of the Inquisition, brought from Lima, and of other rare historical documents, including the colonial archives. I visited the Library one afternoon, and was shown some of its treasures by Director Montt. But the atmosphere of secluded scholarship did not come upon me until in a remote recess I met the Orientalist of the institution, a priestly bookworm in his clerical *sotana*, a skull-cap covering his tonsure, keen eyes peering from the spectacles across a large inquisitive nose, — altogether a striking figure of the recluse in the midst of the musty wisdom of the past.

Some sections of the capital city are shabby. A walk in the poorer parts — and they cover much territory — disclosed to me even more than shabbiness, grinding poverty. Across the Mapocho, the walled and bedded river, is a church with a gaudy blue front and a dreary triangular plaza. Penury stretches on all sides. The dwellings are low, with floors below the street level and in the cold and rainy season under water. The interiors are repulsively forbidding and unsanitary. The comforts of life, let alone the decencies, cannot be acquired in such squalid surroundings. No subject of municipal legislation is more pressing than that of sanitary tenements, and no municipality has shown greater indifference to it heretofore than Santiago. Until something is done in this direction, the palpitating social question will continue to palpitate, and purely political issues will have to be decided under the scowl of the proletariat.

The women conductors on the Santiago tramways have been often described. They are not many, and they are not all of them the loveliest of their sex, but they are faithful and obliging. They collect the fares about as rapidly as men would do. The motorists on the trolleys are men.

A pleasing view of the poorer class of the population may be had on a national holiday or a Church celebration. I had it one day when the festival of Corpus Christi was commemorated. Both Church and State took part. In the Plaza de Armas were altars with burning candles. There were the troops in their gayest trappings; the infantry in blue breeches with yellow stripes, wearing white plumes; the cavalry with blue plumes, and the military bands with red plumes, — a gorgeous grouping of colors. It was a fine army showing, more imposing than the priestly conclave which, approaching from the adjoining streets, entered the plaza in front of the Cathedral. The parade was led by the Procession of the Cross, composed of various societies. Delegations from the different parishes followed. Next came the religious communities, — the Franciscans, the Dominicans, the Capuchins, the Mercedarios, and the Augustinians. After them the parochial clergy brought up by the prebendary under the pallium, the archbishop being unable to occupy that place on account of illness. The pallium was preceded by the archbishop's cross, and was conducted by local notabilities.

During the procession some of the women and many of the boys knelt in the streets and a few men doffed their hats, but the crowd as a whole was not devout and the ceremony was not impressive. It partook more of the nature of a perfunctory official function.

Though the snow of the Cordilleras is always in

sight, Santiago does not have a snow-storm oftener than once in ten years. But it rains. During June, early Winter, I saw clear skies on not more than half a dozen days. My Chilean friends told me this was exceptional, and to prove it they brought the verified weather statistics. These showed an average of only 35 rainy days out of 365. The largest proportion was in August, when there were ten days on which rain fell. But the sky is overcast much oftener than this. There are very many days which are described by the expressive Spanish word *triste*, that gives to Nature the element of personality and means sombre and sorrowful. Besides, while the actual rainfall is not so great, there are seasons when the humidity is very disagreeable, and this is in Winter instead of in Summer. In January the relative humidity was 64.6, while in July (midwinter) it was 83.7. The average for the year was 73.29. The temperature is quite variable, and the difference between sun and shade is marked. In January the maximum in the shade was 68° Fahrenheit, and in the sun 85°. In July it was 46° in the shade and 57° in the sun. The mean average for the year was 69°.

The Chilean of the upper class is as indifferent as he thinks the humbler class ought to be to mere physical comfort. He resents the statement that not more than half a dozen dwellings in the capital have chimneys, and he is right in doing so, for that is a libellous exaggeration. Yet the majority of them are without chimneys, and their occupants get through the villanous Winter season with oil-stoves or perhaps even without this means of artificial warmth. I went an afternoon in midwinter to call on one of the local captains of industry. He had a handsome residence, and, happily, a parlor upholstered in warm colors. No other means of getting warm were provided. He came down to see me in his overcoat, and I had gained experience enough not to think of removing mine. " It is only a few months," is the smiling explanation of shivering through the Winter. But the means to provide comfort during those few months are coming. The wealthy citizen now builds his residence with chimneys and open grates.

Life in Santiago — that is, social, professional, and business life — is only for the classes. The gulf between comfort and poverty — for it is simply comfort, since there are few great fortunes — is bridged by ignoring poverty. And it has to be confessed that, with wretchedness blinked out of sight, existence in the Chilean capital is agreeable. The city is both the heart and the pulse of the nation. The commercial habit — hardly industrial, for the factories are few — limits itself to an hour in the morning before breakfast and rather resents intrusion during that hour. Though he is at his office, the business man would rather have you come around after breakfast, since it spoils his midday meal to take up the work of the day before then. Some humorous experiences of my own, some polite postponements, satisfied me of the fixedness of this custom.   In the afternoon there is real activity, concentration which in a few hours makes up for apparent slackness.

In professional and official affairs it is the same. An official appointment or a call of any nature on a public functionary should be made somewhere between half-past two and half-past four. I discovered that the

VIEW OF LOS ANDES

official urbanity was greatest if the call could be made between three and four o'clock.

The social life is more of the clubs than of the home, yet there are many fine homes where a charming hospitality is dispensed. The breakfast, preferably on Sunday, is a favorite social function, beginning at mid-day and conducted with all the formality of an evening dinner. At a breakfast in the home of Mr. Emilio Bello Codecido, a colleague in the Pan-American Conference at Mexico, I met many of the leading people of Santiago, among them Mr. Auguste Matte, another colleague in that conference. Madame Bello is the daughter of former President Balmaceda. Again, Mr. Juan Walker Martinez, the brother of the Chilean minister in Washington, desiring to give me an opportunity to meet some of the principal men of the city, arranged a breakfast at the Union Club. When given on week days, these social breakfast functions presuppose no pressing business or professional engagements during the afternoon.

The Santiagonian is a night-hawk. His club life, and when he is not at the club his family life, does not begin till two or three hours after sundown. Every evening he is found at the Union Club, one of the best associations of gentlemen in South America. It may be that he is going to forego this practice for a few hours and accompany his wife and daughters to the opera or the ball, which celebrates some charity or a public function. Female society is satisfied with these diversions and with church-going. At the opera it is resplendent in Parisian costumes. Charity draws all its members. At a charitable performance in the Municipal Theatre one night I was assured I saw all that was lovely in the capital — and very lovely it was.

The Chilean women are less restricted by traditional Spanish formalities than their sex in other South American countries. They shop by themselves, and many are employed in the stores and similar places, but man is the master, and the women take pleasure in recognizing this. They go to the ball or the opera to be admired, and the strangers admire and continue to admire.

The chivalry of the male Chilean, while formal and precise, is rather commonplace. He gives the lady the inner side of the street, and will politely describe the arc of a great circle and cheerfully step off into the sewer that his gallantry in this matter of etiquette may not be questioned. But this is the limit of his concession, except that if he be of a literary turn he may write sonnets to her black eyes. He extends the first greeting. Without it his most intimate female acquaintance must not manifest the faintest sign of recognition. This custom is intensely exasperating to the visitor, who finds the Chilean women look so much alike that he may have calmly ignored his *vis-à-vis* at a social function while he has greeted with effusive politeness a lady who makes it apparent, though not disagreeably, that she never saw him before.

At the theatre the *zarzuela*, or one-act comedy, is as popular as in Spain. After the performance the clubs find all the men congregated there. The gambling is high. It has been said that the Chilean who forms a part in the social life of the country must be either a soldier, a priest, or a farmer. With the predominance of the army and navy, the first class would be certain. The priest is less an element than formerly, but the farmer is the constant factor. The latter class includes the professional men, lawyers and doctors, and the business men, for all are landed proprietors.

Sunday is the day for society, for drives to Cousiño Park, and to the Quinta Normal or Agricultural Experiment Station, which is also a zoölogical garden. The grounds are extensive and well wooded with sycamores and cypresses, but they impressed me as being badly neglected. Cousiño Park also had the appearance of unkemptness. Chile long ago abolished the bull-fight, and she does not permit a national lottery, though there is no interference with the sale of tickets for the Buenos Ayres drawing. Football and other athletic sports are in high favor. Santiago in this respect is an English town. The great attraction is the racing, and on a Sunday afternoon in the season the Carrera, or Club Hipico, gathers all that is fashionable and all that is animated.

Though Santiago has a delightful Summer climate,— the thermometer never gets above 85° Fahrenheit, — every one who is anybody has a *fundo*, or country estate, to which the family flits at the first approach of the heated season. Later in November all move to the seashore resort of Vina del Mar, near Valparaiso, and play golf.

The English group in Santiago is the largest of the foreign colonies, but it is not so extensive as the many English and Scotch names would lead one to suppose. These names are borne by Chileans whose great-grandfathers were from the British Isles, or a very few of whom were from the United States.

Newspapers in Chile are as much an institution as

in the United States. This is true both of Santiago
and of Valparaiso. *El Mercurio*, " The Mercury,"
which is published in both cities, has fine buildings,
superior in their conveniences to newspaper offices in
the United States, and with provisions for editors,
reporters, printers, and other employees that the Land
of Journalism (I mean the United States) is a century
behind in. Dining-rooms, private parlors, working-
offices with baths, bedrooms, chess, for the working-
staff of a daily newspaper! The Santiago office of
El Mercurio is notable not only for its own facilities,
which are very complete, but for its salons and other
rooms which are maintained for the benefit of the
public. In a newspaper office in the United States
the patron is lucky if he can get standing-room
against any kind of counter or railing in order to
write his advertisement. In Santiago he may have
a table and chair and take his time. In consulting
the files he has all the luxury of a modern library
reading-room. The salons in the " Mercury " building are thrown open to the public for receptions and
similar functions. One afternoon I attended by invitation a concert given by the members of the
visiting Italian Opera Company in the music-room.
Members of the Diplomatic Corps, public functionaries, and all that was distinguished in professional and
social life in the capital were present by invitation of
the newspaper management.

The owner of *El Mercurio*, Mr. Augustin Edwards,
is a young man. He is of the banking family of that
name, is a member of the Congress, and has been
Minister of Foreign Affairs. His journals publish
more foreign and cable intelligence than any two

The Roman Aqueduct on Santa Lucia, Santiago

newspapers in any city of a quarter of a million inhabitants in the United States.

While a large amount of telegraphic and local news is printed, the leader, or editorial on the foremost topic of the day, is a prominent feature of the daily issue, and one that carries great weight with the reading public. One evening at dinner, at the house of Mr. Alejandro Bertrand, the distinguished Chilean civil engineer, who was his country's expert commissioner in the boundary dispute with Argentina, the talk turned on the negro question. There are no blacks in Chile, and one of the guests, a man of prominence in finance and politics, who had lived much in Europe, confessed his perplexity over the negro issue, and wanted to know something about the African race. The clearest exposition that I ever heard of the life-work of Booker Washington, and the most discriminating explanation of the race problem in the United States, were given by Mr. Silva, the leader writer on *El Mercurio*. Though he had spent some years in England, he never had visited the United States, yet he was thoroughly conversant with our national perplexity. It therefore may be understood that the leading problems of the United States are discussed with intelligence in Chile, though Chilean subjects may not always receive the same treatment in the journals of the United States.

Besides *El Mercurio*, Santiago has other vigorous papers. One of them is *La Lei*, "The Law." The name is misleading, for it is merely a daily journal devoted to current topics. It represents radical political tendencies. Its editor, Mr. Phillips, was declared to me to be either feared or loved by every public man in Chile, and the alternations of fear and love were said to be as regular as the seasons.   Here, then, was the ideal editor.   In a call on Editor Phillips I was impressed with this feeling.   His aggressive personality would be bound to make friends and enemies, and his independence in discussing public questions would be certain to insure ideal journalism.

CHAPTER XIV

NITRATE OF SODA AN ALADDIN'S LAMP

Extensive Use of Nitrates as Fertilizers — Enormous Contributions to Chilean Revenues — Résumé of Exportations — Description of the Industry — How the Deposits Lie — Iodine a By-product — Stock of Saltpetre in Reserve — The Trust and Production — Estimates of Ultimate Exhaustion — A Third of a Century More of Prosperous Existence — Shipments not Affected by Panama Canal — Copper a Source of Wealth — Output in Northern Districts — Further Development — Coal — Silver Mines Productive in the Past — Prospect of Future Exploitation.

IS nitrate of soda, the saltpetre of commerce, a national blessing or a national curse?

After the war with Peru and Bolivia, by which Chile added to her territory 1,200 miles of seacoast, including the Bolivian Province of Antofagasta and the Peruvian Province of Tarapacá, a Chilean naval commander was credited with the foreboding prophecy that the nitrates would ruin Chile as they had ruined Peru.

In its political phase the question may be answered according to the bias of the individual. It enters into the subjects concerning which Chileans engage in heated controversies when discussing policies and tendencies, or criticising government expenditures. But this aspect has no direct bearing on the naked economic facts of production and the addition to the nutritious substances of the world's soil.

Nitrates are among the most extensively used fertilizers known to agriculture, and the demand for them
grows. Their relation to the fiscal system of Chile
may be understood when it is known that from 85 to
87 per cent of the total revenues is derived from the
export tax on the saltpetre products. This impost is,
in terms of English currency, at the rate of 28 pence
per 46 kilograms or Spanish quintal of 101.4 pounds,
relatively 55 cents for each 100 pounds. Their ratio
of contribution to the national wealth is shown by an
analysis for a given year, when the total value of the
exports was $73,786,000 gold, of which $53,565,000
was nitrates and the by-product of iodine, while the
balance of $20,221,000 was composed of mineral and
agricultural products and manufactured articles. In
Chilean currency the figures were $202,153,000, of
which the nitrates constituted $146,756,000. In the
last quarter of a century the nitrate beds have yielded
to the Chilean government $273,000,000 gold, and it
is estimated that during the next twenty-five years, on
the basis of the present export tax, the revenue will
amount to $436,000,000.

The first exportations were made in 1832. They
continued on a small scale until the war in which Peru
lost the Province of Tarapacá, and their exploitation
on a large scale may be said to have begun in 1882
under the Chilean administration. In that year the
exportations amounted to 10,701,000 Spanish quintals.
In the period inclusive from 1832 to 1904 the total
reached the enormous sum of 602,438,000 quintals,
or 61,087,213,200 pounds, equal to 27,271,077 long
tons of 2,240 pounds. The personal histories of the
individuals who engaged in the exploitation of the

saltpetre deposits are as romantic as the experiences of the bonanza mining-kings. Nitrate kings have risen and thriven and have held their courts with titled courtiers in their train. Colossal fortunes have been made and plain commoners have become peers of England treading the golden path which was paved with saltpetre.

So little is known about the nitrate industry that I venture to repeat the substance of a description which I found at once entertaining and instructive.[1]

The saltpetre or nitrate zone embraces the extension comprehended between the Camarones in south latitude 19° 11′ on the north and parallel 27° to the port of Caldera on the south, 450 miles in length. The distance which separates it from the coast varies. In the northern part the sea is only 15 miles away; in the South it is 93 miles distant.

The deposits of saltpetre situated in the Province of Tarapacá occupy the small folds and the gently rising hills which extend from the west of the pampas of Tamarugal. To the south of the Loa River these deposits follow no lode, and they are met with in the midst of the great pampas as well as in the folds of some hills. But they extend always in a zone which runs to a distance varying from 37 to 93 miles from the coast. The short space that separates them from the sea makes easy the access to the neighboring ports by means of the railroads through the ravines which traverse the Cordillera of the coast.

The saltpetre is found mixed with other substances

---

[1] For the facts here given I am indebted, through the courtesy of Minister Walker Martinez, to Mr. J. J. Campana, of Iquique ; but the opinions are my own.

and forming an irregular layer, frequently broken up into barren parts, in which generally common salt dominates, or simply a conglomeration of clay, gravel, and sulphate of soda.

The layer or covering which contains the nitrate is encountered at a very slight depth, covered by a fold of the conglomeration indicated, and which in general is altogether sterile, though in some parts, principally in the North, it contains a regular vein of nitrate.

The vein of nitrate of soda in the layer which contains it is quite variable, the highest proportion being in the Province of Tarapacá, where in some points the medium quality amounts to 60 per cent. In the southern region this quality of *caliche*, or crude material, diminishes, and does not exceed an average of 30 per cent.

The name *caliche* is given to the raw material which contains the saltpetre that is found in the beds of deposits mixed with common salt, sulphate of soda, clay, and other foreign substances. The thickness of the layer is decidedly variable, and fluctuates between a few inches and three feet. Deposits of greater thickness exist, but these never have a great extension.

The height above sea-level at which these deposits are met with varies from 3,600 to 13,000 feet.

The layers composing a saltpetre deposit are:

1st. *Chuca.* — This is formed by clay mixed with earth very fine and evenly spread. The thickness of the *chuca* generally does not exceed an inch and a quarter.

2d. *Costra.* — This layer, which forms the immediate covering for the *caliche*, has a thickness fluctuating between four-fifths of an inch and several feet.

3d. *Caliche.* — This is the layer which contains the saltpetre, and its thickness varies greatly in different places.

4th. *Conjelo* and *cova.* — This is the last layer, which rests upon the rock. It is formed by a mixture of common salt, various sulphates, and other salts, but contains no saltpetre. Its thickness is also very variable.

The limpid *caliche* is taken to the finishing establishments, where it is submitted to a process of purification which is founded on the great solubility of nitrate of soda, superior to the other salts which are in combination with it, in water heated to the boiling-point. The solutions which result are carried by means of troughs to great vats, where the nitrate of soda crystallizes along with the potash, which exists in small quantity together with a little common salt and a small amount of sulphates and impurities.

The quality of the saltpetre thus crystallized is 95 per cent of nitrate of soda, and it is known by the name of ordinary or current saltpetre. Refined saltpetre of the grade of 96 per cent is also obtained by submitting the warm solutions to a light and short decantation, by which there is left a part of the salt and the impurities. The refined product is passed immediately to the crystallizing vats. For this process powerful machinery is used which can refine 1,000,000 pounds of saltpetre daily. The residue of the nitrate of soda is known by the name of *ripio.* Its percentage of saltpetre is estimated below 15.

The saltpetre zone is served with railways. These leave the various ports and ascend to a height of 4,000 feet above sea-level, with the exception of those of

Caleta Buena and Junin, which stretch from the summits of the neighboring Cordillera to the sea and are united with the ports by means of automotors. The automotor *plano* of Junin has a vertical height of 2,145 feet, and those of Caleta Buena 2,430 feet.

The Granja or Challorcollo road traverses the pampas of Tamlugal, and reaches the foot of the hill of Challorcollo. From this point there is a hanging railway, which reaches the mines in the summit of the hill at a height of 4,600 feet and is two miles long.

An important factor in the production of nitrates is coal, which is used in large quantities, the consumption being not less than 400,000 tons annually. The prices fluctuate from 22 to 28 shillings per ton. Generally English coal or that from Australia is used. Chilean coal is not employed to any extent. The home production is hardly sufficient for the needs of the railroads and the industries in the southern part of the country. Besides, the ships which carry the nitrates to foreign ports return with coal as the cargo. The freight rates to Europe for the nitrates vary from 20 to 30 shillings per ton.

In all the deposits iodine is found formed of salts with the base of soda. The salts of iodine dissolve along with the nitrate of soda, and later are extracted from the mother waters which have remained after the crystallization of the saltpetre. The process is simple and cheap, and the iodine is obtained in the metallic state and perfectly pure, in which condition it is a commerical commodity.

The small consumption of iodine in the industry has caused the producers of the entire world to form a combination to limit the production and fix its relation to consumption. The agreement obliges all the saltpetre establishments of each country to withdraw only a very small part of the iodine which their properties contain. At some future period the refuse of the saltpetre will be worked to extract the iodine.

The annual production of iodine is approximately 4,200 Spanish quintals. The price of the substance is about 5½ pence per troy ounce. The total export tax varies from $150,000 to $100,000.

To the east of the ports of Punta de Lobos and of Hurmillos is a great salt field extending over an area of 32,000 *hectares*, or 80,000 acres. It is covered with common salt, or chloride of sodium. The salt is perfectly pure and crystallized. The analyses have given 99.99 per cent of chloride of sodium. The thickness of this salt layer is not known. The deepest wells have reached 82 feet. In a recent year 220,000 quintals were exported to the interior of the country. The good quality of this salt allows it to be used in every class of industry and also for domestic purposes. Besides the great salt bed named, there are various others, but these are not so important.

The number of laborers employed in the nitrate industry varies from 20,000 to 25,000 according to the activity of the season. Production in some years has been curtailed through the scarcity of labor or through strikes and similar causes.

The principal application of saltpetre is in agriculture, it being employed as manure for land worn out by many years of continuous cultivation. Some crops give 25 per cent to 30 per cent more than those which are raised without fertilizing the ground with nitrates. In special cases the returns have been much larger, and it is on this account that this fertilizer has obtained so considerable an increase in all markets.

The stock of saltpetre was calculated for the entire nitrate zone as of January 1, 1900, approximately as follows:

	Spanish Quintals
Tarapacá — Private properties	407,160,000
State properties	165,888,513
Total	573,048,513
Toco — Private properties	138,112,000
State properties	87,726,769
Total	225,838,769
Aguas Blancas and Antofagasta — Private properties	153,000,000
Taltal — Private properties	151,984,500
Grand total of nitrates	1,103,871,782

To this calculation should be added the nitrates which may exist in the pampas without having been discovered up to this time both in Tarapacá and in the districts of the South. In Tarapacá are the pampas of Orcoma, in which have been found layers of saltpetre of low grade, but which later may prove worth developing, though not while deposits of greater importance exist and while the present prices are maintained.

There are also deposits of saltpetre to the north of Pisagua in the pampas of Tacna, but in small quantity and in isolated beds.

Deducting the output from the time the calculation was made to 1905, the total would be 951,754,000 quintals then untouched. The nitrate fields which have not been reconnoitred have been estimated at 500,000,000 quintals, but that is rather a guess than a calculation. A safer assumption would be 300,000,000 quintals. The Antofagasta district has come up to expectations. Approximately, then, it may be said that in 1905 Chile had a nitrate reserve of a billion and a quarter (1,250,000,000) quintals of fertilizing material for the world's needs. That is a prodigious quantity, but not an inexhaustible one. In the eleven years from 1894 to 1904 inclusive the exports increased at an average rate of 1,000,000 quintals annually. They were 23,947,000 in 1894; in 1904, 32,387,000 quintals.

The industry is in every sense a modern one, for it is controlled by a combination, or trust. This arrangement has one good feature: it insures reliable statistical data. The prospect as to production may be readily grasped when the explanation is made that the output for the year which ended with the first quarter of 1905 was placed at 36,000,000 Spanish quintals as against 32,387,000 the previous year. This means a direct revenue of $20,000,000 gold as long as the rate of production is maintained. A lowering of prices might cause the output to be lessened a few million pounds, but the world's demand is steady enough to assume that for the present period these figures may stand substantially without change.

In the entire nitrate zone there are about 100 *oficinas*, or clarifying establishments. The original combination of the producers, or trust, was for five years, and began March 31, 1901. The amount of saltpetre which the *oficinas* may produce is fixed annually by a directorate. The exportation cannot be less than the previous year's consumption.

If the rate of production fixed by the combination

during recent years should be maintained without further change, there would remain 33 to 35 years more of nitrate exploitation on the present scale. Nothing, however, is more improbable. The product will be increased as rapidly as good prices can be obtained, and the experience of the last ten years has shown that the consumption grows fast enough to justify the larger output. No combination of producers can keep new capital from coming into the nitrate fields, for no vague fear of the future will be strong enough to cause the government to withdraw from rental for an indefinite period its nitrate properties. The new capital wants quick returns on the investment. It urges advertising, spending more money in the propaganda maintained to educate the world in the value of saltpetre as a fertilizer.

Against constant pressure for widening the market may come competition from artificial products, or new discoveries of nitrate fields in the desert of Sahara or in California that will terminate the monopoly of production and cause the export tax to be lowered. But while the profits might be lessened from some such cause, it does not follow that the production would be curtailed. It would the more likely be swollen. Expert opinion is that the existing *oficinas* could double their output. The profit which now accrues from an annual production of 35,000,000 or 36,000,000 quintals could be spread over 50,000,000 quintals and still show a margin of gain. Thus in any view the quantity of saltpetre extracted is likely to grow with each year, subject only to temporary checks or fluctuations.

Studied in every light, Chile's Aladdin's lamp

flickers, for the life of the nitrate industry as a national wealth producer draws to a close. A third of a century to forty years reasonably may be fixed as the term of its existence. After that will remain the debris of the industry, and possibly before the beds approach exhaustion, irrigation will make the dead pampas blossom with the luxuriance of tropical agriculture, and the present sparse and artificially sustained population will be supplanted by populous farming communities.

In the opening chapter I have stated that the Panama Canal in its ultimate economic influence will not affect the nitrates or be affected by them, because their life is limited to the infancy of the waterway, while, during the period of their existence that may remain after it is opened to traffic, the bulky nature of the cargo which must pay the tolls counteracts the possible shortening of the distance. It may develop that other commercial considerations will cause some diversion of the nitrate carrying-trade through the Canal, but this will be chiefly for the gulf ports and the Atlantic coast of the United States. It is not likely to become important, since the market for saltpetre fertilizers is mainly in Europe. England takes directly and for the Continent between 7,000,000 and 8,000,000 quintals annually, Germany about 1,000,000 more, and France 5,000,000 quintals. Other European countries import from 500,000 up to 2,000,000 quintals. The east coast of the United States imports 5,000,000 quintals, or not more than 15 to 20 per cent of the total production, though the consumption is a growing one and is stimulated by systematic advertising. This proportion may increase without materially lessening the cargoes of nitrates which will be transported through the Straits or around Cape Horn to Liverpool, Hamburg, and Havre.

After the nitrates, copper is the most productive source of mineral wealth, and is the most important element in metal mining. The output ranges from 30,000 to 35,000 tons each year. The heaviest output is in the northern region, where the outlet is through the ports of Coquimbo and Antofagasta, but the single district of Lota in the South has a larger output than either of them. It contributes from 7,000 tons upward in bars and ingots. The Guayacan mines in the Department of Ovalle have a similar output. In the district of Chuquicamata, which is in the volcanic Cordilleras, 160 miles from Antofagasta by the railway and 9,000 feet above sea-level, are half a dozen copper mines producing 18,000 to 20,000 tons of ore which averages 18 per cent. The area is 8 square miles of country rock of pure granite with true fissure lodes, and it is estimated that there are 15,000,000 tons of decomposed rock averaging one-half of 1 per cent of copper. In the Capopo district are a group of copper mines which have a monthly output of 2,500 or 2,600 tons of ore, the sulphides predominating in most of them.

The copper industry of Chile has been a reasonably profitable and steady one, and without doubt it is capable of a considerable expansion by the application of modern methods and the more general adoption of improved machinery. The bulk of the shipments is in the form of fine bar copper, though both regulus and copper ores are exported.

The coal mines are located in the Provinces of Concepcion and Arauco, the most productive veins being at Lota and Coronel. This is utilized on the railways and in local industries as well as in coaling vessels, but the output does not equal the demand, and Chile may be looked upon as an importer of coal for an indefinite period. There is lignite to the south toward the Straits, but its commercial value has not been demonstrated.

Iron ore has been found in the Province of Coquimbo and elsewhere, but the production is light. The government made valuable concessions to a French company which agreed to establish an iron industry in Valdivia.

The gold that exists in the North, where the lodes are quartz, and the *lavaderos*, or washings, in the alluvial soil of Tierra del Fuego are not likely to become important sources of national wealth, though new discoveries which prove worth working are reported from time to time.

In times past, Chilean silver mines have been quite productive. The most famous were the Chanarcillo and Chimbote in the Copiapo district, which a few years ago were declared to be worked out. A group in the Iquique region includes the mineral section of Huantayaja. The total output from this group during the ten years preceding 1892 was placed at $22,000,000. After that the production decreased, though it was said to average $400,000 annually. The depth of workings in these mines varies from 200 to 2,000 feet. The general character of the ore is chlorides, and the formation of the rock is porphyritic and calcareous. White silver about 95 per cent pure and the very rich ores are found in pockets near the contact of the calcareous porphyritic rocks.   Near these mines is the mineral section of Santa Rosa which includes the Consequencia and the Pansio.   The latter is said to have produced $1,600,000 during the last ten years.

In the Province of Antofagasta are the two silver districts known as Caracoles and Inca Caracoles.   The former is 110 miles from the coast.   These mines were discovered so recently as 1869.   The lodes were of extraordinary richness.   The ores were chiefly chlorides, iodides, and mixtures of chlorides and sulphides. The ore deposits were superficial, and the ore generally was found in pockets.   The shafts were from 300 to 600 feet deep, though one of them had a depth of 2,500 feet.   Deep mining was abandoned, as it was shown that the veins split up into small fissures. The output of the Caracoles group was estimated at 60,000,000 ounces of fine silver up to the time when the mines were practically abandoned.   At present the output is said not to exceed a few thousand ounces.

The Inca Caracoles mines are situated near the town of Calama, 150 miles from the port of Antofagasta.   The country rock is porphyry, and the lodes range from 3 to 6 feet in width.   The ore is chiefly chloride, and averages 40 ounces to the ton.   Heavy freights and the absence of water have prevented the development of this group, and the prospective output cannot be accurately estimated.   However, it seems to have great possibilities.

Neither copper nor silver ever will suffice to make up the deficiency in the national wealth caused by the gradual exhaustion of the nitrate beds, yet increased transportation facilities and the application of the newer processes give promise of a revival of the mineral industry and an appreciable addition to the productive resources of the country.

CHAPTER XV

CHILE'S UNIQUE POLITICAL HISTORY

National Life a Growth — Anarchy after Independence — Presidents Prieto, Bulnes, Montt, Perez — Constitution of 1833 — Liberal Modifications — The Governing Groups — Civil War under President Balmaceda — His Tragic End — Triumph of his Policies — Political System of To-day — Government by the One Hundred Families — Relative Power of the Executive and the Congress — Election Methods Illustrated — Ecclesiastical Tendencies — Proposed Parliamentary Reforms — Ministerial Crises — Party Control.

CHILE has a political history that marks an isolated chapter among the Spanish-American Republics. Its unique and significant feature is four successive and peaceful presidencies of ten years each. The phenomenon is worthy of study. The tributes which the Chileans pay themselves are merited. Their national life has been a growth and not a series of spasms.

After independence was achieved through O'Higgins in 1818, the Liberator was sent into exile, because he sought to exert kingly powers as a dictator under the merest crust of republican forms. The riot of liberty followed for ten or twelve years with frequent revolutions, changes of rulers, and unavailing efforts to form a stable government. The anarchy of license under the mask of popular institutions reached its height during the period from 1828 to 1833, when the Liberal party — that is, liberal in name — was in power.

Then came the Conservatives, or reactionists. They forced the adoption of the Constitution of 1833, which remained unchanged for thirty-seven years. Order and tranquillity was the motto, and genuine republicanism was choked in order that a government of law might live.

Under this Constitution the colonial despotism differed only from that of Spain in that it was exercised by family groups, who controlled the Executive, rather than by a viceroyal representative of the distant monarchy. It was easy to suspend the Constitution and to put the whole country under martial law. The promptness with which this was done in the emergencies undoubtedly prevented the series of revolutions that cursed other South American countries. It was constitutional for the Executive to abrogate the organic law when the opposition got too active. The party in control under this Constitution of 1833 always was known as the Conservatives, and the opposition in a general way as the Liberals. Sometimes a faction of the Conservatives would split off and attempt a revolution ; sometimes the conservative element was really liberal in character, but not in name.

From 1833 to 1873 Chile had four presidents, all elected and reëlected under constitutional forms. These chief magistrates were Joaquin Prieto, Manuel Bulnes, Manuel Montt, and José Joaquin Perez. During General Bulnes' administration an army uprising was attempted ; during that of President Montt a revolution started at Copiapo in the North. There were also other disturbances. But all of them were suppressed without long periods of civil dissensions, and though liberty seemed to be smothered under councils of war and the absolute suspension of individual rights, it was a hardy plant and after a brief period would begin to grow again.

Under the Constitution of 1833 the presidential term was five years, and there was no prohibition against a second term. In this manner each president reëlected himself and enjoyed a ten years' tenure. But he could not have done this if the privileged classes, the family groups, had not sustained him. They were aggressive in defending their share in the oligarchy, and their individual independence they maintained as sturdily as did the English barons who forced the Magna Charta from King John. With the national development assured, the country began to chafe under the recognition of the autocratic power which was vested in the Executive, and to feel that the growth which would not have been possible without the colonial despotism under republican form had now reached the full measure. Consequently the agitation for liberalizing the Constitution began and was continued persistently instead of intermittently. In the decade from 1860 to 1870 the Conservative reactionaries were pressed so vigorously and were on the defensive so constantly that the harsh features of the Constitution were modified in the spirit if not in the letter.

During the life of this old parchment and the four Executives who put it into practice, — for there never was a dictator among them, — Chile consolidated her domestic interests, inaugurated the building of railways, and by the navy and other means prepared for the war which it was felt one day would be had with Peru and Bolivia. In view of all that was accomplished, it can hardly be said that the Constitution of 1833 and the power of the one hundred families as exerted under that instrument, were bad for the country. But a change was inevitable, and in 1870 the Constitution was reformed in a manner to bring it within the sphere of modern principles of government and remove its aggressive antagonism to republican institutions. Greater independence was conceded to the judicial power, and larger liberty of action to the municipal authorities, while the electoral right of the citizen was broadened. The presidential term remained at five years, but successive elections were prohibited so that the ten-year tenure could not continue.

Frederico Errazuriz was the first of the Executives to serve under the amended Constitution. His term was peaceful and progressive, but was devoted chiefly to preparing for war by ordering the construction of the armored cruisers which rendered the Chilean navy so formidable. He was succeeded by Anibal Pinto, who had served in the cabinet as Minister of War. A financial and economic crisis supervened during his administration, and in its closing year was fought the war of the Pacific, with Chile as the antagonist of allied Bolivia and Peru. Chile's sweeping victories not only gave her the nitrate territory which she exacted as war indemnity; it made her the most aggressive and the most feared Power in South America.

It is only with the internal political history that I propose to deal. A Chilean historian naively remarks that it had been the practice for the outgoing president to intervene in the elections in order to insure the election of a candidate of his own choosing. President Pinto announced his purpose of repudiating this practice, yet he was succeeded by Domingo Santa Maria, who had held the portfolio of Foreign Relations in his cabinet. President Santa Maria found himself antagonized by the Conservatives and one wing of the Liberals. He tried to organize an administration party and to control the election of senators and deputies in the Congress, but failed. This was a clear manifestation of the inability of the Executive to rule without the consent of the families who composed the various political groups. But the issue between the Executive and the families was to be forced by a more resolute hand. Its outcome was dramatic, a tragedy for the nation and a tragedy for one of the country's greatest men.

José Manuel Balmaceda was chosen president in 1886, after a sharp electoral struggle in which the Conservatives and the reactionary faction of the Liberals opposed him. He sought to conciliate the latter by calling some of them to his cabinet. He had grand plans for the development of the nation, and he wanted a united support.

President Balmaceda strengthened the naval and military establishment out of the nitrate proceeds ; but his guiding ambition was to apply them to public improvements, railways, roads, harbors, and schools. The Conservative-Liberal fusion thwarted him. It prevailed in the Congress, and demanded that he name ministers satisfactory to the majority. This he claimed was in violation of his constitutional prerogatives. The Congress refused to authorize the taxes and appropriations necessary for carrying on the government. When for any reason this was not done at the regular session, the practice had been to convoke the Congress in extra sessions. President Balmaceda, wearied with the controversy, abstained from taking this action. On January 1, 1891, he announced that the appropriations for the current year would be the same as during the previous year.

Bloody, merciless civil war followed. The Congressionalists proclaimed that their contest was against Executive usurpation. They removed to Valparaiso, and took refuge on the warships which had been prepared for them. They named Captain Jorge Montt as Commander of the National Squadron. President Balmaceda declared Montt and the naval commanders who obeyed his orders traitors. The President organized an army, while the navy sailed for Iquique and seized the nitrate provinces.

The Congressionalists instituted their provisional government there to carry on the war against President Balmaceda. They organized troops which were transported to Valparaiso and defeated the garrison. A second victory at Placilla and they were in control of the capital, welcomed by the populace as liberators.

Balmaceda took refuge in the Argentine Legation. Flight across the Andes was open to him, but he disdained it. He waited calmly till September 19, the day on which his constitutional term as president ended, wrote farewell letters to his family and friends, arrayed himself in black, pointed a revolver at his right temple, discharged it, and died instantly. His policies live.

I have recalled these swiftly tragic events without any intention of opening up controverted subjects. My purpose has been to sketch them only in their relations to the political system of Chile as it exists to-day, for they influenced it and caused modifications of the Constitution restrictive of the Executive power.

By the books the form of Chilean government is popular representative. To the foreign observer the wonder grows that a system which gives such inordinate power to small groups of families, who call themselves political parties, and which binds the Executive hand and foot, can prove satisfactory. But it suits Chile, or has suited her, and the country progresses. That is the conclusive answer. If Chile chooses to make a strait-jacket for herself, that is her own concern, and if in that strait-jacket she expands and develops a progressive national life she may be permitted to take her own way and her own time for freeing herself.

But what of the governing classes? Who compose them? The Chilean professional man or merchant or government official will tell you, as he told me, that there are no class distinctions, and at the same time will take pride in drawing himself and his fellows far apart from the masses. It has been said that a hundred families have ruled Chile for seventy-five years. The numeral might be doubled or trebled, but the truth would not be changed. The landed interests, the commercial community, and the Church have ruled the country, and it must be said that they have ruled well. They may accuse one another of being false to their trusteeship, but the foreign observer is not impressed with this charge. All of them have worked together to make Chile the powerful and aggressive little nation that she is, and have secured her the respect that the rest of South America has given her. But they have taken all the benefits for themselves, — the honors and emoluments of public office, the opportunities for wealth that came from the nitrate fields, the chances for careers that have been afforded by the army and the navy. It may almost be said that the army and navy exist for the employment of the one hundred families.

Chile herself is not a country of great private fortunes. One or two families have been enriched by mines, a half-dozen by banking and commercial development, a larger number by the nitrates. But when it is all said, the Chilean hundred families are kin of moderate means. Their main sources of income are from their landed estates. These land-owners do not tax themselves heavily. As in the majority of countries of Spanish America, the government imposts are laid on the revenue from the land and not on the land itself. The landed proprietors contrive that these imposts shall be light.

The existing regimen, as studied on paper, is almost a complete reversal of the regimen under which for nearly half a century Chilean nationality was developed and the little ribbon of a republic was consolidated and made strong. The old form was a colonial despotism, with monarchical powers for the Executive. The present system is congressional despotism without republican powers for the Executive, but under both forms the one hundred families have ruled. The president is selected by electors chosen in the provinces through direct suffrage, since there is no such thing as provincial legislatures.

Intense jealousy of the power of the Executive is shown. Politically the president of Chile is a cipher, though he has vast power in relation to public contracts.

But he can rule only as the instrument of the Congress. Not only does the ministerial system prevail in its most extreme form, so that it is not unusual for the cabinet to be changed half a dozen times within a short period, as happened in 1903 and 1904, but a further limitation is put on the president's authority by the Council of State. He governs through this body, which is composed of eleven members, the majority of whom are selected by the Congress, each branch naming three. The remaining five can be chosen by the president only from designated functionaries, one of them always being the Archbishop. Thus it cannot be said that there are three coördinate powers, legislative, executive, and judicial, in the Chilean government.

In operation there is no equilibrium of executive and legislative powers, because Chile is governed, ruled or misruled, by the legislative branch. The authority of the Congress is very extensive, and it never sleeps on its rights. Usually it keeps the president awake seeing how they can be respected and executive policies at the same time be carried out. An election for Congress is not greatly different from a similar event in the United States. The parties nominate their candidates, usually after a caucus. Minority representation obtains. Electioneering is done through the newspapers, through meetings, and through placards. The placards cut a very extensive figure. The manifestoes of the candidates, their allocutions and appeals to the voters, are printed in type so big that the one-eyed man must see and stop to read.

Election methods in many respects are patterned

after the United States, and it is considered fair politics for the party which gets control of the voting machinery to use its advantage without particular regard for the will of the voters as manifested in the ballots. An example of this was given me which showed that Chilean politicians have a fine sense of humor, — one which would be appreciated by Tammany or by Philadelphia. Mr. George Asta-Barragua, who related the incident, had lived in Washington when his father was minister to the United States, and could enjoy the pleasantries of politics in either country.

The contest was very bitter between two candidates who might be disguised as Lopez and Martinez, those names being as common as Smith and Jones. The friends of Martinez secured a majority in the election board, but Lopez had the privilege of naming the minority member, one Rodriguez. The ballots deposited were evenly distributed. The majority of the board calmly counted all of them for Martinez. Rodriguez protested, but without avail. The Martinez faction had determined that in this precinct there should not be one vote for Lopez. After numerous energetic and violent protests, Rodriguez saw that the game was against him, and only varied the proceedings by violent protests in the nature of shaking his fist under the noses of his co-judges. Finally he contented himself with shrugging his shoulders, and the proceedings went on good-naturedly. His co-judges joked him, and he jested with them.

The last thing to be done was for the judges themselves to cast their ballots. Then Rodriguez made his final stand and delivered a little speech to the other judges. It was in substance as follows : " Gentlemen, I recognize that you are two against one. I won't say that we would n't have done the same if we had been two against one. But now that the farce is nearly over, I have one request to make, which as honorable gentlemen you surely will grant. It would be scandalous if, with myself as the representative of Lopez, the word was circulated that I did not vote for him. Therefore my request, honorable associates, is that I may cast my ballot and have it counted for Lopez."

His honorable associates conceded that it was his duty to cast his ballot. He did it with the name LOPEZ in great black letters. His honorable associates calmly counted the ballot for Martinez. Rodriguez protested energetically. Colleague No. 1 picked up the ballot, remarking, " There is no vote here for Lopez." Then he held it up and said to Colleague No. 2, " Do you see anything of the name of Lopez here ? " Colleague No. 2 slowly spelled out, " M-A-R-T-I-N-E-Z." Rodriguez then gave it up, and the vote of the precinct as returned showed, for Martinez, 267 ; for Lopez, 0.

I was assured that this was an actual occurrence, and it certainly was a fine exhibition of campaign humor.

The Roman Catholic Church is a part of the political system, and is a political power in Chile, although there is no discrimination against Protestant forms of worship. In 1813, during the struggle for independence, Bishop Villadres preached in the name of God war against the patriots. Bishop Andreu preached war against the King's soldiers. Thus the Church was not arrayed wholly against the patriots. They recognized it in the Constitution, and it receives State aid.

While the influence of the hierarchy in the main has been reactionary, the ecclesiastical authorities have been politic enough not to antagonize the ruling family groups. When they have sought to do so, they have been worsted.

The Chilean government is measurably independent of ecclesiastical dictation. It always has insisted on its right to nominate the Archbishop, and when Rome has been unwilling to recognize this nomination the Archbishopric has remained vacant. That was the condition for several years previous to Balmaceda's election as president. Then a compromise was effected by the Vatican recognizing the choice of the administration. A Papal legate is maintained at Santiago, and the intrigues and manœuvres to give him precedence have caused unpleasantness in the Diplomatic Corps. Of late years the Church influence has been decidedly reactionary. This was accentuated on the death of Pope Leo, when the Bishop took occasion to preach a political sermon, aimed not only at the Italian government but at Liberal governments everywhere. The leading public men resented this reactionary tendency. When the priests expelled from France sought an asylum in Chile, they were frigidly received.

The efforts to reform the political system relate both to the executive and to the legislative branches. One group wants the vice-president chosen, as in the United States, to succeed to the Executive functions on the death or incapacity of the president. Under the present form there is no elected vice-president. That functionary is the Minister of the Interior, and usually he is a member of the House or of the Senate. When the president desires to forego temporarily the responsibilities of office or becomes ill, he can withdraw and turn the administration over to the vice-president. The latter official during the interim exercises all the powers of the chief magistrate, but in case of the president's death a new Executive is chosen to fill out the term. The agitation for an elective vice-president is not very pronounced, though it may be made a part of the programme of one or the other of the political groups.

The movement for a change with regard to the Congress is more definite. One phase of it relates to the form. Some want to dispense with the formality which takes place at the opening of Congress when the president is escorted to the hall of the Sessions by the troops, is attended by the cabinet, and delivers his message in person in the presence of the Diplomatic Corps and of distinguished officials. It is not a live question. I attended an opening session in company with Minister Wilson, and thought that the message acquired dignity through its ceremonial delivery.

The vital reform which many Chilean public men think necessary in order that national policies may be carried forward and the government placed in harmony with popular sentiment, is a complete overturning of the present parliamentary system, with its frequent and ridiculous ministerial crises, the consequent cabinet changes, and the interruptions in the Executive's policy. The theory of parliamentary government is carried to an extreme which hardly could be conceived of in England. It would make a Frenchman envious of the ease with which ministries can be upset and new ministries set up to be overthrown in their turn.[1] It is a panorama of lightning parliamentary changes. The consequence of the present system is to continue the power of the family groups who call themselves by various names and who may or may not reflect distinct political tendencies. All of them must be represented in the cabinet. Occasionally by means of a coalition or a fusion the Executive may secure something like a political majority, but it does not hold, because the elements composing it have too many selfish interests and too many individual ambitions to gratify. Sometimes, too, the House may be satisfied with the cabinet, while the Senate refuses to accept it. That was the condition in the Fall of 1904, when the Liberal Alliance was the power behind the ministries.

The leading men who are agitating for a reform are radical in their programme, for they want Chile to adopt the practice of the United States, and nothing can be more opposite than our own system and that which now obtains in Chile. These reformers would have the Executive sustained by a political party in the

---

[1] The Chilean correspondent of a London newspaper gave this illustration: "Valparaiso, February 11. The changes effected in the composition of the Chilean Ministry, and especially the Finance Department, have at times been so frequent that not very long ago both the British and the United States Ministers informed the President that for the future they would be unable to recognize any change. They complained, not without sufficient reason, that no sooner had they entered into arrangements with one Minister of Finance than these had to be suspended and commenced *de novo* with his successor, who, again, at the final stages, referred the foreign representatives to his successor at the Treasury Department."

Congress; but even when he may not have a partisan majority back of him, they would have his administration, chosen as it is for five years, assured the voting of the necessary appropriations and the power to continue the policy on which he was elected. That, they argue, would give continued internal tranquillity and strength abroad. This was lacking to Balmaceda, and its lack caused him to defy the Congress and go outside the Constitution. A long time must pass before Chilean public sentiment can be educated up to the point where a hostile partisan majority in the Congress will not dare to refuse to vote the ordinary appropriations of the government. When that point is reached, there will be simply two political parties instead of half a dozen groups centring around individuals.

When I was in Chile in 1903, there were four parties who were recognized, and these were split into so many sections that it was hard to distinguish them. The parties were the Liberals, the Radicals, the Conservatives, and the Social Democrats, or Populists. But the Liberal party was composed of middle-of-the-road Liberals, moderate Liberals, and liberal Democrats, while the Conservatives were divided into regular Conservatives and clerical Conservatives, with a shading off into minor groups. The general tendencies were clear, and an alignment was forming between Liberals of all shades in order to combat the Conservatives. The growth of the Liberals is a revival of the Balmaceda policies. Their success means reforms in the parliamentary system, more freedom for the Executive, and perhaps a broader foreign policy including the frank recognition of the influence on the Panama Canal on all the Pacific coast of South

America. It is generally assumed that no president can now be elected in Chile who is not satisfactory to the Balmacedists. President Jerman Riesco, who was chosen in 1901, gave a liberal and temperate administration.

But these tentative suggestions of reform in the political system, and even the tendencies in regard to public policies are only surface ebullitions if they are studied without an insight into the deeper social and economic conditions, for Chile has social and economic questions of a more pronounced character than any other country in South America. I defer their analysis for another chapter.

CHAPTER XVI

PALPITATING SOCIAL QUESTIONS

Existence of the Roto Discovered — Mob Rule in Valparaiso — Indian and Caucasian Race Mixture — Disquieting Social Phenomena — Grievances against the Church — Transition to the Proletariat — Lack of Army and Navy Opportunity — Not Unthrifty as a Class — Showings of Santiago Savings Bank — Excessive Mortality — Need of State Sanitation — Discussion of Economic Relation — Changes in National Tendencies — Industrial Policies to Placate the Roto.

IN the fabric of Chilean social organization the warp is the individual unit known as the *roto*. The roto constitutes the mass. *Pelucon*, aristocrat, is a term transmitted from the old *régime*. Violent objection is made to its use at the present day on the ground that there are no privileged classes and that it never had more than a restricted meaning. But it describes the antithesis of the roto since his evolution into the proletariat began, and it typifies a recognized social distinction, so that its use is permissible. *Pelucon* comes within the designation of the governing classes and the one hundred families, and does not require further explanation.

One morning in May, 1903, the Chilean government and the foreign residents awakened to the existence of the roto as an organized element in society, with destructive capabilities and the courage of destructive tendencies. Disputes with the steamship companies had resulted in a strike. That morning the mob seized Valparaiso and took to burning property, pillaging, and killing. It was a wild mob, but it had perception and direction. It burned the offices of the Chilean corporation known as the South American Steamship Company, and undertook to sack one of the newspapers, but it left unharmed the property of the Pacific Steam Navigation Company, which was a British corporation. Its grievances against both companies were the same, but this Chilean mob would give no ground for foreign intervention.

The authorities were blamed for the demoralization which the strike developed. It was charged that the forces were at hand to quell the disorder, and that a firm show of strength would have saved the hundred lives which were sacrificed before the rioting and sacking were ended. The inquiry was made why five hundred marines who were available were not utilized. The sinister reply was that they had refused to be used, that they had been on the point of mutiny when it was attempted to use them. They were of the roto class, recruited from the same ranks as the strikers. The exact truth never got to the public. The Chilean government vindicated its ability to maintain order and by the presence of warships and of troops silenced the clamor of the timid English and French residents who were calling for cruisers to be sent by their own governments.

Ultimately the strike was adjusted. But the conditions along the coast as far as Pisagua also were bad. They were especially threatening at the nitrate-shipping-ports. The national authorities kept a cruiser at Iquique, and moved down from farther north additional troops. An outbreak of bubonic plague and the practical cessation of all industry helped to prevent the repetition of the scenes that had been witnessed at Valparaiso. Yet months afterward the embers of unrest at Iquique were smouldering, and official commissions were reporting "remedies for the grievances of the working-classes." A chain of trades unions under various names, coöperative labor societies, mutual aid associations, brotherhoods of working-men, seamen's unions, was in existence. The social question was the palpitating one. The restlessness of the masses of the population, including the roto classes, found another exemplification in October, 1905, when Santiago for a time was under the control of rioters. The immediate cause was the agitation against the tax on the importation of cattle from Argentine. Back of it was the old-time discontent and the feeling that the government was being managed for the classes at the expense of the masses. The high cost of meat was something that came home to the bulk of the population, and it took to rioting, killing, and wounding as well as to destroying property as the means of showing its dissatisfaction. The rioting was not stopped until the police had been reënforced by the troops.

A generation ago J. V. Lastarria, the Chilean diplomat and historian, asserted: "The Chileans are the most homogeneous, most enlightened, most patriotic, and most united people of Spanish America, and they know how to use in the most practical and most prudent manner their political rights." He also declared that the physical and social elements of his country explained her salvation from the disastrous anarchy which the other Republics had suffered and her progress in all spheres of human activity.

This complacent judgment was not unjust, but in

GROUP OF ARAUCANIAN INDIAN WOMEN

describing his countrymen Señor Lastarria meant chiefly the higher stratum, the governing classes. When he wrote, the robust race mixture was yet going on, the amalgam of peasant northern Spain and of the Basque, after two centuries of transplantation, with the fierce Araucanian Indian blood. Not all of the aboriginal amalgam has been Araucanian. There are ten distinct aboriginal tribes known in Chile, and in the northern part the mixture has been more that of the Indians of the historic Upper Peru or Bolivia. All of these tribes have been habituated to hardship, and the grosser qualities of civilization have been developed aggressively.

The Chilean lower stratum of to-day is far from the refinements of civilization. Its vices and its virtues are equally strong. Among the virtues is native independence. The vices are of crude, half-conscious brute power, with little restraint of the passions.

Out of the race mixing — the mingling of European blood not always of the best and the Indian stock, with the Araucanian predominating — has come the roto. I studied him in various places and under varied conditions. He is not an individual for parlor-car company, or an agreeable companion as to the physical senses in a journey in a second-class train, nor yet so unpromising as usually he is painted. In the ports he is found as a coast product. He is a longshoreman, stevedore, boatman. The English word roustabout in a measure helps to describe the Chilean roto, but insufficiently. It gives too transitory an idea of the personality. The roto is no wharf rat. He is a permanent quantity, a fixture in the social fabric of the State, and he is a trade unionist.

In the agricultural regions the roto class is peon
and is not so marked, but it is the basis of the population.   The day laborer in the towns of the North
who has more of the Aymará Indian blood than of the
Araucanian, and who possesses less instinct of class
organization than the longshoreman, also shows discontent.   This *wanderlust* is one of the characteristics
of the Chilean laborer.   He is born a nomad.   Even
the most highly paid laborers in the nitrate fields
refuse to be content and to stay.   They are forever
moving on.

The outcome of the events of 1903 was that
Chile discovered she had a palpitating social question,
and began to seek the horizon which might bound the
zone of unrest.   Among the social phenomena observed were the disproportion between the deaths and
births, the excessive child mortality, the emigration
of Chilean peons to Argentina, the constant movement
of the migratory mass apparently without aim, and the
popular fever for striking.   In these phenomena were
discovered conditions which showed the actual state of
the lower stratum, but the horizon was not complete.
The Chilean observers did not note the phenomenon
of the roto's slow perception of his own power, and his
dawning conviction that there were classes in the State,
and that in some way his class was down in the abyss.
He was becoming a proletariat.

The roto has many qualities in common with the
higher classes.   His patriotism is fully as deep.   Heretofore he has been willing to fight at the dictation of the
military commander, but the threatened mutiny of the
marines was a warning.   At that very time the conscription was going on, and an uncommon sullenness

was shown by the conscripts in the interior, and a vague resentment against being enlisted to fight their brothers. This was when the necessity of employing the army to break the strike was most openly discussed.

In relation to the nitrate fields the roto fails to see that the high wages at one time prevailing there helped him, and now that the pay is dictated by the trust his resentment grows. He has a vivid grievance in the payment of his wages in scrip. In the early days fortunes were made out of the saltpetre beds by officials and private individuals who already were comparatively rich. English parvenus little better than day laborers also gained riches. But the Chilean laborer developed no successful nitrate operator, no earner of day wages who became a millionaire. He seems to have been treasuring this up until the culmination has come and he is asking the question, How have the nitrates helped *me*? Though he furnishes the chief revenues of the State and though he is not heavily taxed, the proportion he bears is not in ratio to his wealthy employer. This belief, undoubtedly, is one basis of the discontent. It may be summed up that the roto feels that he is no better off than if Chile did not draw an enormous income from the export tax on saltpetre.

He also cherishes a grievance against the Church. Heretofore his devoutness or his superstition has been one of the bulwarks of the hierarchy. It interfered little with his crude morality, his notions of private vengeance, or his general conduct in the affairs of life. In a certain manner he venerated the priest and the symbols of ecclesiastical authority, and could be depended on to do whatever was put upon him. But this submissiveness has gone. The Church is a very large property-owner, and does not pay taxes in proportion to the burdens of the nation. The proletariat has become imbued with the belief that its aggressions are directed specially against him.

This feeling in part may be due to the spread of socialistic doctrines, though the socialistic propaganda in itself in Chile is weak. So far as it has a standing, this is because the roto in his protest finds the movement the only available vehicle of utterance for his dissatisfaction. He is not socialistic by nature, because what he takes by brute force from his weaker neighbor he expects to keep for himself and not to turn over to the vague entity known as society. The falling away of the roto from the Church is because of its goods and property which escape taxation, because of the feeling that his back is bent to the pack in order that a greedy ecclesiastical power which claims spiritual dominion over him may exist and pamper its ministers in luxurious idleness.

Another cause of dissatisfaction, which a foreign observer may note more quickly than a native one, is the feeling of resentment that there is no opportunity for him in the army and navy. He forever must be of the ranks. He must fight the battles, but always in inferior station. The enlisted man never can be anything else. Both army and navy draw the line as severely as in the most exclusive military organization of Europe. The common soldier or sailor is clay, a mud ball, something to be kicked, but never to be recognized as a human being with aspirations and ambitions. Yet it is the sailors of this class, as much as the daring commanding officers, who by their bravery and endurance have given glory to the Chilean navy.

But neither naval commander nor army officer yet realizes that this clay is beginning to think, and to feel that something is wrong in the political organization of the State when he who sustains the State is nothing.

Among the qualities of the roto, whether in the army or the navy or in the mass of the population, is persistence in his prejudices. He is not easily changed from that which is taught him. I was in Santiago during the celebration of the peace pacts with Argentina. The governing classes and the merchants entered heartily into those festivities. They knew that the prevention of war by the treaties had saved the country from bankruptcy, even though war might have brought territorial extension. But it was noticed everywhere that the masses took no part in the demonstrations. They either were surly or indifferent. They had been taught to believe that Argentina was an enemy with whom they would have to make war and from whom they would have a chance to take spoils. They could not readily change about and join in the celebrations of peace.

If the roto in such a persistent manner retains the lesson that has been taught him, how much greater will be his doggedness in adhering to his self-taught lesson that something is wrong in the social order, and that he is the one who is wronged?

In the economic discussion of the social movement, citations will be made of the lack of thrift on the part of the roto classes, and their unwillingness to do anything for themselves. This is loose assumption, which is not warranted. On the seacoast he may be reckless with his wages, but in the interior this is not true, and I question myself whether it is true to the extent claimed even in the seaports. In Santiago the *Caja de Ahorros*, or Savings Bank, has between 49,000 and 59,000 accounts. The total deposits, as shown in a late annual report, amounted to $3,625,000. Out of nearly 50,000 depositors, only 355 had balances of $1,000 and more. Of the depositors under that sum, 1,409 were soldiers; 730 were private employees; 311, servants; 1,020, students; 342, seamstresses; 255, merchants; 102, farmers; 144, shoemakers; 67, laundresses; and 3,225 were set down as without profession. Presumably this meant unskilled laborers. Santiago and its suburbs have a population of 300,000. While the aggregate of the deposits is not great, the very fact that the Savings Bank carries 50,000 small accounts, and some of them very small indeed, indicates no lack of thrift on the part of the mass of the population.

In seeking the horizon of the social question one blot which may be remedied has been laid bare. This is the excessive mortality. A cause of the physical sturdiness of the roto who reaches manhood is undoubtedly to be found in the survival of the fittest. That brutal doctrine is exemplified in him. He endures harsh conditions of life, lack of comforts, want of everything that is decent and helpful, and when he does grow up it is as a robust animal only half tamed by nature.

The figures on this subject are startling. The annual death rate has been placed as high as 70 per 1,000 and frequently it is given as 50 per 1,000. This is correct for the majority of the towns and cities, but does not apply to the country as a whole. The official statistics for a period of ten years, which I examined, did not exceed an average of 35 per 1,000. But even that is nearly double the normal death rate in temperate countries; and Chile, not being in the torrid zone, is not subject to yellow fever and similar tropical epidemics. The figures showed that the birth rate and the death rate were almost balanced, since the birth rate ranged from 35 to 37 per 1,000. In 1895 the total births reported were 110,000, and the deaths 92,000, leaving an excess of 18,000 births over deaths. In 1898 the birth excess was a little larger. But in 1901 the births were 116,000 and the deaths 111,000, giving an excess of only 5,000. In previous years the births were not larger and even have fallen below the deaths. In a subsequent year a more normal condition was shown, the births numbering 115,813 and the deaths 88,607. In the two big cities no natural increase was contributed to the population. In Valparaiso Province with 243,000 inhabitants, during a twelvemonth period there were 9,475 births and 9,674 deaths. One year an epidemic of measles caused frightful ravages. In the year 1900, in the city of Valparaiso, the births were 5,610 and the deaths 7,170, and of the latter 2,245 were infants under one year of age. During this annual period the death rate per 1,000 in Valparaiso was 54.4. In Santiago Province, with a total population of 434,000, the births numbered 16,074, and the deaths 17,798. This excess was due to the city of Santiago, where there were 11,000 births and 12,500 deaths in a total urban population of 262,000. The mean average death rate is a little higher than in Valparaiso, though the latter is subject to the vicissitudes of seaports. In a given year only one city of more than 10,000 inhabitants showed a death rate of less than 50 for each 1,000. This was Antofagasta, in which the proportion was 44 out of every 1,000.

Indifference to personal comfort and the inevitable results of unsanitary living have helped to brutalize the roto, but it is wide of the mark to say that he prefers this existence. Cleanly and sanitary living are not so repugnant to him. What he needs is guidance and example.

On the part of the State there is a remedy for this condition. University settlements and similar movements for bettering the condition of the poor through individual initiative are not yet practicable. In a government where Spanish paternalism is inherited, hygiene and sanitation are emphatically the province of the State and of the municipalities which depend on it, since they do not enjoy a large measure of home rule. A perception of this truth has been shown in the disposition to treat the roto's grievances as a social question rather than as a political issue. When this perception is translated into definite measures, his discontent with the existing order will become less menacing. For the government the lowering of the death rate and the increase of the birth rate per thousand has both economic and political significance.[1]

---

[1] A cabinet minister was thus quoted on this subject in a foreign journal :

" 'You may put in the most up-to-date drainage, and introduce the most admirable sanitary improvements, but you cannot induce the low-class peons, such as form the bulk of the residents of this and other Chilean cities, to use them. The housing arrangements of the poorer classes are simply indescribable, and they live like animals, crowded together in miserable rooms for which they pay an exorbitant price. The people

But is the economic and industrial relation of the roto to the State understood? Yes. How often I heard it discussed, how often I listened to the assertion made by Chileans, that Chile as a nation has a rotten core, that the anomaly of a government riotously rich through a single source of revenue and of a people superlatively poor, cannot long continue!

I sat through one night with Señor A, and listened to his eloquent and passionate indictment of his country and of the class of which he was the exponent, for he was of the ruling families. Another night it was with Señor B until the sun was breaking, and a third time it was with Señor C until the lingering *habitués* of the club were calling for their morning coffee. The talk ran in the same vein. The condition of the poor must be bettered. There must be a change in economic policies; dreams of conquest must be given over; the national revenues must be devoted to internal improvements; foreign capital must

— and especially the respectable class of employees — find it is impossible to secure clean and wholesome accommodation. Even the smallest rooms in the most unattractive houses are set out at absurdly high rentals — say from $10 to $15 (15*s.* 10*d.* to 22*s.* 9*d.*) a month each room.

"'Does the Government, then, do nothing to improve or control the conditions of the poor classes and protect them from the extortions and ill-treatment of the landlords?

"'Unfortunately, no kind of sanitary or habitation laws exist at the present moment; but I have often talked over the matter with the President of the Republic, and both he and I are determined to do something, if we can, later on. Things move slowly in Chile, you know, and, although it may appear rather strange to you, coming from a European country, Chileans are not accustomed to see, and do not expect, radical alterations effected in their country. However, you have touched upon a most important social question, and one which I have had much at heart myself. Perhaps we may be able to do something in the direction of improvement.'"

be encouraged to go into other industries than the
nitrate gamble; the military party must be curbed.

"Then, Señor, there is a military party in Chile?"

"Ah, my friend, there is.   Who can deny it?"

The military party was not a partisan organization,
for it was only reflected in the different political groups
which were at variance among themselves as to the
details of their programme, though not as to the main
purpose.   This was territorial accretion, and the indefinite application of the nitrate resources for military
ends as the means for continuing the supremacy of the
army and navy elements.   The reliance was the aggressive and sacrificing patriotism which is part of the being
of every Chilean, whether high or low; hence the difficulty of combating it.   But it took no thought of the
roto; therefore its weakness.

A series of swift events — some domestic, some
international — checked the militant military tendency.
Through the peace pacts with the Argentine Republic,
Chile found the opportunity of freeing herself from
naval expenditures that were weighing her down.   In
the construction and control of the Panama Canal
by the United States, her conservative statesmen were
enabled to establish the definite lines of both commercial and political relations with the other countries
of South America.   By reason of the acuteness of the
financial and industrial crisis which prevailed in 1903,
the depth of the popular discontent was revealed, and
the imperative need of finding a remedy was disclosed.
The roto had to be conciliated, propitiated, humored,
perhaps bamboozled a little, but always with a view
to bettering his material condition.   A comprehensive
system of public works, railways, harbors, rivers, roads,

and also municipal improvements, was recognized to be the channel into which the national income should flow.

It is the slow process of years during which the palpitating problems sometimes may throb with pregnant intensity, but their solution progresses in the degree that Chile adheres to industrial and commercial policies, and recognizes the true function of the masses in the political and social fabric of the State.

CHAPTER XVII

CHILE'S INDUSTRIAL FUTURE

*Agricultural Possibilities of the Central Valley — Its Extent —
Wheat for Export — Timber Lands of the South — Wool in
the Magellan Territory — Grape Culture — Mills and Factories — Public Works Policy — Longitudinal and Other Railway Lines — Drawbacks in Government Ownership —
Trans-Andine Road — Higher Levels of Foreign Commerce —
Development of Shipping — Population — Experiments in
Colonization — Internal and External Debt — Gold Redemption Fund — Final Word about the Nitrates.*

TRADE and industry in the future will have a
broader scope in Chilean national policies. The
passing of the era of unlimited naval expansion assures
this result. After the peace pacts with Argentina were
made effective, and the building of new battleships
was stopped, it was estimated that $1,000,000 went
into industries of the soil. By the sale of other super-
fluous naval armament to European Powers, more
funds can be released for public works and agricultural
development.

The basis of the agriculture of Chile is the great
central valley. This lies between the Cordillera of
the Andes and the Coast Range. It begins at the
hill of Chacabuco in latitude 33°, and extends to the
estuary at the head of the Gulf of Ancud known as
the Bay of Reloncavi, latitude 41° 30'. Santiago is in
the plain at the upper end of the valley. At the lower
end is the bed of lakes and gulf channels. The central

valley is 580 miles long, and has an average of 31 miles in width, though in the northern section it is not more than 15 miles across, and at the Angostura de Paine in latitude 34° a stone may be tossed from one side to the other. The area is approximately 18,000 square miles.

In this valley are the chief centres of permanent and growing population, as distinguished from the floating population of the nitrate provinces. The region favors all kinds of farming, both temperate and semi-tropical, for the grape, the orange, and the apple are found together. It grows the products which supply the inhabitants of the whole country, and it also has a surplus for export. Wheat and barley are regularly shipped to England in steadily increasing quantities, the £250,000 worth of wheat which Great Britain received from Chile in 1904 having come from this district. Corn, or maize, and linseed also are exported, and some wool is sent abroad. The live-stock industry is a successful one, but its products are chiefly utilized for home consumption.

The central valley is capable of a very large extension of the area under cultivation. The total of land given over to the production of the cereals, alfalfa, and vegetables, is about 9,000,000 acres. One drawback to increase is the tendency of the land-proprietors to keep their holdings intact and to prevent a material addition to the number of small farmers. There are no vast single estates, as in the wheat-growing regions of the United States. But there are many large haciendas, whose owners are content to receive a relatively small return from them rather than sell a part in order to secure capital for developing the remainder. This question enters into the relation of the roto or peon to the State, though not in an acute degree.

When the government and the individual Chilean land-owners succeed in bringing a larger area under cultivation, it will be by means of the small farmers. They will add enormously to the productive resources. While the central valley may not be said to have anything like the present wealth of the deserts of Atacama and Tarapacá, with their saltpetre deposits, yet its founts of production are enduring, and they will broaden and spread while the nitrate beds are being exhausted. This is both an economic and a political fact of vast importance to Chile.

The forest lands in the southern provinces are being gradually developed. Here is another source of national riches, for timber on the Pacific coast is not plentiful, and southern Chile has forests which are capable not only of supplying her own demands, but also of supplementing the needs of neighboring countries. In the Provinces of Arauco, Valdivia, and Llanquihue, the exploitation of the native timber has caused a lessening of the quantity imported from Oregon and California.

Below the central valley is the territory of Magellan, stretching to the Straits and across to the Chilean section of Tierra del Fuego. It comprises 47,500,000 acres, a large portion of which is unusually well adapted to sheep-raising. At the close of 1904 there were 4,250,000 head of sheep in this region. The animals furnish a strong, silky white wool, and there is some commerce in sheepskins. The wool exports range from 120,000,000 to 140,000,000 pounds annually. Great Britain and the United States take the bulk of the merinos, while France shares with them the common and mixed wools. The value of the annual commerce in wool, hides, and skins is about $2,000,000. In a recent year the estimate was that $24,000,000 was invested in new enterprises, chiefly mining companies and cattle-ranches in the Magellan district.

Grape culture is both a profitable and a promising agricultural industry. The capital invested in it is estimated at $17,000,000 to $20,000,000 gold. The area under cultivation is 60,000 acres, and the vine-yards have a production of 1,062,000 *hectolitres*. In a twelvemonth the value of the product was $3,250,000. The government encourages the industry by an export bounty on wines and grape alcohols.

Efforts have been made to introduce the cultivation of beet root into Chile, and government favor has been shown these projects. Yet it is very doubtful whether the outcome is worth the forced aid necessary to nurture the beet-root industry. It is more profitable for Chile to follow along the lines of the agricultural products which do not require a highly artificial stimulus.[1]

---

[1] A different view is taken by Chilean authorities. An article in the *Boletin de la Sociedad de Fomento Fabril* (Bulletin of the Manufacturers' Association) stated :

" The soil and climate of Chile indicate that the sugar industry would prosper in the Republic, if properly exploited, not only to the extent of supplying the domestic needs of the nation with that important product of prime necessity, but also in such quantities as would leave a considerable surplus for export to foreign markets. The sugar beet is one of the tubers that flourish most luxuriantly in the lands of the central zones of the Republic. In addition to the natural adaptability of the soil and climate of Chile for the growth of this tuberous root, the country also possesses deposits of nitrate and guano which are recognized to be the best and most appropriate fertilizers in the cultivation of this highly saccharine-producing tubercule.''

Agricultural exports, in the decade from 1893 to 1902, ranged from $2,000,000 to $4,500,000 annually. The latter sum seems likely to prove the minimum basis for the future.

The industrial resources of Chile are mirrored, though not with completeness, in the Permanent Industrial Exhibition which was opened in 1904. This covers not only the products of the soil, but also the home manufactures that are fabricated either from imported raw material or from half-manufactured products brought in to encourage the home industries. The Chilean policy is protective both by bounties and by duties. The sugar refineries, which import the raw cane sugar from Peru, are among the most stable of the industries. The flour-mills are also profitable enterprises. They grind the native wheat, and have a market for the flour for export in Bolivia and Peru, as well as farther up the coast.

The country has about 8,000 industrial establishments. Among these are 400 engaged in tanning and curing hides, 430 in various kinds of woodworking, 308 in metallurgy, 268 in chemical products, 560 in ceramics or pottery, 1,900 in food products, 1,920 in cloth manufacture and tailoring, 700 in building, and so on. Car-shops are maintained in connection with the State railways. A disposition on the part of foreign capital to engage in textile manufactures has received encouragement, and woollen and

---

The duty on the raw sugar is 6.50 *pesos*, or Chilean dollars, per 100 kilograms, equal to nearly one cent per pound in gold. The duty on refined sugar is about two cents per pound. The output of the refinery at Viña del Mar is 53,000,000 to 54,000,000 pounds, much of which is exported. This refinery, with a capital of $1,500,000 gold, through a period of ten years, paid annual dividends of 10½ per cent.

cotton mills may result. The native labor, judged by the experiments, is competent.

The public works policy has become the programme of all political groups, though the Congress sometimes is laggard in voting the appropriations recommended by the Executive. Railways are its most important feature. No chapter in Chile's history is more creditable to her people than the sacrifices made for building railways, and nothing shows the national instinct better than the perception that was demonstrated of the part which railroads play in both the industrial and the political development of a nation. In 1905, 3,100 miles were in operation, with many new lines under way. The majority of the lines are owned by the government, with the exception of the nitrate roads and the Chilean section of the Antofagasta and Bolivian Railway.

This State ownership is at once an advantage and a drawback. The policy of government proprietorship has made possible the building of links that have been of great value in internal development, and that will be of greater value when they become joined together as parts of one system. The disadvantage is in operation. When a Buenos Ayres railroad president was considering the extension of the Southern Railway of Argentina through the lower Andes to a junction with the Chilean roads, — all of which will come some day, — he made inquiries about the earnings of the Chilean system under government control. He was told that they had amounted to $18,000,000. That was very good indeed, considering the mileage and rolling-stock. " And how much did it cost to operate them last year? " he inquired. " $20,000,000," was the reply. This meant that under State management roads which would have paid dividends showed a healthy deficit. The deficit is not invariable, for in 1903 the government railways showed a surplus of $1,360,000 Chilean currency.

This government administration illustrates the evils of the use of patronage. The management is expensive; there is favoritism, discrimination, losses, unnecessary employees by the hundred. When the national policy is matured, and the country has the railways which are necessary and which would not have been constructed except by the government, the political evils can be overcome easily. The lines can be leased to private companies under a rental which will insure profit to the lessees and a steady revenue to the government. The State railways have an annual traffic of 3,000,000 to 3,500,000 tons of freight, and carry from 7,000,000 to 7,500,000 passengers.

The Chilean aspiration has been shown very clearly in the dogged determination with which the longitudinal line paralleling the coast and the Cordilleras has been carried forward. This policy already has given a section of the central valley the benefits of railway transportation, and in a few years undoubtedly the gaps will be closed so that the through journey can be taken from Santiago to Puerto Montt at the entrance of the Chiloe Archipelago. Also it will bring Iquique and the nitrate provinces of the North into through railway communication with the capital and the South. These northern links will be of marked value in reviving copper and silver mining.

The trans-Andine road, completing the gap from Los Andes through the Uspallata Pass to the Argentine boundary, when completed, will open a new chapter of intercontinental transportation. Promise is held out that the line may be in operation by the end of 1907, but the great spiral tunnel, which is the engineering device for breaking the back of the Cordilleras, may require a longer time. The important fact is that after delays of forty years the Chilean government guaranteed capital to the amount of $7,500,000 an annual return of 5 per cent for twenty years, and let the contract. A colossal bronze statue, resting on a granite column, the Christ of the Andes, at the very pinnacle of the Cordilleras, is a striking monument along this railway line. It is just on the boundary between Chile and Argentina, and commemorates the peace treaty without which the railroad systems of the two Republics would not have been joined. The idea of the commemorative statue was due to Señora Angela de Costa, of Buenos Ayres. The influence of this trans-Andine railway on the mutual commerce of Chile and Argentina by establishing through communication between Valparaiso and Buenos Ayres will be considerable, but it promises to be even more beneficial in bringing the western pampas of Argentina to the Pacific and to Panama.

Chilean foreign commerce reaches to higher levels with each year. Naturally the nitrates form the bulk of the exports, and assure a balance of trade in favor of Chile. On this account, by England and Germany an advantage is maintained; but since the United States is not a large consumer of the saltpetre, the balance of trade is in its favor. For the ten years from 1895 to 1904 inclusive, the United States products imported into Chile aggregated $41,610,000, while her exports to the United States amounted to $26,100,000.[1] Farm implements, builders' hardware, machinery, and mineral oils composed the larger part of the shipments.

This commerce is likely to grow to much larger proportions in the degree that railway building, municipal improvements, and harbor works are carried forward by Chile. A government agent who visited Europe and North America in 1905 in connection with contracts which were to be let, suggested to Pittsburg manufacturers the formation of a company that should give special attention to iron and steel products, railway and road supplies, for the Chilean market. The commerce is certain to grow after the Canal is constructed, because the agricultural machinery, mineral oils, and other products of which Chile is a heavy importer, will best be furnished by the United States, more especially in view of the cheapened transportation. An American bank in Valparaiso, in order to make the United States trade independent of English banking relations, is one of the probabilities of the future.

Chile's dependence on the sea makes foreign trade a vital element of her growth and prosperity. She has an encouraging future in the development of her own shipping. With the hardy marine population of the Chiloe Archipelago and the other seafaring population of the coast as the basis, her advantage on the Pacific is manifest. She will have in the future a much larger share in the coast-carrying trade which will result from the Panama Canal. Efforts to run

[1] The figures are on the basis of Chilean export and import valuations. The United States Treasury statistics place a higher value on the imports from Chile, chiefly nitrates.

"CHRIST OF THE ANDES"

Chilean vessels as far as San Francisco failed a few years ago, because of obstacles which competitors were enabled to throw in the way. This was a temporary check. The shipping along the coast as far as Vancouver will not always be denied her, but after the Canal is opened there will be a more pronounced advantage in passing through it to the Atlantic, and the flag of the Chilean merchant marine will be seen in New Orleans and New York.

The existing navigation has a substantial base for developing the maritime commercial movement. In a recent year the number of sailing-vessels calling at the Chilean ports was 549, and the total registry of these vessels was 797,000 tons. Most of them were British, the number being 302, and the tonnage 447,000. After that came Germany, with 92 ships and 146,000 tonnage. The United States sailing-ships numbered 17, and their aggregate tonnage was 15,000. Chile had the same number, but with a tonnage of 13,000.

The steamships numbered 1,255, with a total registry tonnage of 2,741,000. Of these Great Britain contributed 685, whose total tonnage was 1,477,000; Germany, 381, with a tonnage of 946,000; the United States, 15, with 39,000; and Chile 149, with a tonnage of 224,000. The Chilean government pays a small subsidy to the companies which carry the mails along the coast and to and from Panama. The Chilean merchant marine consists of 136 vessels, with a total registry of 67,936 tons. Next to Chile herself, the greatest volume of the coast trading is done by ships under the English flag.

The population of Chile is between 3,000,000 and

3,100,000. In 1796 an enumeration showed 350,000 inhabitants. In 1810, almost at the threshold of the struggle for independence from Spain, the number was 500,000. In 1866 it was estimated at 2,000,000. The census of 1895, which was taken with care, gave 2,712,000 inhabitants, nearly equally divided between town and country. The urban population was 1,250,000, and the rural 1,472,000.

Measures for adding to the number of inhabitants by means of colonization and other forms of stimulated immigration have not given very encouraging results. The public men and political economists who analyze the causes which prevent the natural increase of population from being normal, also find that the artificial propagation is unsatisfactory. During the ten years ending in 1902 the government spent $100,000, Chilean money, a year in its colonization efforts, and maintained an agency in Paris. The result of that work and the expenditure of half a million dollars was the arrival of 7,000 persons, some of whom went back and many of whom drifted to other countries. During the same period the Manufacturers' Association, the *Fomento de Fabrica*, secured 2,000 individuals. That is to say, in ten years government agency and private enterprise did not succeed in bringing 10,000 permanent immigrants to Chile.

Yet colonies have not always been failures. The German revolutionists of 1848 who settled around Valdivia, Osorno, and Lake Llanquihue, took root and flourished. With their tanneries and breweries they have made Valdivia the industrial centre that it is. After the war with Peru the Colonial Department sought to establish frontier colonists on the lands south

of the river Bio-bio and also in the archipelago of
Chiloe, where cereals grow in spite of the ceaseless rain.
It is doubtful if large groups of foreigners ever can be
settled permanently among those islands, but on the
mainland there is no reason why colonization should
not succeed. The forest clearings in the South and
the opportunities for sheep-raising and wool-growing
should induce an appreciable immigration in those
localities.

The Chilean government is seeking more especially
immigrants from northern Europe, Scandinavians, who
would find the climate cold enough for them but
much less severe than that of their own country.
The climate of Chile has its eulogists, and the eulo-
gies are not undeserved. There are, as the books
say, the three climates, — the dry heat of the North,
the tropical warmth of the Central region, and the
temperate climate of the South. Actually two-thirds
of Chile might be called temperate, and the South,
even in the Straits of Magellan, is not frigid, for the
warm winds of the ocean, not having a whole continent but only the tapering end to sweep over, modify
what otherwise might be Antarctic cold.

Whether the Boer colonies which were established
after the war in the Transvaal will spread is uncertain.
The first colonists were pleased with their surroundings. But there is no *veldt* in southern Chile, no
limitless stretch of level country, and the probability
is that the Patagonian plains and the pampas of Argentina will absorb most of the Boers who elect or
who have elected to leave South Africa for good.

Hitherto colonization has been conducted by Chile
as a government project, but it is an open question

whether better results would not be obtained by making the state ancillary to private enterprise. It also
may be assumed that universal education in hygiene
and observance of sanitary principles, along with the
improvement in the physical condition of the working-
classes, by lessening the mortality, in a single generation would result in a large addition to the permanent
population through the simple processes of natural
increase.

The foreign debt of Chile in 1905 was £16,650,000,
or $222,000,000 in Chilean currency. This debt was
created under refunding and other laws passed subsequent to 1885. Of the total, 83 per cent is held by
the Rothschilds and 8 per cent by the Deutsche Bank
of Berlin, the balance being distributed among various
creditors. Chile has paid very liberal commissions in
securing loans, whether they were temporary or for
refunding purposes. She always has preserved her
credit, but this credit often has been a too ready
excuse for further borrowing.

In the period of unlimited naval expansion and war
preparations, in spite of the regular income from the
nitrates, Chile kept piling up her obligations, and,
abandoning the gold standard, began issuing paper
notes. The latest issue of $30,000,000 made under
the law of December 29, 1904, brought the outstanding paper up to eighty million *pesos*, the value of the
peso being 36.5 cents United States currency. With
the view to getting back to the gold standard, a conversion fund had been established, and when this
paper issue was authorized the gold redemption reserve was close to $13,500,000. The hope had been
to reëstablish the gold basis in 1907, but this law

specifically fixed the date for the conversion of the paper currency at January 1, 1910. The gold reserve is to be strengthened from the proceeds of the sale of nitrate grounds, the sale of public lands in the Straits of Magellan territory, and a reserve of $500,000 in gold monthly, which the government undertakes to hypothecate for the conversion scheme, all of which is to be deposited in first-class European banks and in those of the United States. To these deposits will be added the interest as it accrues.

The Chilean Minister of Finance, at the time of the passage of this law, estimated that on January 1, 1910, the supply of gold would amount to $86,000,000, which would leave the government a surplus of $6,000,000 after the retirement of the paper notes ; but there is no assurance that further issues of currency may not be made in the interval ; and this keeps foreign capitalists and investors nervous, although, since the nitrate taxes are payable in gold, as are also the customs receipts, the position of the country is not a perilous one financially.

The basis of further debt on the part of Chile may be found in providing funds for the Valparaiso harbor improvements and also for the railroad from Arica into Bolivia. The latter project and the guaranty of the payment of interest on other railroads to be built by the Bolivian government, may be considered justifiable, because these railroads are expected to make Chile commercially dominant in Bolivia and to increase her trade very largely.

Notwithstanding the conditions which were held to justify the country in increasing the amount of paper currency, the system, while very profitable to the banks and the money-changers, is unequivocally bad for the merchants. They have to buy abroad in gold and also to pay the customs duties in the same manner, while they must sell on a fluctuating paper basis. With decreasing naval and military expenditures, with improving industrial conditions, and with widening commerce, Chile should return to the gold basis and maintain it.

After this outline sketch of the resources, industries, commerce, and finances of Chile, I am brought back to the question of the nitrates. They form more than 75 per cent of the exports, and they contribute more than 85 per cent of the government revenues. Because their exhaustion is foreseen and the time calculated, does it follow that the Republic rests on quicksand, that the foundation will disappear and leave no solid national superstructure behind? One answer might be found in an historical review of the growth and consolidation of the national life during the seventy-five years before the nitrate provinces were acquired.

Another answer may be found in the newer industrial and commercial life on which the country is entering. The fertilizers have yet in them the means of internal development — roads and railways, harbors, municipal improvements — sufficient for a century's growth. The central valley, the forests of the South, the sheep pastures of the Magellan territory and Tierra del Fuego, the coal of Arauco and Concepcion, the copper and silver of the northern provinces, all have potencies of production while the nitrate exhaustion goes on, and their development may be contemplated with equanimity while awaiting the advance of scientific irrigation to make green at some future period the white refuse of the saltpetre beds. Closer commercial relations with the neighboring countries of South America and wider trade with all the world, the expansion of the native merchant marine until it becomes an international factor in the ocean transport trade, offer the natural outlet for the national energies while assuring the national integrity. With these economic forces recognized and given their proper sphere, the collisions and the cross-purposes of domestic politics need have no deterrent influence on the industrial future of Chile. Agriculture, mining, and trade are better for her than battleships.

CHAPTER XVIII

WAYFARING IN BOLIVIA — THE ROYAL ANDES

Old Spanish Trail from Argentina — Customs Outpost at Majo — Sublime Mountain View — Primitive Native Life — Sun-beaten Limestone Hills — Vale of Santa Rosa — Tupiza's People and Their Pursuits — Ladies' Fashions among the Indian Women — Across the Chichas Cordilleras — Barren Vegetation — Experience with Siroche, or Mountain Sickness — Personal Discomforts — Hard Riding — Portugalete Pass — Alpacas and Llamas — Sierra of San Vicente — Uyuni a Dark Ribbon on a White Plain — Mine Enthusiasts — Foreign Consulates.

I JOURNEYED into Bolivia, the heart of South America, from northern Argentina with pack animals over the old Inca and Spanish trail. The Pacific coast routes for reaching the imprisoned country are by the railroad from Mollendo to Lake Titicaca, and then across the lake and by the little railway from Guaqui to La Paz; by the railroad from Arica to Tacna, and from Tacna by mules to Corocoro, whence a stage may be had to La Paz, 60 miles farther on; and by the railroad from Antofagasta to Oruro, 575 miles, and then by stage to La Paz, 160 miles.

The ancient and historic route from the Atlantic is the one that is followed in the prolongation of the Argentina Railway lines, and in joining the new Bolivian links so as to form a complete section in the Intercontinental or Pan-American system from Buenos Ayres to Lake Titicaca. From Jujuy, 1,000 miles distant from Buenos Ayres, up through northern Argentina, the course is in a double funnel along the great *cañon*, or *quebrada*, of Humahuaca. The trail widens in the valley of Tupiza, and then contracts from Tupiza west and north into difficult mountain passes through the Chichas Cordilleras and the sierras of San Vicente, until the Altiplanicie, or great Bolivian table-land that lies between the granitic Oriental, or Royal, Cordilleras and the volcanic Occidental, or Western, Cordilleras, is reached.

The boundary between Argentina and Bolivia is the Quiaca River. The town of La Quiaca on the Argentine side is the frontier custom house. On the Bolivian border is a big ranch with a row of willow trees. There is a fair road through an alternation of gravelly mountain-sides and rounded tops. The first Bolivian settlement is Majo in the valley, an adobe village of a few hundred inhabitants. This place is the customs outpost. Majo has a government post, or inn, which is called a *tambo*. The *tambo* consists of a corral for the animals and an adobe hut for the accommodation of strangers. Lodging is free. The traveller spreads his blankets on the earth floor or on the mud benches along the wall. The innkeeper, who is a government official, provides him with food. I got chicken, rice, and bread, which was luxurious feasting after ten days' hardships. Fodder was supplied the animals at a fair charge, and a smithy, which was part of the inn, was free for the use of the *arriero*, or muleteer.

It was September when I was at Majo. At five o'clock in the afternoon the thermometer marked 76° Fahrenheit, and at seven o'clock, when the sun had gone down, it marked 46.5°, a noticeable change. At

mid-day at this season the temperature was about 86°.
In the early morning before sunrise I had broken a
film of ice on one of the rivulets in a sequestered
gulch.

But Bolivia is not seen from the little valley in
which the hamlet of Majo lies. After two hours
of going down and up steep hills the eminence on the
edge of an extensive gorge is reached. It is the first
view of the Royal Andes and their sierras. A sublime
sight it is. The change from the arid, half-desert
scenery is startling. The mountains in the foreground
lie in irregular, transverse black and gray masses, and
through the mists the fleecy peaks and pinnacled precipices are visible. The dominating one is Guadalupe,
18,870 feet above sea-level, the Pike's Peak of Bolivia.
Closer at hand the sierras are covered with some
appearance of vegetation, — pale green cacti and russet
brown thorn-bushes or acacias. I followed the ravine
down along the banks of the dried-up river, which
was bordered with pepper trees and willows. In this
valley are a number of attractive small farms. After
leaving it there is another hill climb. Yuruma, the
hill village, is a dilapidated collection of adobe cabins.

Genuine Bolivian life, the primitive and patriarchal
existence, I encountered in the villages of Nazarene
and Suipacha. They lie on either side of the Grand,
or San Juan, River, which is easily forded in the dry
season. It was a rural scene that would have delighted
the poet or the philosopher who wants to go back to
Nature. Nothing more tranquil in all the world than
this secluded nook in the Andes. The women were
washing clothes in the streams, the men and boys
were working in the fields, the flocks of sheep and

cattle grazed placidly in the valley and on the hillside, and everybody had a respectful greeting to
the stranger, sometimes in Spanish, sometimes in
the Quichua tongue. The donkeys wandered about
bearing clay water-jars and apparently without a
driver until a small and wrinkled old man with most
wonderfully patched and brilliantly colored trousers,
screamed to them, and they stopped where a customer
waited. The cabins were of adobe, or unbaked brick.
Some were quite neat and were half hidden in gardens
surrounded by mud walls covered with thorn-bushes.

I never met so many very old people as in these
two primitive villages. Far from the carking cares
and ambitions of the world, they follow their unevent-
ful course until the sands of life literally run out. In
front of one cabin was an old woman crooning over
her bowl of porridge. She appeared to me a vitalized
mummy. I reined my mule before a dwelling a little
farther on and asked, "What is the age of *la viejicita*
(the little old woman)?" "We don't know, sir,"
replied the occupant, civilly. "We think she is more
than one hundred and fifteen years old. Her great-
grandchildren say she is one hundred and twenty-five."
I might doubt the family records of the crone as preserved by the great-grandchildren, yet seeing her it
was easy to believe that her life may have spanned
three centuries, — born in the late years of the eighteenth and stretching through the nineteenth into the
twentieth, — for she certainly was more than one hundred. When the Bolivian census was taken a few
years ago, the enumerators reported 1,261 persons
whose age passed the century mark, and many of
these centenarians dwelt in this San Juan valley.

The gold-hunters at various times have ruffled the placid life of the inhabitants. A ledge of quartz cropping out from the side of the sierra near Suipacha has been attacked viciously, but more promise has been held out by the placer yields. Its sands are not all golden, yet they have yielded enough to encourage the investment of a large amount of capital in companies formed for the purpose of dredging the river-bed. These enterprises have their headquarters in Buenos Ayres. During my journey I found the people impatient for the arrival of the heavy dredging machinery which was at the seaboard awaiting transportation. It arrived later.

After leaving Suipacha there was a very hot and dusty hill climb of three hours, although most of it was along a fine piece of mountain highway, really a splendid triumph of road engineering. The hills all around here seemed to be limestone, and the sun beating on them created the most intense heat that I experienced anywhere. In the morning at sunrise my thermometer registered 50° Fahrenheit. In the early afternoon in the midst of these limestone cliffs it marked 110° Fahrenheit. This was 15 degrees higher than at any other point in the journey. I might have questioned the correctness of the thermometer, but its previous and its subsequent registrations I was able to verify, so that there was no reason to doubt its verity in registering this locality.

But though the glaring sun and the choking dust made the afternoon very uncomfortable, there was compensation. It was almost dusk when we — myself, the muleteer, and the pack animals — descended into the vale of Santa Rosa and found it gloriously

restful. A model ranch spreads through the valley.
The bed of the river is among spur cliffs and broken
mountain walls on either side, out of which plunge
miniature Niagaras. The stream is bordered by willows. It narrows until its course is forced through
a cliff which rises sheer in front to the height of 700
or 800 feet and is known as the Angustora, or Narrow
Way. The needle-point chasm made by the river
has been enlarged by artificial means, and the narrow
way is wide enough for ox-carts.

After the Angustora the course broadens again into
the valley. The stream is very crooked and has to be
forded often. At this season the fording was not difficult, but in January and February, when the rains come,
the only passage is along a trail well up the side of the
precipice, for the river-bed is a tumultuous torrent.

Tupiza lies in this vale of Santa Rosa, the brook
being an affluent of the San Juan and sometimes called
the San Juan. I entered the village by moonlight.
I left it early one morning by starlight. The night
of my arrival fourteen hours continuously in the
saddle had wearied me greatly, yet the physical sensation disappeared in an instant on entering the beautiful valley, bathed as it was in the soft moonlight.
When taking a last look at it, there was the same
impression of charm. The river is fringed by drooping, feathery willows of the softest and most velvety
green. They seem to be taking a perpetual bath in
the dews. There are also the pepper trees. After
a long desert ride the sober verdure of these trees
is always refreshing. It is a harbinger of revivified
Nature, but here in contrast with the glistening green
willows they are the merest drabs.

The mountains which shut in the valley are brown, with granite flanks exposed ; and the sunsets — ah ! the artist would have to penetrate this lovely region to see whether the miracle of silver gray changing into impalpable azure and then flaming into red prairie fire can be transferred to canvas.

Tupiza is the most important place in southern Bolivia. It is the gateway north, south, east, and west. It is 9,800 feet above sea-level. The town has 5,000 inhabitants, and is the head of administration for the department. The church edifice has twin towers and a blue front, with much gaudy and gingerbread ornamentation inside and out. The government building, which includes the custom house, post-office, and telegraph office, is more tasteful. It is of two stories, with brown front and with arcade windows. There are a few two-story houses with narrow window balconies, but the dwellings are mostly of one story, with sloping grass-thatched roofs and whitewashed or dark blue fronts. They have square inner courts, or *patios*, and are without windows opening on the streets. As the street door is kept closed, there is complete seclusion from outside life.

The plaza is ornamented with feathery willow trees, under one of which in the heat of the day the public business is transacted, the desks and chairs being moved out from the government building. I watched the process for a couple of hours one day, and found it a not unpleasing picture of local and patriarchal administration. A fountain in the centre of the plaza at all hours is thronged by the men and women with their earthen water-jars, gossiping and quarrelling. There are many small shops for the sale of fruits, vegetables, and gaudy handkerchiefs. The women venders exercise squatter sovereignty on every street corner.

Ladies' fashions are of so world-wide an interest that I digress to describe them as they were seen at Tupiza, as I had seen them in the primitive villages of Nazarene and Suipacha, as I saw them afterward at Uyuni and other places, including the capital.

The prized possession of the Bolivian Indian woman, and her chief pride also, whether she is pure Indian or *chola*, is her petticoat. Her dowry is in this garment. Like the Dutch woman of tradition, she carries her wealth about her. These petticoats are of all the colors of the rainbow and divers other hues not found therein. I first noticed them at Nazarene, and remarked the love of color, which must be inborn, for the garments were of purple, violet, fiery red, crimson, scarlet, subdued orange, glaring saffron, blue, and green. They were very short, reaching barely below the knee, and no difference was observed between childhood, maidenhood, matronly middle life, and wrinkled old age. Glancing from my window in Tupiza, I thought it was a parade of perambulating balloons.

The more well-to-do of the Indian women have stockings and shoes, but the love of color does not extend to the hosiery. Most of this wear is of ordinary brown or black. There is, however, pride and something like social distinction with regard to the footwear. I was amused on seeing the number of russet gaiters. Later at Uyuni I remarked that the prevailing fashion was high-heeled French gaiters, but in Tupiza and the other villages the extreme was not so great. Nor does the possession of the shoes make stockings necessary. Many of the Indian women with their plethora of petticoats apparently consider the acme reached if they can also have shoes, and do not fret themselves over hosiery.

These women have a habit which the bashful traveller does not at first understand. When he sees one of them calmly removing a petticoat, he is apt to turn away, but he need not do so. It may be that the advancing heat of the day has caused the wearer to discard the outer skirt, but more likely it is the vanity of her sex, and the desire to make her sisters envious by showing what is beneath, for each new vesture disclosed is more brilliant than the one which overlapped it. I sat in the plaza at Tupiza and watched two Indian women try to make each other envious. The first one removed the outer petticoat, which was of purple. This divestment disclosed another garment of blazing red, and after that came a brilliant yellow. The other woman started with a green petticoat, and gradually got down to a mixture of blue and yellow. By that time I had begun to fear for the consequences, and made a pretence of turning my back by strolling to the hotel.

From Tupiza to Uyuni is three days' hard riding with horse or mule, and usually it is nearer four. The region is graphic in its grandeur of conical peaks, Chorolque, Guadalupe, Cotaigata, Ubina, eternally snow-covered, which hold beneath their granite domes a mass of mineral wealth that is for the centuries. The trail by which one passes is along the torn flanks and through the harsh passes of the Chichas and the San Vicente ranges.

SANDSTONE PILLARS NEAR TUPIZA

The morning we left we followed the river-bed, passed some good farms and mud huts, and continued through a pasturage on which were grazing goats, llamas, and sheep. The vegetation was of yellow mustard flowers in bloom, pale cactus stalks, brown thorn-trees, and clumps of russet grass. There are a big, gaudy ranch-house, which looks like an imitation French castle, and an ornate little chapel at the head of the valley before it narrows into a chain of crooked gorges. The mountains seem to lie squarely across the way in irregular masses, like gigantic wedges, but there are abrupt hatchet gashes in the sides and many defiles, crevasses, and chasms.

A few miles from Tupiza the geological formation is very curious. At a distance the appearance is that of an old city of crumbling brown cathedrals, towers, buildings, and solitary sentinels. The sandstone formations resemble brown instead of crystal stalagmites. Some of the figures are strikingly grotesque. It is really a series of crenellated mud mountains which have been worn by the atmosphere and the water cutting down and washing away the earth.

The first stopping-place is the hamlet of Ingenia. This place has a *tambo* and a mud chapel and church. The Indian natives were blear-eyed, dirty, and the most repulsive that I met anywhere, but they were devout and hospitable. They escorted me to the chapel to see the image of the Virgin, which had some special history, and they got some fresh eggs for me. The altitude of Ingenia is 10,200 feet. I set out in the early morning with my pack animals and muleteer, all of us in ill humor because of a bad night's entertainment. The day's journey to Escariano, the next lodging-place, was not a long one. Beyond Ingenia the river course is narrow, and allows no room for ranches or even farms of the ordinary size, though there are some pasturage and a weedy kind of grass, scrub fir, or juniper. I was surprised at the number of quail which started up from every bush, and also at the variety of song-birds that hardly would be looked for in a treeless country.

Two or three hours from Ingenia the thread of the trail along the margin of the ravine narrows until it is not possible for animals or persons to pass. On entering the long *cañon* it is necessary to call out and make sure that no one is coming from the opposite direction. The echoes rumble through the gorges and finally die away. If no answering call is heard, it is safe to go forward along the edge of the sloping precipice. Sometimes *tropas*, or droves of burros and llamas, get into this gorge from both entrances, and then there is a controversy, and also a difficulty about backing out until space can be found for passing.

The *cañon* opens into a circle of slaty limestone hills, which have to be climbed and descended with considerable care. There are some white cactus bulbs with yellow flowers, and also in this locality some abandoned mine shafts. The cost of fuel and of freight transport made it necessary to close the mines until a railroad shall be built.

An incident of the day is thunder and a threatened rain. A ragged purple curtain hangs over the summit of Guadalupe, but that is far away and the clouds pass. They are followed by a soft wind which grows almost into a gale.

These winds are said by the Indians to cause the

siroche, which is the dread both of the natives and of travellers. Some authorities claim that the illness is due to the presence in the earth of minerals, which are exhaled like gases and poison the atmosphere. I had been warned especially against this sickness when crossing the sierras between Tupiza and Uyuni, but during my travels in the Andes I experienced only one attack of *siroche*, and this was before reaching Tupiza. It had been a long morning climb and ride across sandy plains and among the cactus and fir underbrush. Coming up gradually from the sea-level and by slow stages, I had not felt any serious apprehension, though somewhat troubled by a neuralgic headache and by just the appearance of bleeding at the nostrils.

That morning the wind was blowing so softly that it seemed to cradle itself. A feeling of intense depression came over me. It was purely mental, because the day had not advanced far enough for the physical fatigue to manifest itself. I was out of temper, and my nerves were on edge. At noon, taking the observation of the temperature by means of a Centigrade thermometer, I found myself in a hopeless muddle in trying to reduce it to Fahrenheit. The method was absolutely clear in my mind, — "divide by 5, multiply by 9, add 32," — but at every calculation the result was different, though I was certain I was following the rule. Finally I turned to the muleteer and asked him crossly, "Loreto, what's the matter with me?" "It's the *siroche*, sir," he explained. "The wind is very bad to-day, but if you can keep on for a few hours we'll be all right." Then he looked at me a little suspiciously and said, "I don't think we had better stop here."

I had no desire to stop there under the savage sun,
while the wind was forming white mantles of sand on
the fir bushes, and told him we would go on. We
kept on, and I began to feel myself again, though for
a period of perhaps six hours I was in a condition of
collapse similar to that which I often had experienced
following attacks of sea-sickness. In my own case,
however, there was none of the nausea which accompanies that distressing malady, and which with most
persons is also an incident of *siroche*. My muleteer's
fear was that I would insist on stopping or on turning
back. He had had that trouble with two or three
persons whom he had guided over the mountains,
and, as he told me, they had given him a great deal
of worry by their whims.

Having had this attack, I was a little apprehensive
with regard to crossing the *punas*, or table-lands, from
Tupiza to Uyuni, and I could see that my *arriero* also
was watchful. But I felt not the slightest symptoms.
Mining engineers who make that journey two or three
times a year told me that they always suffered from
the *siroche*. Animals likewise suffer from it. The
horse is of little use in these altitudes, and the mules
are not immune. My own pack animals gave out
twice.

My greatest annoyance was from the blistering and
bleeding of the lips due to the dry wind. The natives
grow expert enough to save themselves by means of
scarfs while riding, but I found that this method gave
me no protection. My lips were swollen unnaturally,
and local applications did not reduce the swelling or
the pain except temporarily at night. It was weeks
before they became normal, and this I found was the

gravest inconvenience in traversing the *punas*. My nerves also were under intense strain. That tension is unavoidable so high up, but it is something that gradually can be overcome. After living a month at an altitude of 12,000 to 14,000 feet, I experienced little annoyance from keyed-up nerves.

The increased heart movement is something which no one can escape, and it varies only in degree according to the individual. Jogging along comfortably on the back of a mule, the accelerated action is not appreciated, but let the traveller get off to rest the animal by walking and he quickly discovers the limit of his exertion. In my own case I found it easier to climb the hills afoot than to descend them, the heart apparently pumping with more regularity on the up-grade. But at night, after a hard day's travel, on lying down to sleep it would be half an hour to an hour before the trip-hammer beating would lull itself away into slower and more regular palpitations.

From Escariano to Tambilla is a wearying ride. The course is across gorges and chasms, up the dry river-bed, then down for a good many hundred feet and again up into white plains covered with scrub. The longest climb is up the corkscrew height of Portugalete. It would be not only cruelty, but physical impossibility, to surmount this summit on the back of a mule, and I trudged it at an even pace with the panting pack animals. The pass or gateway of Portugalete is 14,137 feet above sea-level. Through this pass the railroad will wriggle its way.

After the divide was reached the descent was fairly steady, though abrupt. Guadalupe was in sight part of the day, and there were also glimpses of other peaks, snow-covered, while in some of the transverse gorges which the sun did not penetrate I saw the perpetual ice and snow. I stopped two or three times to gather a handful of snow, and then climbed back on the mule, passing in a very brief space of time from temperature below freezing to 90° or 95° Fahrenheit. On this slope were pasturing many alpacas and other sheep as well as goats and llamas.

During that long day we passed just two human dwellings, adobe huts, and reached Tambilla after nightfall. Tambilla lies in a valley, but its altitude is 12,900 feet. The Indians who kept the *tambo* were very indifferent to our comfort. They were having some kind of a celebration, and at first professed not to understand Spanish. As the *arriero* knew a little Quichua, he went after them in the Indian vernacular, and I swore some Spanish oaths, which were not nice but which brought out sullen rejoinders and the promise of something to eat. This was prepared in time, — the usual *chupé,* — but having seen its preparation, my stomach revolted, and I went to bed after partaking of hot coffee and crackers. During the night a freight train arrived, burros laden with dynamite for the mines, and I felt satisfaction in hearing the freighters, all of whom were natives, take possession of the sleeping quarters of the inmates of the *tambo.*

It was a relief to get away in the early morning long before sunrise. The sun disclosed the edges of a vast mountain plain, with sand-dunes and scrub breaking its monotonous stretch and a rim of chalk-white mountains enclosing the whole basin. This was the Sierra of San Vicente. Again I noticed the presence of both quail and song-birds. About noon we

BOLIVIAN INDIAN WOMEN WEAVING

AYMARÁ INDIAN WOMAN AND CHILD

reached a bend in the dry river-bed and even a rivulet
of water. A ruined cabin and a corral fallen into
disuse were here. In front were two graves marked
by stones and a rude cross. My muleteer mused a
moment. He pointed to the cabin, then to the
graves, and shook his head. " I was here a year ago,
Señor," he said, "and they [pointing to the graves
as though he could see their tenants] were there
[pointing to the cabin] then."

The afternoon was a gradual but steady climb among
vast sheep pastures which were still peopled with many
flocks, although nearly all the huts had been abandoned by their human dwellers. Toward evening after
another long ascent we crossed an easy gradation of
summits and then down to Amachuma. It is 12,444
feet above sea-level. The Indians at Amachuma were
indifferently hospitable. At first they professed ignorance of any language except Quichua, but later, when
the government innkeeper appeared, we got passable
accommodations, one of the mud benches along the
wall being cleared of the dogs and the natives in order
that I might spread my blankets.

From Amachuma the next morning we rode for two
hours up and across the chalk-white hills, and then a
dark ribbon forked out on a vast plain below. " That
is Uyuni," said Loreto, my muleteer, simply. It lay
against the horizon like a frozen sea. For the first
time in weeks Loreto became enthusiastic. " There
[to the north] is Oruro; there [to the south] is Antofagasta; there [to the east] the Potosi silver mines;
here, Huanchaca silver mines; but, Señor, there is no
water in Uyuni for my mules. I shall have to lead
them back here to-night."

Uyuni is a waterless oasis on the salt pampa.

Two hours descending through the white sand and scrub and we were on the outskirts of the place. The most prominent spot which we had seen proved to be the cemetery. The town is a staked, plain kind of settlement, without shrub or tree. The railroad yard, enclosed by a corrugated iron fence stockade, takes in most of the municipal territory. Caravans of llamas and droves of burros and mules filled the streets. Much of the freighting is done by the llamas. There are many small shops and several very extensive warehouses and supply stores.

Uyuni is an outfitting and shipping centre. It is on the edge of one of the most productive and varied mineral districts in Bolivia. In 1885 there was almost no settlement, but the development of the Huanchaca and the other mines made a town necessary. Huanchaca is nine miles away on the railroad spur. Though the company a few years ago was compelled to spend a large amount of money in pumping out the Pulacayo mines, the output was diminished only temporarily. It furnishes the bulk of the freight down the railroad to the coast at Antofagasta.

Everybody in Uyuni is an enthusiast on mines. I felt myself in Colorado or the Black Hills when the local judge and a party of citizens came to welcome me. The judge drew a rough map of the district. " Here," he said, " is tin ; there, gold ; yonder, silver ; over there, copper ; out this way, borax ; off here, bismuth ; this way, lead ; a little beyond, antimony." He and his fellow-citizens were very anxious for the railroad to be built to Guadalupe and Tupiza, so that the mineral industry could be assured of transportation facilities.

In strolling about I observed all the characteristics of the native Indian race, and of the *cholos*. The fondness of the women for bright petticoats and French gaiters I have recounted. It affords a lesson to the political economist by showing that artificial wants can be created and goods sold in remote communities. Not only were French gaiters in demand, but gaudy handkerchiefs for head-dresses and also much jewelry that was not gaudy. Many of the women had finger-rings and ear-rings of gold. They appeared superior to the men, who are given to imbibing alcohol. But I would not be too censorious. I had seen these men in the desolate, lonely passes and on the dreary sand-plains, and was not sure, if my life from New Year's to New Year's had to be passed in the same way, that whenever I got into Uyuni with a chance for human companionship, I also would not get drunk.

Uyuni is intensely cold, lying, as the town does, at an altitude of 12,100 feet under the snow mountains which send down their icy breath, and on the salt plains which, when the rays of the sun are off them, are scarcely less chilling. The legend told every new-comer is of going to bed with a bottle of hot water to keep the feet warm, and waking up to find the glass in fragments and the ice retaining the perfect form of the bottle. I did not have this experience, but in September, which is in the beginning of Spring, the cold was penetrating enough to make me believe the story.

I noted on Sunday several foreign flags flying over various consulates ; and this was a reminder that Uyuni, through its commercial and mining interests, is a kind of international centre.   The Italians, French, Germans, and Chileans have the largest interests among the foreigners, though a fair proportion of the business is in the hands of Bolivians.   Some of the foreigners originally came over the trail from Argentina.   More of them followed the routes of travel from the Pacific.

CHAPTER XIX

WAYFARING IN BOLIVIA.—THE CENTRAL PLATEAU

A Hill-broken Table-land — By Rail along the Cordillera of the Friars — Challapata and Lake Poöpo — Smelters — Spanish Ear-marks in Oruro — By Stage to La Paz — Fellow-passengers — Misadventures — Indian Tombs at Caracollo — Sicasica a High-up Town, 14,000 Feet — Meeting-place of Quichuas and Aymarás — First Sight of the Famed Illimani Peaks — Characteristics of the Indian Life — Responsibility of the Priesthood — Position of the Women — Panorama of La Paz from the Heights — The Capital in Fact — Cosmopolitan Society.

THE Altiplanicie, or Great Central Plateau, because of its mineral riches, was called by the geographer Raimondi a gold table with silver legs. Once the bed of a vast inland sea, the table-land now forms the Titicaca basin and lies between the Oriental and the Occidental Cordilleras. Its surface is broken by many conical hills and small sierras, supposedly the result of volcanic eruptions, yet it comes within the definition of level country as level country is understood in the Andine regions. The southern zone of the Altiplanicie has been aptly described as a solid cape of salt.

From Uyuni, in the lower corner of the great plain, the railway skirts along the mountain range known as the Cordillera of the Friars. The road crosses the salt pampas and winds among the foothills and along the Marques River into agricultural lands, chiefly

grazing, with pasturage for some cattle, donkeys, and
llamas, and many sheep. There are a number of villages, always with a little church in the centre. The
September day on which I took the trip the people
were making a *romeria*, or pilgrimage, from hamlet
to hamlet, to celebrate one of the numerous religious
holidays.

During the first three hours weather changes were
swift and sharp,— heavy clouds, thunder, the first rain
I had experienced for weeks, a whirling dust-storm,
thunder again with looped lightning, pelting hail, and
finally blinding snow. My fellow-passengers were
Bolivian business men and their families, and English
and German mining superintendents. An excellent
breakfast was served in the station at Sevaruyo.

The principal town on the line is Challapata, near
the borders of Lake Poöpo. Challapata is a starting-
point for Sucre. Sucre is the old capital of Bolivia,—
an historic city and a very rich one, lying in a fertile
valley but very remote from the highways of travel.
Few foreigners or natives in Bolivia know how to find
it. The most confusing directions are given in regard to reaching it. A trail or cart-road of a very
hard kind to travel runs from Tupiza to Sucre, and
in La Paz I was gravely told that to get there I
would have to go to Tupiza. Other directions are
as vague. The shortest way from either La Paz or
from the coast is to proceed to Challapata and then
procure mules to Sucre, though for two days the journey may be followed by means of a stage or similar
vehicle.

Lake Poöpo is a teacup beside a soup-tureen in
comparison with Lake Titicaca; yet it receives the

waters of that lake, which is not an evaporating pan, through the Desaguadero River, and then loses them in the Laca-Amra, a disappearing and reappearing stream. Only one gallon in a hundred of the water drained into Lake Poöpo by the Desaguadero is carried off by other streams. The Titicaca current is 23.73 metres per minute, and the volume of the Desaguadero is 4,822.5 cubic metres per minute.

From Poöpo on to Oruro I noted a succession of smoke-stacks from the smelters, and very apparent evidences of the mining industry. After that it was all mine sights and mine talk. There is a large foreign colony, which includes Yankees, Englishmen, Germans, and Chileans. The town is a bare sort of place, with the shafts gaping from the mountains all around. It has a population of 10,000, a newspaper, two banks, and some extensive commercial establishments.

Oruro is an old town, and still shows many Spanish ear-marks. The Jesuit chronicles say that in the height of the mining fever, in the seventeenth century, it had 70,000 inhabitants. The streets are narrow, and the buildings have balconies and overhanging eaves. The local administration is progressive, and the plaza is an evidence of local public spirit. It has a fountain in the centre, and some effort at adornment has been made by fencing in the flower-plats. The pilgrimage of women and children to and from the fountain with their water-jars is an endless one. There is a military garrison and a *Cabildo*, or municipal headquarters. In the market are the women venders, decked out in their brilliant petticoats, selling onions, fruits, fish, rock salt, and

the other commodities of humble life. Here, as in
Uyuni, I observed many kindly and intelligent faces
among them, and they seemed to me superior to
the men. The latter are the *cargadores*, or burden-
bearers. They travel around with their backs bent,
pedler fashion, even when they have no burden.

Oruro's climate cannot be made a subject of local
pride. It is raw and rainy, with snow in the morning
which melts quickly under the sun. The mean average
temperature as I gleaned from the local records is 43°
Fahrenheit, but in the month of November the extremes are 68° and 34°. An ordinary year has 54
days of rain, 8 days of heavy snow, and 52 days of
sleety winds. The mineral resources of the sub-
Andine region, of which Oruro is the centre, com-
pensate for its lack of genial temperature. The most
important of the mines is the San José, which produces both tin and silver.

La Paz by the stage route is 160 miles from Oruro.
When the railroad is completed, the distance will be
shortened a little, though the same general course will
be followed. I left Oruro one September morning
in the diligencia. The transportation had been controlled by a pair of Scotchmen, and it was generally praised for the service, but they turned it over to
local management and then there was nothing to
praise. We had a dozen passengers, though only
room for ten. They included a Peruvian gentleman
and his Chilean wife; two Chilean rotos, or rough-and-
ready workers who were going to La Paz to take jobs;
a party of Italian pedestrians who walked in this
manner; a German drummer; a native merchant,
and myself. The route followed the pampa along

the edge of the mountain range, and as there had been local snow-storms the regular line of white silhouettes glistening in the sunlight presented a most exquisite sight. But the road was very heavy, and our six mules had difficulty in pulling the stage from one mud hole to another.

At noon we were mired. It rained and hailed throughout the afternoon. One of the Italians, after a long parley with the driver and the Indian postilion, took a mule from the traces and started for the hamlet, which lay eight miles farther on, to see if means could not be found for transferring us.

About nine o'clock through the darkness we heard shouts, and found that a *carreta*, or two-wheeled cart, with four mules had been sent to our rescue. No promise was held out to us of reaching the village, but the stage was so uncomfortably crowded that some of us felt bound to make room for those who preferred to remain. We clambered out, and the outrider took us on his shoulders and waded through the mud till he was able to drop us into the cart. He had been picked up somewhere along the way. Without him we would have had to pass the hours till morning in the open *carreta*. The wind was biting, and though wrapped in heavy overcoats and blankets, we could not keep the chill from our marrow-bones.

The night was so black that nothing could be seen ahead except the moving silhouette of the Indian guide. I learned on this occasion of the endurance of this class of natives. Our postilion was barefoot, clad only in thin cotton trousers and some kind of shirt, yet he plunged through the ponds, waded the creeks, and marked out a course for the mules, urged by their hoarse, screeching driver, to follow. When they got mired, he was at their heads or at their heels, yelling at them in the Aymará tongue with the heartiness that a muleteer on the Western frontier will put into his coaxing of the same animals. After seeing him set the pace, I could readily understand how these men could travel all day on foot and keep the animals going at a good pace. Two or three times we thought we were hopelessly lost, but at last he brought us into the village of Caracollo and to the *tambo*, or inn. The breakfast had been waiting since eleven o'clock in the morning. We sat down to it at a quarter of an hour before midnight. After enjoying the repast we went to bed commiserating our companions who were huddled together in the stage somewhere back on the pampa.

The next morning I made a little study of native life as seen at Caracollo, chiefly in the plaza, which was more in the nature of a market-place. It was under water, but the Indian women were squatted about selling their wares with stoical indifference to personal comfort. The priest was fat, good-natured, and more intelligent than others of his class whom I met. He told us that the Indian tombs or tomb dwellings which we saw on the edge of the village were at least four centuries old and were still venerated by the natives. I strolled up the hillside to have a closer view of them, and found that they are now put to baser uses. The veneration of the natives apparently is shown by finding the shady side in order to take a snooze at mid-day. Half a score of the Indians were enjoying their siestas.

The tombs are oblong in form, from six to twelve

Scene in the Plaza at Oruro — Ancient Tombs at Caracollo —
Primitive Methods of Tin-crushing

feet high, and are hollow. Some are open at the
top, but more are closed and have a kind of arched
roof. All that I noticed opened or faced toward
the east. Some have openings on each side. The
straw and mortar seemed to be so fresh that it was
hard to conceive of these monuments of the past
being centuries old, but of the fact there is no
question.

The stage managed to pull itself out of the mud
and reach Caracollo at noon. We set off at once.
At Villa Villa, a dreary spot, the eating-house had
nothing ready for us because we were running off
schedule time. Yet the Frenchman and his wife who
kept it managed to provide us a mouthful. They
were from Marseilles. "How did you get away off
here?" I incautiously asked him. He shrugged his
shoulders.

We reached Pandura at nightfall to find that the
stage coming from La Paz, also running off schedule
time on account of the rains and the bad roads, had
arrived there ahead of us. Pandura, which consists
of three or four mud structures, by squeezing itself
could just shelter one set of passengers. There was
no possibility of accommodations for us, nothing
we could do except to continue our journey over
dangerous roads. The more fortunate passengers,
however, were very considerate. We could not ask
them to give up their beds, but they themselves vol-
unteered to forego their dinner. It had been ordered
before our arrival and would be ready in an hour.
Since they had the whole night before them, they
could wait for another dinner to be prepared. We
accepted their offer, and after the meal had been eaten

with gluttonous appetites, we plunged off in the darkness. The animals were utterly worthless and could
barely drag us along. Where fresh mules were in
waiting they were already blown, and the local *tambo-
keepers* refused to let us have the animals which
were reserved for the government mail. Usually after
alternate threatening and cajoling we would get the
post mules, sometimes taking them forcibly, and then
proceed a little better. But it was a nightmare of a
journey.

In the morning we reached Sicasica. Sicasica is a
town of consequence and the centre of a silver-mining
district. It is one of the highest inhabited places in
Bolivia, the altitude being 14,000 feet. It has an old
Jesuit church, built in 1622, notable for the fantastic carving on the lava stone exterior and for some
passable paintings on the interior walls as well as a
fine altar.

Sicasica is notable in another way. It is the
meeting-place, as it were, where the two distinct Indian
races, the Aymarás and the Quichuas, come front to
front. Heretofore in southern Bolivia it was the
Quichua race I had met and their language I had
heard, but from Sicasica on the Aymarás were my
study. Both these Indian idioms are spoken, and
neither race learns the tongue of the other, nor do
they have a common medium in Spanish. The local
innkeeper told me that few of them knew any Spanish,
and that the little intercourse they had with one
another was more sign language than anything else.
Aymará was predominant, and its barking sounds
were heard in sharp contrast to the softer accents of
the Quichua. I wandered into a girls' school, where

the little maids were seated on vicuña skins and, rocking forward and backward, were conning their lessons aloud while the woman teacher accompanied their sing-song, standing. There was neither bench nor desk of any kind. The primer was in Aymará, and seemed to correspond to Noah Webster's spelling-book.

In the afternoon we reached Ayoayo, where a small garrison of soldiers is maintained. Ayoayo is historic for an uprising which was instigated by the priests against foreigners. It resulted in a massacre. The place also was the headquarters of a stubborn Indian uprising against the authority of the Bolivian government. That was many years back, and I do not know that the maintenance of a garrison at this time has anything to do with past history. The officers were bright, fine-appearing men; the soldiers were stolid-looking, but apparently were under excellent discipline. There are Indian tombs in the neighborhood of Ayoayo, though not so many as at Caracollo.

After leaving Ayoayo is the sublime sight of the peerless Illimani, — a vision to my mind equal to that of the famed Sorata seen from Lake Titicaca, and unsurpassed among the many glorious panoramas of mountain grandeur which the Bolivian Andes afford.

The Continental Andes fork northwest of Lake Titicaca in latitude 14°. The Occidental Cordilleras trend south to the Pacific coast. The Oriental Cordilleras extend in a general direction from northwest to southeast. They are marked by three series of peaks, — the Cololo, which is in Peru; the Illampu; and the Quisma Cruz, or Three Crosses. The greatest of these are the Illampu, which begin with the towering

glacier peak of Sorata and end with the grouped pinnacles of the Illimani. The heights of the summits
according to the best estimates vary from 21,200 feet
to 21,700 feet. It is this region which entitles Bolivia
to be called the roof of the world fully as much as
Thibet.

On the Illimani the snows of yesterday are the
snows of to-morrow. Their sublimity cannot be
grasped at close view. It is necessary to see them at
a distance such as that afforded after leaving Ayoayo
in order fully to appreciate their magnificence, for from
this point the lower flanks, brown and barren, are not
visible. A great wall of marble whiteness, with turrets
and minarets surmounting it, stretches along the horizon. When the turn in the road is made and the sloping sides are in sight, the view is grand enough, but
nothing like the first vision. The chain extends more
than a hundred miles. The cold from the Illimani is
felt very sensibly, yet it is a clear and crisp cold and is
not disagreeable.

The night was spent at Calamarca, where we found
an unusually good *tambo* with the rarest of innova-
tions — two or three camp bedsteads — and excellent
food, well cooked by the wife of the innkeeper, a
very intelligent *chola*.

We left Calamarca on the fourth day, though we
should have been in La Paz at the end of the second
day. The approach to the capital is across a great
meseta, or mountain plain. It swarms with Indian
life. All the region between Oruro and La Paz
seems to be as thickly populated as the land will sustain. The stage road not only passes through many
villages, but there are more of these to the right and

A Drove of Llamas on the Pampa

to the left a short distance from the highway. Some of them are not unattractive collections of adobe huts, and several of the groups are rendered picturesque by the big oval ovens or kilns almost as large as the cabins themselves.

The life is a primitive, pastoral one. Sheep and some cattle, alpacas, llamas, and burros are raised and graze on the plain and in the valley. Maize, or Indian corn, and a little wheat are grown along with barley, and the native cereal known as *quinua*, which is like millet. The crops appear scanty, and the vegetation at this height is not exuberant.

The native existence, while not a joyous one, does not appear to be too sombre. The religious festivals are celebrated with undeviating punctuality. No matter how small the collection of huts, somewhere among them is a church, and each group of cabins has its own *curé*. I remarked everywhere the grass cross over the dwellings. It was very rare to find a hut without this symbolism. It seemed to indicate great devoutness, but what I had already seen of the *curés* and their flocks made me doubt whether this was the correct explanation. The cross, I was told, was blessed by the priest, and then it kept out the rain, which at times is very heavy. One old man, who, after pretending that he knew nothing but the Aymará tongue, had talked very well in Spanish, was asked if the crosses really did keep out the rain. He replied gravely, "Yes, if the roof is a good one."

Whether the orthodoxy of the Indians is more than a crust of superstition I do not profess to know, but I have the conviction that a true missionary priesthood would work a vast improvement in their condition, and would produce the evidences of genuine belief in the doctrines of the Church which is demonstrated by the practice of those doctrines. They have had Roman Catholicism for four hundred years, and another form of worship would be meaningless to them; but what they need is the vital principles of the Catholic worship, and not the abuses of unfaithful servants of the Church.

I had heard that the Indians in the depths of their natures preserved the old traditions, and that they still secretly worshipped the White Spirit of the Illimani. Several persons whom I asked replied that they knew nothing of this belief. One of them, a Peruvian who had spent much time among the Indians, said the only spirit they worshipped was the spirit of alcohol.

Among the native population the *cholos* are easily distinguished. They are the migratory classes who live in the larger towns and some of whom work in the mines. Many of them are freighters. They have charge of the pack trains to and from the mines. They have a distinctive dress, — the loose cotton trouser, widening below the knee and with a V-strip of different cloth in either side. They are a political power, for, while they take little part in the elections, they are not unready to share in a disturbance.

The aboriginal native yet preserves many customs distinct from the *cholo*. He wears a cap, or *gorro*, which was worn in the time of the Incas, and he contents himself with a blanket instead of trousers if he cannot afford the latter. The pure-blood Indians are the best for the freight caravans where the llamas are employed, for they can manage those whimsical beasts of burden as no one else can. The llama feeds as it goes along, and a born manager of animals is needed to handle a *tropa*, or drove, of them, and keep them moving in regular order. The life of the freighter is a hard one, tramping all day and at night sleeping in the corral with the beasts.

The Indian woman in Bolivia occupies a plane on an equality with the man. She has no lord and master, as has the American Indian woman in the noble red man of the West. She works, but he also must work. She accompanies him with the pack trains, all the while that she is trudging along twirling her spools and winding the wool into yarn. It is rare to see an Indian woman without her spools unless she is weaving at the loom. Walking and talking, gossiping and scolding, shouting at the llamas, tramping over the sharpest mountain-pass or plunging down into the gorges, she manages to keep the spool always twirling. It is a most peculiar process, and would drive a small boy who has a notion of spinning a top on the end of his finger wild with emulation, though he hardly would be able to imitate the process.

Marriage bonds among these Indians are not loose ties. In all the settled communities where the little church has been planted, the priest sees that the ceremony is performed, for it means a fee to him. But when the man wanders away for work and is gone for years, as sometimes happens, it is no interruption to the family bond that on his return a brood of children greet him. He resumes the matrimonial relation and accepts the children without question.

There is a prevalent delusion that in these altitudes the birth rate is very low, and, moreover, that many

of the children come into the world deaf or lose the
sense of hearing soon after birth.   While the families
are not so large as in the tropics or lower altitudes,
they are numerous enough, and I was not surprised
to be told that the report about deafness and the
excessive rate of infant mortality does not bear the
scrutiny of scientific investigation.

To reach La Paz from Calamarca it is necessary to
cross several *quebradas*, or wide ravines.   Then the
gravelly plain spreads out and stretches to the precipice of the circular basin in which lies the city.   La
Paz spreads along the inner sides of a rocky amphitheatre, a panorama of red roofs, blended blue and
white buildings, church towers, and parks of willow
and eucalyptus trees.   The greenest and most refreshing spot in the mountain bowl, the one which gladdens
the eye and rests the mind while filling it with pleasing
anticipations, is the cemetery.   But from the Heights
no one guesses that this oasis is a graveyard.

A splendid highway leads down to the city, which is
1,400 feet below the level of the great plain.   At
first it is a straight slanting road at an angle of
45 degrees.   Then it winds and becomes very crooked
and abrupt.   This is the coachman's hour of triumph.
He sends the mules at a full gallop, and if a spill does
not happen the plaza is reached in half an hour.   In
passing, there is a blurred impression of steep mountain sides with burros, llamas, and men and women
slowly climbing the precipitous paths.   This vision
becomes more substantial when the level is reached
and it is possible to look back and see what appear to
be countless processions of two-legged and four-legged
ants losing themselves on the ridges and steep slopes.

VIEW OF THE CATHEDRAL, LA PAZ

La Paz has a plaza and an alameda and two or three smaller parks which are not uninviting. The Chuquiyupu, or La Paz, River winds through the town. The hillsides on which the buildings are located are very steep. The Plaza Murillo is a sort of terrace or level between the river and the ridge. There is an old cathedral, — one of the few in South America about which I know nothing, for I did not even enter it. The market-place in front affords the best examples of native life. La Paz, notwithstanding it is the commercial centre and has the largest Spanish and foreign element, is still the home of the native race. The town has a population of 60,000, of whom 40,000 are said to be Aymarás, 10,000 *cholos*, and the remainder of European, chiefly Spanish, origin. The *cholos* learn to speak Spanish, but the Aymarás will not.

Though no act of Congress has formally made effective the provision of the Constitution which allows the capital to be shifted, Sucre no longer is the seat of government. The President has his residence in La Paz, it is the headquarters of the army, the national custom-house is there, and the Congress meets there. When Sucre was the actual capital, it was isolated from the rest of the country. The foreign ministers lived at La Paz. Some of them during their term of office never visited Sucre, but contented themselves by sending their credentials by messenger or through the mails.

La Paz is notable for the international character of its society. At a dinner at the home of Minister Sorsby I met a Bavarian mining capitalist and his wife, an English railway manager married to an Argentine lady, the wife of a Greek mining engineer who had come out from Constantinople on her bridal trip, a French financier, a Spanish merchant, two or three Peruvian gentlemen, as many Americans, and a Brazilian. This is the cosmopolitanism of a mining country in any part of the world. Mr. Mathieu, the Chilean Minister, I had known in Washington when he was Secretary of the Legation. Mr. Ignacio Calderon, afterwards Bolivian Minister to the United States, at the time of my visit was the Secretary of the Treasury. A pleasant incident was a breakfast with his family and a talk of home affairs, for his wife was a Baltimore lady.

A resting-place after weeks of wayfaring, a vantage point for digesting information and maturing impressions of the imprisoned country and her people, a preparation place for further wayfaring, — all these La Paz was for me.

CHAPTER XX

THE MEXICO OF SOUTH AMERICA

Depression and Revival of Mining Industry — Bolivia's Tin Deposits and Their Extension — Oruro, Chorolque, Potosi, and La Paz Districts — Silver Regions — Potosi's Output through the Centuries — Pulacayo's Record — Mines at Great Heights — Trend of the Copper Veins — Corocoro, a Lake Superior Region — Three Gold Districts — Bismuth and Borax — Bituminous Coal and Petroleum — Tropical Agriculture — Some Rubber Forests Left — Coffee for Export — Coca and Quinine — Cotton.

BOLIVIA, in the character, variety, and extent of her resources, is the Mexico of South America. Her mines yielded the precious metals for hundreds of years. She was the casket of gems held in pawn by the Spanish Crown. She poured the riches of prodigal mother Nature into the lap of the mother country.

Nor was the largess limited to the colonial epoch. The prosperity continued until world conditions, the fall in the price of silver, the depression in the baser metals, bore with crushing weight on an industry which after centuries of ceaseless exploitation must show exhaustion. Lack of transportation facilities discouraged capital from meeting the stress of lowered prices by replacing primitive processes with modern methods. Mining was not abandoned, but it did not advance. Fresh discoveries did not follow exhausted ore beds.

But the dawn of the mining revival came. It was heralded by the basis of all modern industrial development, — railways. The country will have means of communication. The impulse will be given to working old mines and developing new ones, and the progress for the next quarter of a century promises to parallel that made by Mexico during the last twenty-five years. Much of it will be due to the policy initiated by General José M. Pando, and followed by his successor, President Ismael Montes. The understanding of the prospect will best be had after knowledge of what constitutes the mineral resources of the country. From 83 to 85 per cent of the exports are of this class.

Bolivia has not only the precious metals. She also possesses tin. So few countries in the world produce tin, and the article maintains so steady a price, that it is surprising enterprising capital has not made greater efforts to exploit the Bolivian deposits. This mineral is found all through the eastern fold of the plain lying between the Oriental and the Occidental Cordilleras. It extends from the vicinity of Lake Titicaca to the southern boundary of the Republic. The richest and most productive zone of this region is between south latitude 17° and 19°, but the tin fields cover an extent of 300 miles. The most common formation is of slate and gravel, tin being found in the igneous rocks. The best known districts are Milluni; Huayna-Potosi, where the mines are worked more than 17,000 feet above sea-level; Colquiri, where the early Spaniards found tin concentrates, and other sections of the Province of Inquisivi; Oruro; parts of the Province of Poöpo, and the districts of Chayanta, Potosi,

Porco, Tacna, Chorolque, Chocaya, and Cotagaita. The three latter deposits are in the vicinity of Uyuni.

The productive districts are known as La Paz, in the north; Oruro, in the centre; Chorolque, in the south; and Potosi, in the east. Some of the deposits are superficial and thinly spread out over a great extent, while others have been followed to a depth of 1,000 feet and are still continued. The thickness of the veins varies from a few inches up to 10 feet. In some of the mines the mineral is found comparatively pure, containing 40 or 50 per cent and even as high as 65 per cent of the metal. In others the oxide of tin nearly pure is encountered in the form of crystal grains and nodules of a kind of sticky iron sand.

In the northern district between the Illimani and Sorata, and not more than 20 miles from La Paz, is the beginning of the tin deposits of Huayna-Potosi. The tin is found in combination with bismuth, iron pyrites, silver, galena, and even with gold. Milluni is a few miles north of Huayna-Potosi. It has a group of parallel lodes, running east, north, and south, which are composed of quartz impregnated with fine earth, more or less crystallized, and oxides of iron pyrites. There are also veins, running in a westerly direction, which have galena, blends, and carbonates of iron. The greater part of the workings have been at slight depths where the mineral is easily extracted. Chocaltaga, which is within 12 miles of La Paz, is operated under similar conditions. It forms part of the single deposit of Huayna-Potosi and Milluni. The ore extracted from this group is exported by way of Lake Titicaca and Mollendo.

The Oruro region is the most important, as appears

from the comparisons of production. The output of
the different districts for a series of years is shown
in the following table, in terms of metric quintals of
220.46 pounds:

District	Metric quintals					
	1897	1898	1899	1900	1901	1902
Oruro . . .	14,256	17,215	44,256	82,269	100,206	96,981
Chorolque .	8,680	10,960	20,615	40,146	68,998	56,201
Potosi . . .	8,361	9,153	19,826	29,979	39,175	13,365
La Paz . . .	6,198	6,632	8,097	9,948	10,780	9,536
Total . .	37,495	43,960	92,794	162,342	219,159	176,083

This shows that the production rose from 37,495
metric quintals, in 1897, to 176,083 in 1902. The
value as expressed in *bolivianos* mounted from 2,986,-
000 to 8,783,000, or from $1,255,000 to $3,689,000.
Since then the output has grown continuously. The
Potosi district has increased its production steadily, but
the greatest development is in the Oruro zone. The
tin is exported mainly to Liverpool, though a variable
quantity goes to Hamburg. It is subject to a small
export duty, the rate being 1.60 *bolivianos* for each
46 kilograms of bar tin and 1 *boliviano* for the mineral
in the spongy form known as *barilla*, or black tin. For
the bar this is about 70 cents per 100 pounds, and 43
cents for the *barilla*. The latter is the form preferred
for export. In a recent year the exports through the
port of Antofagasta were: *barillas*, 29,583,000 pounds,
and bars, 4,686,000 pounds.

In every sense the tin-mining industry may be said to be one of the future, notwithstanding that it has been worked for years chiefly with a view to securing the pure tin and without much regard to the silver associated with the deposits.   In the Oruro region some oxidized ores from near the outcrops are operated for tin, but the bulk of the mineral comes from the sulphide zone.   From 2 to 4 per cent of tin has been obtained by concentration and lixiviation tailings.   In Potosi there are also silver amalgamation tailings. The past development of the industry was due to the building of the railroad from Antofagasta to Oruro. This provided means of transportation which made it profitable to work the tin deposits within the limited zone where lower freights could be assured.   The company granted a special tariff for the transport of machinery, fuel, and ores.   By the llama or other pack animals it cost about $1.25 per ton for each mile of transportation to the concentration mills.   The freight to Europe for each metric ton of 2,204 pounds averaged 35 *bolivianos*, or $14.90, the proportion charged by the railroad from Oruro to Antofagasta being about 4.89 *bolivianos* per metric quintal of 220 pounds. Other transport and shipping charges were about 3 *bolivianos* for each quintal.

Of the world's total tin output, say 100,000 tons, the Bolivian production under present conditions may be placed at from 9,000 to 10,000 tons, or more than equal that of Cornwall and Australia combined.   Since the United States consumes 43 per cent of the entire production of tin, the importance of the development of the deposits in Bolivia and of the transportation facilities should be appreciated.

The richest silver-producing districts of Bolivia are in the western part and along the metalliferous zones of the central plateau which form the base of the great plain.   Toward the north, south, and east the ore deposits crown the summits of the Andine sierras sloping to the west.   The region is divided into three sections which differ fundamentally in their geological composition.   The Department of Potosi is the most abundant in silver ores.   In it are situated the deposits of Huanchaca, Aullogas, Colquechaca, Porco, Guadalupe, Chorolque, Portugalete, and Lipez.

The famous, though not fabulous, silver field of Bolivia was the Potosi.   It is said that there may be people in the world who never have heard of Bolivia, but there can be no one to whom the name Potosi is unknown.   "Were I to pay thee, Sancho," said Don Quixote to his squire, when the servitor was bargaining to inflict lashes on himself in order to disenchant the knight's Dulcinea, "in proportion to the magnitude of the service, the treasure of Venice and the mines of Potosi would be too small a recompense."

The discovery was made by an Indian herder, named Gualca, who was pasturing his drove of llamas when he came upon what seemed to be a white metal cord. It was silver.   The *cerro*, or conical hill, of Potosi at the apex is 4,780 metres, 15,675 feet, above sea-level. The configuration is volcanic.   The veins run from north to south, with an average inclination of 75 degrees crossing to the east.   The igneous rock which composes the interior mass of the *cerro* is impregnated in all directions with metallic substances, — lead, tin, copper, and iron.   It is distinguished principally by the abundance of silver in the state of chlorides and sulphides.   The great system of lagoons or canals was finished in 1621, and cost $2,500,000, or what would be equivalent to-day to $12,000,000.   Originally there were thirty-two of these canals.

A chain of authorities from Humboldt to Soetbeer have estimated the silver production of the Potosi district through different periods.   From 1545 to 1800 these mines rendered to Spain $163,000,000, which was the tribute that the Crown exacted of one-fifth of the production.   This would fix the taxed output at more than $800,000,000, but historians are agreed that this was far from the actual amount.   In 1611 the Spanish authorities tabulated 160,000 inhabitants in this district.   In 1905 the population was 12,000.   This measures the decadence of the industry.

The carved stone head which marks the entrance to the old mint, the one established by the Spaniards in 1585 and kept in operation for more than two centuries, now grins on the few Indians who gather around the fountain under it with their droves of llamas.   The grinning head seems to mock their present meagre burdens with the memories of the silver caravans of the past.   But it does not follow that those days have gone forever.   The Potosi mines await the railway to replace the llama, and they want also modern methods to restore the riches that defy the old processes of mining.

The most productive silver mine in South America is the Pulacayo.   It is located in the Province of Porco in the Huanchaca district, and is operated by the Huanchaca Company.   The height is 15,153 feet, and the entrance is through a tunnel, or *socavon*, known as the San Leon.   The claim is made that this mine as a silver producer is the second in the world, the first being the Broken Hill of Australia. From 1873 to 1901 the production was 4,520 tons of silver, and the value of the output was estimated at $116,000,000. Formerly the ore was smelted at Huanchaca, Asiento, and Ubina, but now much of it is carried down to Playa Blanca, near Antofagasta. The company employs 3,200 laborers.

In the Chorolque district is said to be the highest mine in the world, 18,696 feet above sea-level. The altitude of the colossal conical peak is 21,156 feet. In this mountain and its environment are veins of silver, tin, bismuth, lead, copper, bronze, kaolin, and wolfram. It is in the region of eternal snows, of never-ending winds, of intense cold, and of rarefied atmosphere. It is operated through a tunnel known as the San Bartholomew and an aerial railway, half a mile long, by means of which the workingmen descend and return to outer earth. A drawback to the exploitation of this region is the lack of transportation facilities, the nearest railroad junction, at Uyuni, being 95 miles. This difficulty will be overcome when the railway is built from Uyuni to Tupiza, as a short spur will enable connection to be made with Chorolque.

The mines in the neighborhood of Oruro were discovered in 1575. In the beginning of the eighteenth century, just before the War of Independence, in three years they paid to the Spanish Crown as the tax of one-fifth, $40,000,000, which would mean an admitted production of $200,000,000. In the district of Oruro are said to be nearly 5,000 abandoned silver mines. In the immediate vicinity of the city a score of silver and tin mines are in operation. The most important of these is the Socavon of the Virgin. This is owned by a Chilean company. The smelting, or amalgamation, works are located at Machacamarca. Since 1898 the process employed has been the use of hyposulphide lixiviation. The San José mine is located in a basin two miles from Oruro. It is controlled by a Bolivian company, is electrically lighted, and has a smelting establishment employing the Wetherill system by means of electro-magnetism. During several years the value of its annual output amounted to $1,000,000.

Under the law the mines are obliged to deliver in silver bullion the fifth part of the exploitation to the national mint for coinage, and the price is fixed monthly by the Secretary of the Treasury. When the drop in silver continued, Bolivia lowered its export duty, and finally, in December, 1902, silver bullion and minerals were freed from export payment. The present Bolivian silver production, which is 8,000,000 to 9,000,000 ounces annually, forms a very small proportion of the world's total output. But with the building of railroads and the assured decrease of transportation charges, it is a safe prophecy that within a few years the output will be doubled, if not quadrupled. Here Mexico again furnishes the illustration. In 1877 Mexico's total silver production was $25,000,000, while in 1902, or a quarter of a century later, it had risen to $73,000,000, and this increase had been brought about very largely through the facilities afforded by the railroads, causing many old mines to be worked profitably and new ones to be discovered.

The copper deposits follow principally the course of the Andes from the Atacama desert through Lipez,

Porco, Chayanta, and Calchas, northeast to Corocoro.
The most important field is that of Corocoro in the
Department of La Paz, 13,000 to 13,200 feet above
sea-level.   It is the Lake Superior region of Bolivia.
The form in which the copper is most commonly met
with is in small, irregular, spongy grains which are
called *barilla*, and which are from 70 to 80 per cent
pure.   The native metal varies from the microscopic
grains, or *barilla*, to great masses of almost pure copper
which the miners call *charqui*.   Other metals are found
in combination.   An analysis made in Hamburg gave
the following results :

Copper	329
Nickel	175
Silver	9
Zinc	117
Other substances	370
	1000

At times the mines of Corocoro have been exploited
chiefly for the silver deposits, and their auriferous character also has been an element in their value.   The
claim is made that enough gold exists in the copper ore
to pay the freight charges to Europe.   The town has
15,000 inhabitants, and is the capital of the Province
of Pacajes.   The copper layers of this region are
known in an extension of 35 miles.   The mines are
owned by Chilean, French, English, German, and
Bolivian capitalists, to whom American syndicates
make regular offers.

The production of the Corocoro district, in spite of
discouraging markets, has mounted steadily.   In 1879
it was 20,240 metric quintals, but in 1886 it had
dropped to 10,000.   In 1900 it was 25,636, and in
1902, 42,014 quintals, or nearly 1,000,000 pounds.

The freight charges have been a heavy drawback to the industry. The two outlets from Corocoro are through Desaguadero River to Nazacara on Lake Titicaca, across the lake to Puno, and thence by the railroad to Mollendo and by ship to Europe; by pack animals to Tacna, and thence by rail to Arica and by ship to Europe. To Mollendo the cost of freight and insurance was 1.87 *bolivianos* (78 cents), while to Arica it was 2.24 *bolivianos* (96 cents) per quintal. The ocean freight to Europe from either point was about 2.78 *bolivianos* ($1.17). The building of the railroad from Corocoro to Tacna will afford the copper mines cheaper freights.

The government exacts a small export duty on the copper ore. The industry has promising possibilities in other regions, in addition to the increased development that may be looked for in the Corocoro district. The best paying of these is in Lipez, where the white native copper is produced and the ore treated simply by concentration.

There are three gold regions. The first extends from the western borders of the Republic, beginning in the basin of the Inambari River, to the upper Paraguay. It includes the mountain zone of Caupolican, Munecas, Larecaja, Cercado, Yungas, Inquisivi in the Department of La Paz, continues through the Department of Cochabamba, and is prolonged through Santa Cruz. There are some famed placer washings in this district, including the Suches and the Tipuani. The Suches is promising both for quartz and for placers. American gold-miners undertook to dive for the gold washings in the Tipuani, and they are said to have had a fair degree of success.

The Larecaja placers of Tipuani are historic. They have been worked since the time of the Incas. The Portuguese began to test them in the middle of the sixteenth century, and introduced negro laborers from Brazil. The Villamil family from 1818 to 1867 obtained 151,000 ounces of gold from the Larecaja properties controlled by them. The placers of the Yani River are also given considerable importance. The best-known mine in this section is the Elsa. The German mining engineer, Stumpff, estimated the quartz here at 61,000,000 tons, giving 36 cents of gold for each ton.

The city of La Paz lies in the gold gulch of the river Chuquiyupu. This is an Aymará name, meaning inheritance of gold.

The second gold-producing region, generally called the Chuquisaca, commences at Atacama and Lipez on the border of Chile, and runs through the southern section of the district of Chayanta, Sur Chichas, Mendez or Tarija, and Chuquisaca, extending to the plains of Santa Cruz. The best-known placers are in the bed of San Juan River, known as the Gold River of St. John. A large amount of money is invested in dredging machinery for the exploitation of this river. In the Province of Chayanta many gold-mining claims have been filed, but few are worked.

The third auriferous region, and the one believed to be the richest, is in the far north of the Republic, along the limits of Peru, and following the water-courses of the Madre de Dios, the Acre, and the Purus Rivers. As this zone is occupied entirely by savages, its wealth of gold has not been exploited and is more or less fabulous.

The gold production of Bolivia which is accounted for is very small, though the calculation of Humboldt and others is that from 1540 to 1750 it amounted to £420,000,000. No reliable statistics regarding present production are obtainable, for, notwithstanding the very light export duty, which is 20 cents per ounce, there is reason to believe that full reports are not made by the mines. In 1901 the output of which the government had account was 550 kilograms, and in 1902, 580 kilograms.

In the production of bismuth Bolivia claims to lead the world. The King of Saxony takes the product in order to protect his own monopoly. The geological formation and the geographical distribution of bismuth follow the same direction as tin, the deposits being in the transverse folds of the eastern slope of the Andes. It is found mixed with the veins of tin and silver, and occasionally it is encountered in the native state. The tin and silver beds of Chorolque contain bismuth. The deposits in this district have sulphurs of copper and iron which are easily separated. The most recent discoveries have been in the Province of Inquisivi. The production in 1901 was 4,925 metric quintals; in 1902, 3,450. The value the latter year was about $350,000. The government imposes a very slight export duty.

Among the mineral substances not metallic, which Bolivia counts as a source of wealth, is borax. The chief deposits are situated in the Province of Carangas, in the Department of Oruro. The principal field there is the Chilcaya, which has an extent of 30,000 acres. The Chilcaya borax is said to be of the best quality, with 47 per cent water. Its exploitation is quite primitive. Chilcaya is 120 miles from Arica, which is the export port for it.

Geologically, and in general terms, the carboniferous zone is described as extending south toward the Pilcomayo. Bituminous coal and petroleum exist, but their commercial possibilities have not been established. Petroleum is found in the peninsula of Copacabama and other points along the shores of Lake Titicaca, but these deposits are not important. Coal veins of uncertain value exist in the northern chains of the Cordilleras, extending from the Tinchi River to the border of Peru. In the Province of Caupolican the crude petroleum is used by the local population.

Coal and petroleum also are found in some districts of Tarija, Cochabamba, and Santa Cruz. An analysis was made in 1904 by the French geologists, under direction of the government, of the coal beds in the Chimoré and Apilla-pampa districts. It showed for the Chimoré samples volatile substances, 24 per cent; carbon, 47.5 per cent; ash, 28.5 per cent. In the Apilla-pampa specimens an appreciable quantity of sulphur was found. Specimens from both districts burned well, although not free from slate. Preference was given the Chimoré coal as containing a greater quantity of coke and volatile substances. It was declared to be capable of utilization in industries and particularly in the production of gas. Since the central plateau and the most thickly populated regions are above the timber line, and recourse has to be had to the llama droppings for fuel, if further exploitation of the Chimoré region shows the presence of coal in large quantities, it will be a decided economic gain to the country. But the indications do not favor it.

As regards tropical agriculture, Bolivia is also similar to Mexico. Rubber was a great fount of prospective income until the value was compounded in the form of a cash indemnity of $10,000,000 from Brazil, when all title to the Acre territory was yielded. But there are other regions yet left, and Bolivia may still look upon rubber as a source of national wealth. She retains some gum forests in the Madre de Dios zone, which has its outlet through Villa Bella at the confluence of the Beni and Mamoré Rivers, and which includes the Madidi, Orton, upper and lower Beni, and Manuripi Rivers. Another region is comprehended in the districts of Chalanna, Songo, Mapiri, Huanay, Coroico, and a part of the Province of Caupolican. This district has its outlet through Puerto Perez on Lake Titicaca. Its rubber product already is exploited to a fair degree. The Germans have large interests in this region.

A district which is practically unexploited is in the northern and eastern part of the Department of Santa Cruz, formed by the provinces of the Velasco and Magdalena, and bordering on the Brazilian State of Matto Grosso. The gum forests here are along the rivers Paraguay and Verde. They are very remote and practically unexploited, but in time undoubtedly they will be opened up. In the region of Yuracares, in the Department of Cochabamba, there is also a species of rubber tree.

Bolivia has a complete code of legislation governing the production and export of rubber, including the imposts to be paid. The gum trees are national property, and neither natives nor foreigners have the right to exploit them without special license, preference being given the one whose discovery claim is filed first. In the Territory of Colonias, which included Acre, each person was permitted to acquire 500 trees, while companies could acquire 1,000.

Of Bolivian agricultural products for export, coffee is entitled to a chief place. Its cultivation is carried on chiefly in the district known as the Yungas, or hot lands, but the shipments for the world's consumption cannot be large in competition with Brazil and other countries. Coffee is exported to northern Argentina and to Chile with profit. The European shipments of late years have been unimportant, notwithstanding that the excellent quality of the exported product had given it a trade standing. With the coffee lands given railroad transportation, the Yungas product, whose flavor is as fine as that of Arabia, may regain its foreign market.

It is a question whether coca is a blessing or a curse to Bolivia. This is the plant from which cocaine is had, and from the similarity in name is often confused with cacao, or chocolate. The natives have chewed the leaves for hundreds of years, and the students of racial atavism profess to see in its qualities stupefying effects which have brutalized the existing Indian race. It is, however, an important agricultural industry. The shrub grows from two to eight feet high. It is cultivated in the lower plains of the eastern slope of the Andes at heights varying from 1,100 to 5,300 feet. Its cultivation is the leading industry of the Yungas district, in which there are many fine plantations. A plantation lasts from thirty to forty years if handled with care and intelligence. The last year for which figures were given, the coca product was placed at

GATHERING COCA LEAVES IN THE YUNGAS

3,450,000 kilograms (7,890,000 pounds), valued at $1,250,000. The government taxes the production, and draws considerable revenue therefrom, since the home consumption is so common. The exportation is through the ports of Mollendo, Arica, and Antofagasta, and also through Argentina by way of Tupiza. France is the chief buyer. The exports amount to 556,275 kilograms on an average each twelvemonth, but the foreign market is uncertain, and in some years the quantity sent out of the country is much smaller.

Sometimes it is forgotten that when the British government secured the cultivation of the cinchona tree in Ceylon and India, the quinine industry was not entirely transplanted from Peru and Bolivia. Annually from 250,000 to 325,000 kilograms, or 715,000 pounds, of cinchona bark are shipped through the ports of Mollendo and Arica. In the eastern Andine region 6,000,000 trees are said to be under culture, there being a large number of the groves on the broken mountain-sides at altitudes of 3,200 to 6,500 feet. The Bolivian product gives from 30 to 32 grammes of sulphate of quinine for each kilogram, and, it is claimed, is superior to other South American bark.

Cotton-growing without question has a future in the Santa Cruz and Chimoré region. It has been claimed that this district can produce 375,000,000 kilograms,— at least, this was the pretension of some enthusiastic railway promoters. They estimated that one *hectare*, or 2½ acres, would grow 1,600 plants, each of which would yield two pounds of ginned cotton, and that 50,000 families could be colonized in this region who would cultivate each six months 15,000 pounds. While experienced cotton-growers smile at these fanciful figures, the experts who have studied the possibilities of the soil and climate in this region credit it with undoubted cotton capabilities.   It is another illustration of Bolivia's varied resources and of her similarity to Mexico.

CHAPTER XXI

BOLIVIAN NATIONAL POLICY

Panama Canal as Outlet for Mid-continent Country — Railways for Internal Development — Intercontinental Backbone — Proposed Network of Lines — Use Made of Brazilian Indemnity — Chilean Construction from Arica — Human Material for National Development — Census of 1900 — Aymará Race — Wise Governmental Handling of Indian Problems — Immigration Measures — Climatic Variations — Political Stability — General Pando's Labors — Status of Foreigners — Revenues and Trade — Commercial Significance of Treaty with Chile — Gold Legislation — A Canal View.

MID-CONTINENT country though she is, Bolivia realizes the value to her of the Panama Canal. For a great many years the larger part of her exports must be ores and metals. The mineral regions lie chiefly on the Pacific side of the Royal or Oriental Andes. A portion of the output in the southern district may find its way profitably down through Argentina, but the overwhelming bulk of the mineral products will have the shortest transit, and therefore the cheapest outlet by the West Coast, through Antofagasta, Arica, and Mollendo, all within the waterway radius. This also will be the route for the machinery and the merchandise imported.

The future of Bolivia is so intensely an industrial one, that the public men who came into power when General Pando became President keenly appreciated that they must secure the means of internal development. This could be fostered only by building railways. In relation to the general subject of rail communication and transportation the Bolivian plans fit intimately with the Intercontinental or Pan-American railroad idea. To have a complete national system of railways it is essential that there shall be a through trunk line from Lake Titicaca to Argentina, though the branches toward the Pacific themselves partake of the nature of main lines. In the political aspect the motive is to secure such domestic progress as in time will enable Bolivia to obtain a seaport of her own. Yet a patriotic policy of forethought for all contingencies forbids her to be dependent entirely on the Pacific outlet. Out of this feeling grew not only the determination to complete the connection with the Argentine system, but also the purpose of combining railroad and water transportation, so that the great river basins of the northeastern region shall have through communication with the capital and with the interior of the country, and afford an Atlantic outlet by means of Villa Bella and the Amazon River.

In this manner Bolivia helps to maintain her independence and to free herself from too heavily leaning on her Pacific coast neighbors. Nevertheless, geography decrees that her earlier stages of development for a quarter of a century, perhaps for half a century, shall be to obtain the fullest advantage of the extension of the Panama Canal zone along the West Coast.

The political, geographical, and economic conditions which, in the view of President Montes and the progressive public men of Bolivia, are necessary for the development of the nation, involve the construction of railway lines somewhat as follows:

1. Viacha to Oruro.
2. Uyuni to Tupiza and Quiaca.
3. Oruro to Cochabamba.
4. Cochabamba to the Chimoré River.
5. Chimoré to Santa Cruz.
6. Uyuni or Sevaruyo to Potosi.
7. Potosi to Sucre.
8. Sucre through Padilla and Lagunillas to Santa Cruz and Yacuiba.
9. Tarija to junction with Argentine lines.
10. La Paz to head-waters of the Beni at Puerto Pando.
11. La Paz via Corocoro to Tacna and Arica.
12. Oruro to Potosi.
13. Potosi to Tupiza.

This scheme is very general, yet it has a solid basis. When visiting Bolivia in the Autumn of 1903 on an official mission, the plans were explained to me, and the prospective events on which were founded the expectations of realizing them. Concurring circumstances followed swiftly. At the beginning of 1905 Bolivia was in the possession of cash capital of $10,000,000, — the indemnity received from Brazil for the Acre rubber territory; Chile, for patent reasons of national policy, by a treaty agreement had obligated herself to construct the line from Arica to La Paz, and also to advance funds to Bolivia, as a guaranty for further railway building; the Peruvian Corporation, to insure its share of future traffic to the Pacific, was engaging in various projects, and minor enterprises were advancing under the encouragement given by the government.

A rough calculation of the cost of railway building was $20,000 per mile in the central plateau, $24,000 in the valleys, and $32,000 in the mountain regions. The latter estimate was too low, but taking the topography of the country in its entirety and making a general engineering reconnaissance of the proposed routes with a maximum grade of 3 per cent, it may be assumed that the 700 miles of railway which are reasonably sure to be constructed can be built for an average cost of $35,000 per mile, or $25,000,000. Half that amount of capital might be said to be in the control of the Bolivian government at the beginning of 1906. The ultimate extension projected in order to league all the parts of the country together is about 1,700 miles, but that is a matter of many years.

When the 128 miles of the Pan-American system between Viacha and Oruro are completed, there will remain only 125 miles from Uyuni to Tupiza, and then the through links will exist from Lake Titicaca to Buenos Ayres, for the Argentine government will have completed the prolongation of its line to Tupiza, the section within Bolivian territory, 55 miles in length, being constructed and operated under a special treaty. Three-fourths of the traffic of the Southern Railway from Puno to Mollendo is furnished by Bolivia, and it is important for the Peruvian Corporation, which operates that railroad, to make sure that its Bolivian freight shall not be diverted. The traffic by way of Lake Titicaca and Mollendo is about 25,000 tons annually.

The network of railways in project includes the section between Uyuni and Tupiza, and the line from Uyuni or Sevaruyo to Potosi, and from Oruro to

Cochabamba. The commerce of Cochabamba is considerable, yet the most pressing national need is to furnish the Potosi mines with transportation facilities. After the convention with Chile for the construction of the line from Arica to La Paz the American engineers who were making the reconnaissance indicated a preference for the routes from Oruro to Potosi and from Potosi to Tupiza as the complement of that system.[1]

How soon the territory of the Yungas, that is, the head-waters of the Beni, will be opened up may be a matter of conjecture; but the very great advantage resulting to the Bolivian government from having this rich tropical territory developed, which among other things would help to provide the capital with fuel, insures the building of a railway of some kind. The success attending the electric road from the Heights of La Paz down into the city may afford some test of the feasibility of using the waters of the Inquisivi River as the means of traction to Puerto Pando, for the water-power of this stream is almost unlimited. Once the head-waters of the Beni are reached, the way will be open for navigation to the confluence at Villa Bella of the Mamoré and the Madre de Dios, which later reach the Amazon. When the Brazilian government carries out the long-postponed plan of building a railway around the Madeira Falls, Bolivia's course to the Atlantic will be shortened.

This Amazon outlet is likely to become practicable long before the route by way of the Paraguay and the Plate is opened.

[1] *Reconnaissance Report upon the Proposed System of Bolivian Railways*, by W. L. Sisson, C. E. La Paz, 1905.

The Antofagasta and Oruro railway, with its $2\frac{1}{2}$ feet gauge for the whole 575 miles, has been a very profitable enterprise, and indicates the prospective profit of other railways. The government guaranteed 6 per cent annually on the cost of the Bolivian section, that cost not to exceed £750,000, but it never has been called on to meet the guaranty, the net earnings being sufficient to pay all fixed charges and handsome dividends. The railway between Viacha and Oruro, when built, will be of the 1 metre gauge (3 feet, $3\frac{3}{8}$ inches) which is the gauge of the line between La Paz and Viacha. Ultimately the Oruro and Antofagasta line is bound to be widened in conformity with it.

There may be halts in the policy of the Bolivian government. Changes may occur. Unexpected obstacles may postpone the fruition of all these national hopes. Yet during the period when the Panama Canal is building between $35,000,000 and $40,000,000 is likely to be employed in railroad construction, and this will mean collateral expenditures in other directions. It may be guessed that $50,000,000 will be spent in internal development during the next twenty or twenty-five years. That would not seem much in the United States, but in a country such as Bolivia it is an enormous sum.

What is the human material for this development, the mineral and other physical resources being understood ? Taking the Acre region from it, and averaging the territory which will be given Bolivia in the settlement of the boundary disputes with Peru and Paraguay, the country may be said to have an area of 400,000 square miles. A reasonably trustworthy census was taken in September, 1900, and this placed the total number of inhabitants at 1,816,000. Of these the classification was made:

Aboriginal Indian race	1,028,000
Mestizos, or mixed blood	560,000
Whites	215,000

The remainder was composed of negroes and blended nationalities.

The relative number of inhabitants in the different political divisions of the country was:

DEPARTMENT	INHABITANTS
Chuquisaca	196,434
El Beni	25,680
Oruro	86,081
Tarija	67,887
Cochabamba	326,163
Santa Cruz	171,592
Potosi	325,615
La Paz	426,930
Territory of Colonias	7,228
	1,633,610
Not enumerated	182,661
Total	1,816,271

A curious circumstance is the even ratio of the sexes. Of the 1,633,610 enumerated population, the males were 819,247 and the females 814,363. The Indian woman fills so important a function in the industrial economy of the country that her numerical standing is of consequence.

This census of 1900 showed that the foreigners domiciled in Bolivia were few. The total was 7,400, and it was made chiefly of Argentinos, Peruvians, and Chileans. The Europeans — Italians, Spanish, Germans, French, Austrians, and English — numbered 1,500. Substantially it might be said the Republic up to the present is without a foreign population large enough to influence its national character and development. The native inhabitants are the economic element of growth.

The whites are of Spanish origin. The *cholos* are more Indian than Spanish, but they have shown considerable capacity for civilization and progress. The Indians are very largely the Aymará race. Possibly one-fourth may be of Quichua stock, but certainly not more. Included in this aboriginal people are a large number of unclassified Indian tribes, and some of these, particularly the savages, have no affiliation with Aymarás or Quichuas. The number of savages is placed at 91,000, though that is hardly more than an estimate. They are found in the river regions of the East and Northeast. The Quichuas are in the South along the Argentine border, and in the North along Lake Titicaca. The great central belt is Aymará, and the mixed blood there is Aymará and Spanish, somewhat more virile than the Spanish Quichuas.

The Aymarás, though conquered by Spain and recognizing that they were vanquished, have resisted absolutely the imposition of more than the thin layer of Caucasian civilization upon them. They are said to have aspirations for independence, but the uprisings which have taken place never have been general and usually have been due to local causes. Their most marked characteristic is the tenacity with which they have held to their language. It would seem absurd to say that a majority of the inhabitants of La Paz do not understand Spanish, because their intercourse with the Spanish-speaking classes must be assumed to give them some knowledge of that language, yet some experiences of my own showed that it was useless to depend upon Spanish. In the interior there are a few persons among the Indians who understand the language of the government, but the mass of them resolutely refuse to know it. The wife of a mining engineer, whose camp was only a few miles away from La Paz, told me her experience with the household servants. She had had to acquire enough of the Aymará tongue to give the ordinary household orders, and her children had picked up more, so that they got along very well. But no persuasion had been sufficient to secure the consent of the Aymarás to learn a little Spanish. In other mining camps there was the same difficulty. The miners always master a few phrases of Aymará and get along in that manner.

It is not unusual to hear reports of uprisings, or attempted uprisings, by the Indians. I witnessed one of these occurrences at Guaqui, on Lake Titicaca. The Indians were said to be coming down a thousand strong. But when the local authorities exerted themselves, and made a show of a few extra soldiers, what had been a noisy, drunken demonstration quieted quickly. However, there are instances in which the Indians give trouble, but in most cases the disturbances are purely local. The testimony is that the Indian population is to be feared only during periods of political tumult, when the government is divided into factions, or when one leader is fighting against another leader, and the bonds of authority are loosened. Then there is danger. The Indians make a pretence of joining one faction or the other, but it is only with the purpose of freeing themselves from restraint.

Considering that the European race is relatively so small a part of the population, the Bolivian government has handled the Indian problem very well, — much better than it has been handled in the United States. Without question, the army, which is an army of conscription, has been of great benefit, not only in the military control of the natives, but in the training it gives the Indians and the *cholos*.   Military service is compulsory, but it is evaded by many of the Aymarás, and discriminating state policy does not seek to enforce it too rigidly.

In spite of the commonplace and stereotyped talk about the worthlessness of the aborigines and their laziness, all my observations led me to believe that the Bolivian Indians are an appreciable element in the economy of the State, and are capable of assisting the national development.   In the *puna*, or mountain regions, where most of them are found, Nature has not been so prodigal that they can live without work.   They do labor in the mines, in tilling the fields, in tending their flocks, and as freighters.   Their endurance is remarkable.

But this native population is not enough for the development of the mines which may be expected during the next ten or twenty years.   A mining population will have to be brought from other lands, and if not from neighboring countries, then from Europe, possibly Galicia, in Spain, and the northern districts of Italy.   The white race endures the cold, and works in the rarefied air of the mines, 12,000 to 15,000 feet above sea-level, without serious impairment of its vital powers.   I noted this from individual experiences and from what mining superintendents told me.

The Bolivian government has a very liberal policy with respect to immigration and the public lands. Hopes are entertained that a scheme of European colonization on an extensive scale will be inaugurated within a few years. This must come with the development of the *chaco*, or tropical prairie and forest region, which extends from the eastern slopes of the Royal Andes to the Paraguay River. Some of the *chaco* is swamp desert, and some is baked soil, covered with thorny scrub; but much of it is fertile, and the climatic conditions are not unfavorable. Several years ago the government granted a railway concession, known as *L'Africaine*, to the French Bank of Brussels, with the special purpose of securing the peopling of this region. The railway enterprise has not advanced rapidly. In time it may be carried forward and bring the *chaco* district into railway communication, not only with Santa Cruz, which is the tropical capital, but also with Sucre and the whole network of railways. Santa Cruz has encouraging possibilities for the European immigrant.

The agricultural region in the Southeast, of which Tarija is the capital, is now partly settled, but there is room for a much larger number of tropical farmers in that locality. In proportion as the mining population grows, colonization may be encouraged, because there will be the inducement to the agricultural production which supplying the mining camps will demand. There also will be an overflow into farming and pastoral industries.

The climate of Bolivia is so modified by the configuration of the country that more than a general statement is not possible. Lying within the torrid zone, the altitudes are to be taken into consideration as modifying influences. Fully 80 per cent of the population lives at altitudes above 10,000 feet, and not less than 60 per cent may be said to exist above 12,000 feet. That is the height above sea-level of

La Paz, which is the largest city, and of the central plateau. The mean temperature between 12,000 and 13,000 feet varies in different years from 57° Fahrenheit to 59°. Above 15,000 feet it is 43°. The seasons, wet and dry, are of more consequence than the temperature. The central plain, the regions of the Cordilleras, and the *chaco*, are all in their climatic character hospitable to natives of the temperate zone.

There are three distinct climatic belts or zones in the Bolivian territory, according to the altitude of the respective regions. These are called *yungas*, or hot valleys; *valles*, or valleys; and *punas*, or cold lands. *Cabecera de valle*, or head of valley, is a subdivision of the main valley division. The *puna brava* is also a subdivision of the *puna*. The mean temperature and the production of the several zones are as follows :[1]

Zones	Altitude	Mean temperature	Products	
			Vegetation	Animal life
	Metres	C.		
Snow region	5,000	1.3°	Valerian and other Umbelliferæ	The condor or Andean eagle
Puna Brava	4,787	6.4°	Cryptogamia	Llama, vicuña, alpaca, chinchilla
Puna . . .	3,614	12.1°	Stipa bromus, bacaris, bolax glebaria, ocsalis tuberosa, quenopodium	Cattle, sheep, horses, donkeys, bears
Cabecera de Valle . .	3,058	15.2°	Wheat, vegetables, trees	Improved species of the same stock
Valle . . .	2,500	17.9°	Fruit-bearing trees, corn, pulse, etc.	All kinds of domestic animals
Yungas . .	1,688	21.0°	Thick woods, coffee, cacao, sugar-cane, coca, rubber, cinchona bark, and fruits of all kinds	Puma, tapir, and birds of beautiful plumage

[1] *Sinopsis Estadictica y Geografica de la Republica de Bolivia*, La Paz, 1903.

The average annual rainfall is shown in the following table:

Latitude	Temperature	Rainfall
	c.	mm.
0	38.00°	836
5	35.34°	818
10	32.68°	800
15	30.02°	782
20	27.56°	764
25	24.90°	746

Bolivia has only had one revolution in a quarter of a century, that is, since the Constitution of 1880 was adopted. The revolution took place in 1898, when General José M. Pando, the head of the army, superseded President Alonso. It was not a very serious affair, and the tranquillity of the country was not long disturbed. The foreign interests favored the change, for the one issue was whether the populous and progressive Department of La Paz should be held back by the unprogressive sections of the country. Since then the Pando policy has prevailed, and has been continued by President Ismael Montes, who was elected as the candidate of the Liberal party with many evidences of popular approval, and was inaugurated in August, 1904. Previous to that time he had been Secretary of War in Pando's cabinet. He has made the policy of railway and industrial development the principal programme of his administration. Señor Villazon, the Vice-President, was formerly Minister of Foreign Relations, and his election was very satisfactory to the foreign interests. Señor Fernando Guachalla, former minister to Washington and one of the leaders of the Liberal party, is looked upon as a prospective president. He has had wide experience in European diplomacy and in conducting negotiations with neighboring South American Republics, and enjoys an international reputation. His success at some future election would be very satisfactory to the foreign interests.

The president is elected by popular suffrage, or, in case there is no election by the voters, by the Congress. His term is for four years. A body of 35,000 electors substantially constitutes the political power of Bolivia. The vote for president in the last three or four elections has varied little from these figures. The Congress is composed of 16 senators and 72 deputies.

The country is divided into eight political divisions, called departments. These are La Paz, Oruro, Beni, Santa Cruz, Potosi, Chuquisaca, Tarija, and Cochabamba. There is also the national territory of Colonias, which is of lessened importance since the Acre district that was part of it has been yielded to Brazil. The departments are subdivided into provinces, and these in turn into cantons or counties. The administration is highly centralized. Each department is governed by a prefect, the provinces by sub-prefects, and the cantons by officials known as *corregidores*, or magistrates. There are also *alcaldes* in the municipal divisions known as the vice-cantons. Municipal councils are elective, but the administrative officials are named by the higher authorities.

The school system I thought, from observations in

PORTRAIT OF ISMAEL MONTES, PRESIDENT OF BOLIVIA

different places, a creditable one. The country has 700 schools, with more than a thousand teachers and with between 35,000 and 36,000 pupils. It has 15 institutions called colleges, the pupils of which number 2,200. There is also the national university. President Montes hopes to have an American school established as one of the measures of his administration, and has been assured by Washington officials of the coöperation of educators in the United States.

Bolivia now observes only one national holiday. This is the 6th of August, the anniversary of independence from Spain. The Church takes many days for its celebrations, and General Pando, when he was President, thinking that they formed sufficient rest and recreation for the population, abrogated various occasions which were celebrated as national holidays.

The Bolivian legislation with regard to foreigners is satisfactory. They enjoy all the civil rights of natives, and are not subject to military service. They may acquire political privileges and be naturalized after a year's residence in the country. The recognition of the rights of non-citizens with reference to mining claims is quite specific in the revised mining code. Foreigners get along very well in Bolivia, even in the remote localities, when they choose to adapt themselves to their surroundings.

There is no prejudice against North Americans, who, in fact, are preferred to Europeans. For a while Englishmen were not welcome, — it was after one of the dictator presidents had set the English minister on a donkey, with his back to the animal's ears, and sent him out of the country. Great Britain did not feel that she could afford to land forces and cross the

Andes in order to secure reparation for the insult, but for many years thereafter she refrained from sending a minister. Diplomatic relations, however, never were suspended, because the interests of British citizens were looked after by the ministers of the United States. In 1903 Great Britain accredited Mr. Beauclerc, her minister to Ecuador and Peru, to Bolivia also. He presented his credentials and was warmly received. The aggregate of English investments in Bolivian mines is large. In 1905 Germany accredited a minister to Bolivia.

The national revenues are derived from internal taxes and from both export and import duties. The chief source of internal revenue is alcohol, which is farmed out to a private company as in Peru. Under this arrangement the government does much better than when it itself undertook to collect the alcohol duties. As the export taxes were on the minerals and on rubber, the low state to which they fell during the world-wide depression of silver and copper is not difficult to understand. The controversy with Brazil cut off almost completely the returns from the rubber district. Now that source of revenue is gone for good, yet there is enough rubber territory left for Bolivia to expect a fair return from the domestic impost and the export tax. With the revival of the mining industry, the country may expect that the financial condition will improve, because a small export tax on the various minerals will bring in a good revenue. The weakness of the Bolivian fiscal resources, however, comes from the nation's isolated position without a seaport. Under its treaties with Peru and Chile, their products, both natural and manufactured, were admitted free of duty, but in 1905 Bolivia gave notice of her intention to terminate the commercial arrangement with Peru, this being a result of the convention with Chile for railroad construction.

The international commercial movement shows a balance of trade in favor of Bolivia. For a ten-year period, ending in 1905, the total foreign commerce ranged from 34,000,000 to 54,000,000 *bolivianos* annually. In a recent year the value of the exports was 25,170,000 *bolivianos*, and of the imports 16,253,000 *bolivianos*, or, on the computation of 1 *boliviano* as equal to 42.6 cents, $10,571,000 and $6,826,000, respectively. Germany and Great Britain have even shares in the foreign commerce, but Germany's advantage is in the merchandise she exports to Bolivia. Sometimes the United States does not appear in statistical abstracts as an exporter, but this is because consular invoices are made out for the Peruvian and Chilean ports through which the merchandise is entered. According to the Bolivian figures, goods to the amount of $400,000 to $500,000 are imported annually from the United States, but it is doubtful if this is anything like the full sum. Railway enterprises carried on by American capitalists would mean largely increased importations of equipment, mining machinery, and merchandise.

The treaty between Bolivia and Chile which was ratified in 1905 and put into effect, has a highly important commercial and industrial significance. By its terms Bolivia formally yielded all claim to the littoral, or coast strip of territory, which was taken from her by Chile as a war indemnity in 1881. The principal feature of the treaty is the agreement of Chile to

construct at her own cost a railway from the port of
Arica to La Paz, the Bolivian section to be transferred
to Bolivia at the expiration of fifteen years from the date
of completion, Chile also giving Bolivia, in perpetuity,
free transit through Chile and the towns on the Pacific.
Bolivia is authorized to constitute customs agencies in
the ports which may be designated for her commerce.
Under this treaty Chile further agreed to pay to Bolivia a cash consideration of £300,000, and to discharge
various liabilities recognized by Bolivia for certain
claims both Chilean and American.

Another provision of the treaty is that Chile will
pay the interest, not exceeding 5 per cent, which
Bolivia may guarantee on the capital invested in the
construction of railways from Uyuni to Potosi, Oruro
to La Paz, and via Cochabamba to Santa Cruz, La
Paz to the region of the Beni and Potosi via Sucre,
and Lagunillas to Santa Cruz. It is stipulated, however, that Chile shall not be required to disburse more
than £100,000 a year, that the aggregate disburse-
ments shall not exceed £1,600,000, and that the
undertaking shall be void at the end of thirty years.
The terms of this guaranty are somewhat indefinite,
and their vagueness may give rise to controversy in
the future. The present, immediate, and prospective
value of this treaty to Bolivia is in securing a railway
outlet from the interior to the Pacific at Arica, and
thus being assured of a commercial artery which is
bound to become a great highway of commerce. Its
relation to the Panama Canal through the port of
Arica I have explained in previous chapters.

In order that the country's fiscal growth may keep
pace with its industrial and political development, the

government has sought to insure financial stability by recognizing the gold standard, somewhat after the manner of Peru. An important step in this direction was taken when, notwithstanding the silver production and the coinage of the white metal by the national mint, a monetary commission was created. This body matured a plan for the adoption of the gold standard. The report was accepted and recommended by the government to Congress at the Autumn session in 1904, and was enacted into law.

The financial system of Bolivia, as fixed by this legislation, may be said to be an approach to the gold standard. The basis of the currency is the silver *boliviano* of 25 grammes, 900 fine, and supposed to equal 100 *centavos*, or cents. In United States terms the *boliviano* is equal to 42.6 cents. In a recent year 19,187,610 kilograms of silver were coined into 866,592 *bolivianos*. The law of November, 1904, fixed the value of Bolivian silver currency in terms of the English pound sterling. It declared that the pound sterling, or English sovereign, should thenceforth have a cancelling value of 12 *bolivianos*, 58 *centimes;* also that from January 1, 1905, 50 per cent of the customs duties should be paid in gold coin at this rate, or, if a whole or part should be paid in silver, this quota should be subject to a surcharge of 5 per cent. Amounts less than one pound sterling may be paid in silver without being subject to the surcharge. By this law the Executive was empowered to suspend, should it become necessary, the mintage of silver coin; the exportation of silver coin was declared free, and its importation into the Republic was prohibited under the penalty of confiscation.

This gold approach law apparently caused no in-convenience to domestic trade, while it was a great help to Bolivia's international commerce and to her credit abroad.

In 1905 the outstanding issues of the four banks which had the authority to emit notes was 9,144,000 *bolivianos*. The paid-up capital of these banks was 7,350,000 *bolivianos*. German and Chilean banks established branches in Bolivia in 1905. By a law passed in November, 1904, an issue of bonds was made to the amount of 2,000,000 *bolivianos*, to cover government obligations to the banks. They bear 10 per cent interest, and the amortization, or refunding, is to be at the rate of 6 per cent each year, 320,000 *bolivianos* being included in the national budget for interest and amortization.

The chapter is becoming long. The conclusion shall be short. The treatment of the topics has been paragraphic. If it were not so, further chap-ters would be necessary for the exposition of the guiding motives of the Bolivian national policy. Much of it is as yet only national aspiration. But the basis is industrial and, therefore, sound. Bolivia shares with her West Coast neighbors the stimulating influence of the Panama Canal. Its economic effect is her industrial and commercial opportunity.

CHAPTER XXII

NEW BASIS OF THE MONROE DOCTRINE

John Quincy Adams' Advice — Canning's Trade Statesmanship — Lack of Industrial and Commercial Element — Excess of Benevolent Impulse — Forgotten Chapters of the Doctrine's History — The Ecuador Episode — President Roosevelt's Interpretation — Diplomatic Declarations — Spectres of Territorial Absorption — Change Caused by Cuba — Progress of South American Countries — European Attitude on Economic Value of Latin America — German and English Methods — Proximity of Markets to United States Trade Centres — Conclusion.

WHEN John Quincy Adams was Secretary of State, he issued instructions to the minister accredited to Colombia after that country's recognition as an independent Republic. They related to the negotiation of a commercial treaty with a single nation, but their blunt advice might have been given to all Spanish America. "Let Colombia," wrote Secretary Adams, "look to commerce and navigation, and not to empire."

I have shown in the preceding chapters how the West Coast countries are looking to navigation, and to the commerce that comes from the railway which was undreamed when Secretary Adams issued his instructions to the minister to Colombia. They have laid the bases of industrial development in public works and private enterprise. They have prepared the approach to financial stability which is demonstrated by the adoption. of the gold standard and the very marked success of some of them in maintaining it. They have given a hint of the possibility of refunding national obligations and of the profitable employment of reproductive savings. They have sought to induce the currents of immigration, which in the case of South America never will rise with the phenomenal flood of the great West, but which may be expected to grow in depth and movement. They have given the proofs of political progress in the substitution of civilian presidents, bankers and sugar-planters, for the old-time military dictators, and they are working out their own destinies after their own manner.

But what of the United States?

The United States, in its relations with South American countries during the eighty years since the monitory words of John Quincy Adams were written, has not dreamed of political empire, and, unfortunately for its international prestige, has not looked to trade dominion. The lack of a commercial and industrial basis for the Monroe Doctrine never has been fully appreciated by the nation which promulgated it and accepted the responsibility for maintaining it, though some understanding of this defect has been felt in the countries to which the Doctrine applies, and a keener realization has been shown in Europe.

Canning, by patient and adroit manœuvres, was able to consolidate the mercantile classes as a counter-irritant to the prejudices of the English aristocracy, which sympathized with the Holy Alliance in its war against republican institutions. His cold and calculating intellect perceived that the commerce which

Spain had monopolized in her colonies was drifting to Great Britain as a result of their revolt, and he was resolved that it should be held. The threat was made to France that the independence of the colonies would be recognized in case Spain should seek to restore her former monopoly system and should attempt to stop the intercourse of England with them. When the British trade instinct began to manifest itself, the edifice of aristocratic intrigue crumbled. England supported the United States in the recognition of the revolted Spanish colonies, the Holy Alliance failed, and British merchants and manufacturers sought the channels which Canning's statesmanship had opened for them. They never have ceased to follow those channels. Much later came Germany. But the United States always has been indifferent.

If they gave the subject any thought, public men failed to grasp why there was not invariably a warmer welcome to their promulgations, and why the grateful South Americans did not buy more goods in the United States. Now, sentiment alone does not bring trade. The Monroe Doctrine, beneficent as it has been, at no period has caused the sale of a dollar's worth of merchandise in Southern markets. Nor in their most benevolent and belligerent moods, when ready to fight all Europe in behalf of some other Republic, have the North American people ever ordered an extra ship's cargo from these markets. Fraternal sentiment does not change the currents of commerce, but commerce sometimes strengthens brotherly relations. And in this manner it will strengthen the Monroe principle by increasing the material interests of the United States, which in the

23

past have been so immaterial in comparison with Europe. When they see and come in contact with the concrete Yankee nation as represented by trade and by industrial investments, the South Americans will understand better what the Monroe Doctrine is and why it is. The Panama Canal extends the responsibility of the United States. It enlarges the commercial opportunity commensurate with the increased responsibility, and the rest remains for the enterprise and the initiative of the individual citizen.

Since these commercial and industrial elements cannot be entirely divorced from political subjects and international policies, a brief review of the Monroe Doctrine in its historic and political aspect may be permitted.

Has national polity ever been more bragged about and less understood than this Doctrine? It was dogma, creed for the American people, but with the vaguest ideas of what it meant. Heretofore one fundamental error has obtained in the United States, — an error which explains why South America did not always welcome our paper assertions of it. In the loose discussion and affirmation of the principle we usually assumed that it was purely philanthropic, and that our national benevolence was to be exerted solely for the good of the weaker nations of the hemisphere, — an altruistic, even quixotic, mission on our part. Internationally our motives are benevolent, but the Monroe Doctrine was asserted in the first place for the welfare and the self-protection of the United States. When John Quincy Adams told Russia that the Western Hemisphere was not to be used territorially for the extension of monarchical institutions, he made the declaration for our own safety. When that official pronouncement was applied to the Spanish colonies which lately had secured their independence, the fear that the establishment of kingships on this continent would threaten the United States was what gave the declaration force as the will of the American people. Protection of the neighboring infant Republics was secondary. The United States was no more disinterested than was Canning in giving effect to the will of British commercial interests rather than to the prejudices of the British aristocracy against republican government.

Nor were the revolted colonies themselves in that formative period so averse to European alliances. Some of them began their republican careers under dictatorships, but others turned to Europe. O'Higgins, the liberator of Chile, would have had another viceroyalty with a deputy monarch from some European Power. La Plata, which is the Argentine Republic of to-day, sent the Rivadiva mission to Europe to borrow some member of a reigning house. It was Canning's perception that the effort to maintain a balance of South American power by lending European princes as rulers would only add to the difficulties of preserving the European balance that caused the Rivadiva mission to be discountenanced.

I recall this forgotten chapter of history very briefly in order to show that in their infancy not all the South American countries were averse to monarchical institutions, and that therefore the objection by the United States to such institutions because of the danger to itself was the more marked. The Monroe Doctrine in the beginning was enlightened and necessary national selfishness, with incidental benefit to the nations protected.   It is only within the last half-century, since Maximilian was overthrown in Mexico, that the American people have learned they have nothing to fear from kingdoms and empires in the New World, and it is during this period that the Latin-American Republics have reaped the substantial and most disinterested results of the original assertion of the policy of the United States.

Nor has aggressive South American support of the Monroe Doctrine been lacking.   It was during the French occupation of Mexico that the Peruvian Foreign Office invited an interchange of views and an agreement on a general policy repudiating European interference.   Argentina and monarchical Brazil did not at that time join heartily in the proposed concert of action, and Ecuador actually was trying to consider herself under a French protectorate.   A coterie of individuals there had proposed an arrangement with Napoleon III, the Dictator-President of Ecuador favored it, and the Emperor had assumed that the protectorate was a fact.   When a proposition was made to incorporate Ecuadorian territory into Colombia, the French minister at Bogota formally protested, under directions from his government, that this could not be done, because France had paramount interests of sovereignty in Ecuador.   This episode is one of the most interesting of all the forgotten chapters in the history of the Monroe Doctrine.

In Chile in 1864, at the period of Maximilian's attempted usurpation of Mexico, the Chamber of Deputies passed a resolution asserting the historic Doctrine.

The Monroe principle, as it has been interpreted by President Roosevelt's administration, has two phases. One was asserted quietly and without calling out special comment. It was that no European military power should be established within striking distance of the American Continent. This assertion would apply to the Galapagos Islands and to naval coaling-stations in the Caribbean.

The second phase, and the one which received more attention, was the President's declaration that the Doctrine was not to be used as a shield to prevent the collection of just debts. This interpretation sometimes has met with prompt acceptance, and sometimes has been received with mild interrogation. The direct statement was given most specific endorsement by the distinguished public man who has had so much to do with shaping the policy of the United States in recent years. This was in the address of Mr. Elihu Root, when, as a private citizen, he proclaimed the rights of the United States as a police power over the affairs of all other Republics on the American Continent.[1] He was referring especially to claims and international obligations, and the responsibility of the United States for redressing wrongs. In substance this was not different from Secretary Olney's declaration during the administration of Mr. Cleveland, that the United States is practically sovereign on this continent, and its fiat is law upon the subject to which it finds its interposition. At that time Lord Salisbury could find no support in international law for the Monroe Doctrine, but Great Britain afterward, for reasons affecting her policy in

[1] Annual dinner of the New England Society in New York, November, 1904.

other parts of the world, became willing to accept the
Olney-Root interpretation, even to the point of letting
her holders of Latin-American bonds look to the
United States for the collection of their debts, though
that responsibility never has been accepted by the
United States, and never should be.

Germany's acquiescence in the Monroe Doctrine
has not been so complacent or so sudden, but this
acquiescence may be accepted as a fact.   A statement
was attributed to Baron von Sternberg, the German
Ambassador in Washington, that the Kaiser would
not accept territory within the Monroe Doctrine's
jurisdiction if brought to him on a silver platter.   An
interview with Chancellor von Bülow, published in a
South American organ of German interests, was even
more positive.[1] " We know," the Chancellor was
quoted as saying, " that commercial relations are ce-
mented by peace and confidence. . . . We have absolutely no political aspiration in the New World, but
since we possess extensive industrial interests we desire
to obtain the greatest possible participation in South
American commerce."

While the declarations of diplomats sometimes may
be accepted with reservation, the conditions in South
America are such that no reason exists why their pro-
nouncements with reference to the Monroe Doctrine
should not be given full force.   Except as to debts
and debt collections, at most the question is an aca-
demic one and has little practical bearing.   In the
matter of the international obligations, while the
American people approve President Roosevelt's position that the Doctrine shall not be construed to

[1] *Deutsche La Plata Zeitung*, 1903.

enable debtor countries to avoid paying their just obligations, nevertheless in practice probably they would expect the national administration to question whether it is necessary for a European government to occupy any portion of the territory of a Latin-American Republic for debt collection.

The United States is justified in fearing that the repression shown by the landing of troops for purposes of debt collection might assume the form of indefinite territorial occupation by a Power not American, and that would be acquisition. The actual circumstances would have to be considered; but official disclaimers of such intention might not be sufficient. Nor would the experience in the reference of the Venezuela claims to The Hague Court be likely to convince the American people that territorial occupation and administration could be permitted pending the settlement of the disputed questions.

The excessive timidity with which the United States Senate approached the sane and sensible provision for a receivership in Santo Domingo, which was a sure way of preventing this question of European occupancy from arising, indicated that further education was necessary before this perplexing phase of the Monroe Doctrine could be assured of full support along the lines proposed by the national administration. But speaking in terms of actuality rather than of speculation, the perplexity relates chiefly to the West Indies, the shores of the Caribbean, and possibly some of the Central American countries. The West Coast republics, in their great industrial strides and their immense advances toward financial and political equilibrium, give little reason to expect that the question will arise with reference to them.

The Venezuela imbroglio in its influence on South American sentiment has to be understood in the light of the agitation which had been going on for the abrogation of the Monroe Doctrine. This movement had supporters in the United States as well as in Europe. The argument was, that, since we had gone to the Philippines, and since Europe had great interests in South America, we no longer had a right to say to the European Powers that they should keep hands off. Instead, they were to be told to carry out their colonizing aims, which only could be successful by territorial acquisition. Until the United States undertakes to exercise sovereignty on the European Continent or along the Mediterranean, there can be no comparison. And until the continental Powers adjust their balance of greedy and mutually distrustful ambitions, so that the Balkan States may enjoy the privileges of civilized government, their mission to civilize South America and establish a balance there cannot be expected to receive serious attention.

And let not the notion obtain that there can be a geographical limitation of the responsibility of the United States. After the war with Spain, when our new duties pressed heavily on us, the suggestion was made that we might draw the line, say at the Equator, and that we should not go farther afield. It was an impracticable suggestion, and does not need discussion now. Having the isthmian canal to protect, we could not, if we would, limit our responsibilities by a line anywhere through South America.

Another aspect of the same subject may be considered in brief space. This is the figment of territorial ambition and territorial absorption on the part of the United States. It is a phantom to the well-informed Northern mind, yet to the South American imagination it is a spectre. In the Republic of Washington and Lincoln are two classes. One talks vaguely on the Fourth of July, and other occasions of national boasting and self-gratulation, about the destiny of the rest of this hemisphere to become a territorial appanage of the United States. The majority of these talkers have the vaguest possible notion of the geography of the Southern Continent, of the physical conditions, and of the political relations. If they knew more, they would talk less. At home their outgivings receive little attention, but in South America they are given undue importance, and often distorted into supposed policies of the government.

The other class not only entertains no idea of territorial absorption, but dreads the notion of the due and just exercise of our influence. It looks on South America as a nest of revolutions with which the United States should have nothing to do, ridicules the possibilities of commerce, and professes disbelief in the capacity for progress.

After the war with Spain, in Latin America the same idea was entertained of the good faith of the United States that was held in Europe. The belief was that in relation to Cuba it would be a case not only of England in Egypt, but of outright annexation. This class of prophets have not fully recovered from the staggering effect of the withdrawal of the United

States from Cuba. It made a deeper impression in dissipating their jealousy and fear of the giant Republic of the North than any of them were ready to admit. Yet I have heard South American public men of the reactionary group, who would have been loudest in condemning the United States for staying in Cuba, and would have used it as an object lesson to terrify their people with the shadow of the North American Colossus, seriously argue that we should have remained, that annexation is inevitable, and that this should have taken place at once instead of being allowed to await the normal evolutionary process. My friend Don X, whom I had known in Mexico, when I met him in Buenos Ayres pointed out to me the errors of my own contention, that in getting out of Cuba we had kept the national faith and had done our duty. "Cuba," he said, "belongs to you. You should have taken her. We would have used it as an awful example against you,· but we would have known you were only doing what you had a right to do."

Thus it appeared that the reactionary South Americans held it as a grievance against the United States, that we did not give them an example of overweening territorial ambition. But the proof that we were not greedy permeated all classes; helped to convince the intelligent population, and even the unintelligent mass, that there could be such a thing as a nation with disinterested purposes, and that nation the Yankee Republic.

The position of the United States with reference to absorption was set forth so fully in the letter of Secretary Hay to Minister Leger of Haiti, and this position was approved so fully by the American people, that no further declaration is required.[1]

That the attitude of the United States is better understood and better appreciated in the farthest countries of South America was shown during the presidential campaign of 1904, in an article on the views of the two candidates, which was published by an influential Chilean paper.[2]

In considering the economic effect of the Canal on the West Coast countries it has not been my thought to discuss in detail its political influence. Moral influence is the better term. This is one of the great forces that counts in their industrial development. The United States is on the Isthmus. It is there to stay

---

[1] DEPARTMENT OF STATE, February 9, 1905.

DEAR MR. MINISTER, — In answer to your inquiry made this morning, it gives me pleasure to assure you that the government of the United States of America has no intention of annexing either Haiti or Santo Domingo, and no desire of acquiring possession of them, either by force or by negotiations, and that, even if the citizens of either of these republics should solicit incorporation into the American Union, there would be no inclination on the part of the national government, nor in the sphere of public opinion, to agree to any such proposal. Our interests are in harmony with our sentiments in wishing you only continued peace, prosperity, and independence.

Very sincerely yours, JOHN HAY.

Mr. J. N. LEGER, &c.

[2] "In reality, it is to the interests of the United States that the South American Republics should look up to them as their best friend, so that they may gradually open their markets to the enormous products of North America, and that the overflow capital of the great Republic may find good investments, so that they may hope some day to expel entirely European capital. All violent measures which may bring forth the distrust of South Americans and European intervention are entirely against the best interests of the United States, and would be considered in that country a great political blunder and an attempt against its economic development." — *El Mercurio, Santiago.*

for all time. Its presence, rightly understood, gives no support to those who dream of territorial aggrandizement, or to the other class who see spectres and have nightmares. But its authority, fully established in the control of the Canal Zone, does give assurance of increased stability to the various governments, and this stability is the greatest inducement that they can offer to the investment of foreign capital. The Monroe Doctrine became automatic from the ownership of the interoceanic waterway by the United States; yet the influence on the Pacific coast countries will be even more beneficial in relation to their internal affairs than with reference to their protection from possible European aggression. What is needed is for the Fourth of July orator who ignorantly hints at territorial absorption, either to inform himself on the subject and to understand how the Panama Canal becomes the greatest factor in enabling the Spanish-American Republics to work out their own destinies, or else for him to confine his ambitious dreams to Canada. Let Canada be his theme, while Latin America solves her own problems.

In the analysis of the South American countries credit should be given them for what they have accomplished and are accomplishing among themselves. A very competent observer in an exhaustive volume has noted the change in the Spanish character in the South American countries, the modifying influence of environment, and the growth of the constructive element.[1]

It may be said that every boundary dispute is either settled or in process of settlement. The inheritance of these controversies from the Spanish and Portuguese colonial epochs was a grievous one, because in the

[1] Charles E. Akers, *South America, 1854–1904*, London, 1904.

vast interior regions it was impossible to have positive knowledge of the limits. The doctrine of *uti possidetis* was wittily translated by a Spanish diplomat as meaning that the territorial possession of the discovering nation extended from the coast as far as the eye could not see, to whatever frontier the discoverer could imagine. But no serious difficulties have arisen over the application of this principle. The respective parties in interest are settling these border disputes without going to war. All the boundaries will be delimited before the interoceanic waterway is completed.

Their limits fixed beyond dispute, the question of the permanent relation of the countries to one another becomes important. South America for South Americans is a wholesome doctrine, so long as they are willing to work in their respective spheres for the advancement of the whole continent. As some of their writers have pointed out, it never can mean a continental alliance.

While much is made at times of the distrust of the United States, a state of mind which is disappearing, it is usually overlooked that there is just as much distrust of one another among themselves. Though it cannot be said that racial antipathies exist, there are national jealousies. The little Republics fear the big ones. When the talk was loudest about an alliance of Chile, Argentina, and Brazil, the other South American commonwealths refused to believe that such an agreement would not mean their own destruction. At least one of them caused representations to be made to Washington, asking whether it could not be taken under a United States protectorate. And it was a faraway Atlantic coast country, too. The smaller and weaker nations feel that, like the fowl in Voltaire's fable, they might express their preference as to how they should be carved up, but in objecting to be carved up at all they would be told they wandered from the question.

There is really only one acute South American question, which is that between Chile and Peru relative to Tacna-Arica, and since it does not enter into the economic conditions of political progress I omit its discussion here.

In the European attitude with regard to the commercial and industrial bases of the Monroe Doctrine has been much that is both grotesque and humorous. But at the bottom of it all is the full appreciation of the economic value of Latin America. France frequently chides herself for her failure to profit more by the moral influence of Latin ideas and literature on the neo-Latin countries. "We know," wrote one authority,[1] "the grand scheme of economic absorption of the Latin Republics by the imperialism and the industrialism of the North."

The imperialism may be dismissed, but the industrialism of the United States, when it once ventures into South America and becomes rooted, is worthy of the attention which European economists give it.

Though Germany and Great Britain are engaged in a ceaseless struggle for supremacy, the French writer bewailed the Anglo-Teutonic commercial movement as if it were a joint one. He proposed Latin-American leagues; the Spanish moral and economic re-conquest of the colonial empire with the aid of France; a kind of family pact, Hispano-Americanism as opposed to Pan-Americanism or Germanic-Anglicism. On their

[1] *La Vie Latine*, Paris, 1904.

side the Germans complain of the loss of German prestige in South America, and some of their writers advocate a European trade combination against the Yankee invasion of the Southern Continent, just as a similar combination is proposed in Europe. Each nation in the international trust would expect to get the lion's share of the benefit. John Bull occasionally has a tearful period of brotherly affection, and asks Uncle Sam to poke his long fingers into the hot coals where the English walnut has been dropped.

With regard to these suggestions it may be said that in international commerce racial affinity counts for as little as do sentimental ties. The presence of English, German, or French capitalists and immigrants in any foreign country naturally draws some home trade, but this has little influence on the general volume. European colonization of South America need not mean Europeanizing it commercially any more than politically. In spite of the large German colonies in southern Brazil, Germany lost commerce with that nation, while she gained it with other South American countries. It is often remarked that much of Germany's profitable traffic is with British colonies.

In an analysis of European interests in South America it is necessary to distinguish between the securities or various forms of national debts and the actual investments in trade and industry, including railways and mines. While the statisticians vary widely in their estimates, it is reasonable to conclude, from an examination of the leading ones, that Great Britain has $2,000,000,000 in South American investments, of which $300,000,000 to $350,000,000 may be assigned the West Coast; Germany has from

$475,000,000 to $500,000,000, with possibly $150,-
000,000 in the Pacific countries; and France, with
about the same amount, has West Coast investments
reaching $100,000,000, her Chilean holdings amount-
ing to $42,000,000.

The relative characteristics of the two principal
European competitors in South America are very
marked. The Germans are slow, cautious, persistent; taking few pioneering risks, but always on the
ground, filching markets and industries on a thoroughly scientific system. They are very largely in
the commission trade and in banking. It may be said
without injustice, that, in proportion to the amount
of actual capital risked, Germany has contributed the
smallest share of all the leading European nations to
South American development, and has done least for
industrial projects.

Great Britain on her part has gone in with her capital, roystering and swaggering, and always has blun-
dered boldly and courageously. The personnel of
her enterprises has been honeycombed with younger
sons, dependants of the London directors, and the
whole class of inefficient parasites which clog the administration of English industrial undertakings abroad.
Her capitalists have built railroads in the mountains,
where the tropical torrents require enormous resisting
works, just as though they were constructing lines
across the plains of India or from London to Liverpool. The stolid and dogged British investor has
paid for it all, and has kept on pouring more money
into these enterprises. So it came that he floundered
into the untold wealth of the Peruvian guanos, stum-
bled into the nitrates with their incalculable riches,

drifted into the golden stream of mining lotteries, and even fell upon fortunate and undeserved surprises in the way of profitable railway projects; while the expansion of his banking facilities, sometimes undertaken with a recklessness that would paralyze conservative bankers, brought him returns that justified further plunges into doubtful financial enterprises. As a whole, this blundering, or even stupid, English policy of investments has paid pretty regular dividends, — in all probability greater in proportion to the capital than the timid and over-cautious German investor has received. When the United States fully appreciates the field which the Panama Canal opens on the West Coast of South America, her captains of industry will be as bold as the Britishers, but not so recklessly stupid, in their preliminary plunges.

These observations bring the subject back to the point that in international rivalry the country does best that meets its competitors on the vantage ground of better and cheaper goods, rather than by dependence on racial sympathy or fraternal sentiment. The great point for the United States is the very marked advantage in which it is placed with reference to the West Coast countries of South America by the Canal. The trade centres of the Eastern States and of the Mississippi Valley will front on the Pacific, as they now front on the Atlantic and the Caribbean. Proximity of markets is a clear gain, and it will help the ..e of the United States to adventure abroad. ..at sense, for a section of South America it definitely enlarges the commercial basis of the Monroe Doctrine.

But proximity alone is not enough. The United

States enjoys no extensive barter with the Caribbean countries, notwithstanding their nearness. Brazil and Argentina are as close to Europe as to the United States. The need of expanding the home market will be stronger in the future, and when that is felt more keenly the north and south trade-wave will deepen its channel.

Always there will be resourceful, persistent competition. The Pacific coast does not become a *mare clausum*. The United States would not and could not make it a closed sea. The foreign commerce of South America is approximating $1,000,000,000. Of this amount relatively $600,000,000 is exports and $400,000,000 imports. The ratio of the West Coast to the entire continent is about 25 per cent; that is, on the basis of $1,000,000,000 it will have $250,000,000 foreign commerce. The United States is in this trade to the amount of $175,000,000. In one year its exports were $53,000,000 and its imports $140,000,000. The disproportionate balance was caused largely by the coffee and rubber imports from Brazil. But on the West Coast the balance is in its favor.

I have written this chapter as though the admonition of John Quincy Adams had been addressed to my own country instead of to another commonwealth. But it again may be said that empire is not the national thought of the United States, and lust of territorial dominion is not a serious malady with the strongest South American republics. Commerce and navigation are based on agricultural and industrial development. The interoceanic waterway renders certain the permanent influence of United States capital

on the industrial and commercial life of its southern
neighbors. It is for them to reap the larger benefit
in the increased development of the national resources
and the more stable political institutions. Some of
them chafe under the implication that the Monroe
Doctrine will be necessary in the future, and view it
as a shadow rather than a shield. The new basis, the
economic basis, of that doctrine which is provided by
the Panama Canal furnishes the foundation on which
its evolution may begin, so that they may get out from
under the shadow while enjoying the sheltering protection of the shield.

The lessons in physical and commercial geography
embraced in these chapters have shown that the geographical sphere of the Canal includes the Amazon
basins, the Argentine wheat plains, and the Andes
treasure box of mines from Panama to Patagonia.
They have shown how railroad progress is crowd-
ing mule-trail civilization, how the arteries of trade
are lengthening, how fresh commercial currents are
developing, how the new industrial life is unfold-
ing, and how the problems in the political conditions of the Western Hemisphere are being solved.
They give promise of the deferred realization of
Henry Clay's population prophecy. Finally, they
bid the citizen of the United States to look out
from the windows of his own self-contained nation
down the South American Canal line, and, accepting the responsibility which that grand enterprise has
brought, to share in the opportunity which it has
created for contributing to the civilization that comes
through the spread of commerce and industry.

APPENDIX

The relation of the Panama Canal to ocean transportation routes is best exhibited in the painstaking tables prepared by the Hydrographic Office of the United States Navy. These show, in terms of nautical miles, the comparative distances, which are as follows:

WEST COASTS OF NORTH

San Francisco	Monterey	Santa Barbara	San Diego	San Blas	Guaymas	Acapulco	Salina Cruz	San José	Corinto	Puntarenas (Costa Rica)	Panama	Esmeraldas	Guayaquil	Paita	Pacasmayo	Callao
0	90	295	451	1430	1510	1836	2189	2446	2671	2916	3277	3395	3608	3552	3709	4012
....	0	220	376	1355	1435	1805	2124	2371	2596	2841	3227	3320	3528	3477	3634	3937
....	....	0	164	1166	1246	1616	1935	2182	2407	2652	3038	3131	3339	3288	3445	3748
....	....	....	0	843	923	1493	1812	2059	2284	2529	2965	3008	3216	3165	3322	3635
....	....	....	....	0	500	520	780	1074	1310	1534	1948	2033	2254	2210	2374	2680
....	....	....	....	....	0	954	1251	1508	1774	1968	2382	2467	2668	2644	2808	3114
....	....	....	....	....	....	0	300	563	799	1023	1437	1532	1762	1720	1889	2189
....	....	....	....	....	....	....	0	291	529	765	1160	1302	1538	1535	1615	1989
....	....	....	....	....	....	....	....	0	238	474	888	1026	1298	1281	1453	1759
....	....	....	....	....	....	....	....	....	0	284	698	830	1130	1126	1302	1608
....	....	....	....	....	....	....	....	....	....	0	490	640	947	948	1125	1431
....	....	....	....	....	....	....	....	....	....	....	0	475	842	849	1031	1337
....	....	....	....	....	....	....	....	....	....	....	....	0	409	416	600	906
....	....	....	....	....	....	....	....	....	....	....	....	....	0	226	415	721
....	....	....	....	....	....	....	....	....	....	....	....	....	....	0	200	506
....	....	....	....	....	....	....	....	....	....	....	....	....	....	....	0	310
....	....	....	....	....	....	....	....	....	....	....	....	....	....	....	....	0
....	....	....	....	....	....	....	....	....	....	....	....	....	....	....	....	....
....	....	....	....	....	....	....	....	....	....	....	....	....	....	....	....	....
....	....	....	....	....	....	....	....	....	....	....	....	....	....	....	....	....
....	....	....	....	....	....	....	....	....	....	....	....	....	....	....	....	....
....	....	....	....	....	....	....	....	....	....	....	....	....	....	....	....	....
....	....	....	....	....	....	....	....	....	....	....	....	....	....	....	....	....
....	....	....	....	....	....	....	....	....	....	....	....	....	....	....	....	....

AND SOUTH AMERICA

Pisco	Islay (Mollendo)	Arica	Iquique	Antofagasta	Copiapo	Coquimbo	Valparaiso	Talcahuano (Concepcion B.)	Lota (Concepcion B.)	Valdivia	Punta Arenas (Sandy Pt., Chile)	
4115	4451	4579	4645	4770	4885	5036	5140	5272	5287	5410	6199	San Francisco
4040	4376	4504	4570	4695	4802	4964	5065	5197	5212	5335	6124	Monterey
3851	4187	4315	4381	4506	4620	4745	4870	5002	5017	5142	5945	Santa Barbara
3728	4064	4196	4258	4368	4501	4626	4747	4879	4894	5019	5822	San Diego
2784	3126	3254	3321	3444	3582	3713	3724	3993	4008	4139	4976	San Blas
3218	3560	3688	3755	3878	4016	4147	4285	4427	4442	4573	5410	Guaymas
2303	2647	2775	2842	2973	3113	3253	3398	3554	3569	3708	4580	Acapulco
2109	2317	2493	2688	2794	2966	3086	3254	3412	3424	3566	4510	Salina Cruz
1871	2193	2354	2421	2550	2704	2864	3224	3203	3218	3378	4295	San José
1720	2042	2203	2270	2399	2553	2713	2879	3069	3084	3255	4186	Corinto
1543	1866	2026	2093	2222	2376	2538	2702	2894	2909	3071	4019	Puntarenas
1449	1771	1932	1999	2128	2282	2444	2608	2801	2816	2979	3932	Panama
1018	1340	1501	1568	1697	1851	2013	2177	2370	2385	2548	3501	Esmeraldas
833	1155	1316	1383	1512	1666	1828	1992	2185	2200	2363	3316	Guayaquil
618	940	1101	1168	1297	1451	1613	1777	1970	1985	2148	3101	Paita
430	754	913	990	1109	1267	1442	1608	1808	1823	1987	2949	Pacasmayo
127	452	622	689	807	965	1139	1309	1514	1529	1697	2666	Callao
0	335	511	578	703	861	1033	1204	1413	1428	1597	2550	Pisco
....	0	139	222	428	604	790	967	1196	1211	1384	2370	Islay (Mollendo)
....	....	0	110	323	538	697	881	1102	1129	1301	2294	Arica
....	....	....	0	222	437	600	784	1005	1032	1204	2185	Iquique
....	....	....	....	0	229	392	576	797	824	996	1981	Antofagasta
....	....	....	....	....	0	179	361	582	609	781	1705	Copiapo
....	....	....	....	....	....	0	198	426	450	623	1613	Coquimbo
....	....	....	....	....	....	....	0	240	266	437	1425	Valparaiso
....	....	....	....	....	....	....	....	0	39	222	1210	Talcahuano } Concepcion Bay
....	....	....	....	....	....	....	....	....	0	207	1194	Lota
....	....	....	....	....	....	....	....	....	....	0	1011	Valdivia
....	....	....	....	....	....	....	....	....	....	....	0	Punta Arenas (Sandy Pt., Chile)

EAST COASTS OF NORTH

New York	Portland	Boston	Quebec	Halifax	Charlottetown, P. E. I.	Philadelphia	Baltimore	Newport News	Charleston	Savannah	Bermuda	Key West
0	362	300	1404	581	828	229	404	281	629	699	676	1171
....	0	111	1161	343	575	529	693	567	901	971	739	1400
....	....	0	1205	383	627	477	641	515	849	919	696	1348
....	....	....	0	861	570	1558	1739	1613	1904	1978	1505	2377
....	....	....	....	0	273	735	836	710	1077	1147	758	1568
....	....	....	....	....	0	982	1137	1011	1323	1393	852	1807
....	....	....	....	....	....	0	355	229	594	664	729	1093
....	....	....	....	....	....	....	0	156	550	620	759	1049
....	....	....	....	....	....	....	....	0	424	494	633	923
....	....	....	....	....	....	....	....	....	0	88	816	598
....	....	....	....	....	....	....	....	....	....	0	830	569
....	....	....	....	....	....	....	....	....	....	....	0	1090
....	....	....	....	....	....	....	....	....	....	....	....	0
....	....	....	....	....	....	....	....	....	....	....	....	....
....	....	....	....	....	....	....	....	....	....	....	....	....
....	....	....	....	....	....	....	....	....	....	....	....	....
....	....	....	....	....	....	....	....	....	....	....	....	....
....	....	....	....	....	....	....	....	....	....	....	....	....
....	....	....	....	....	....	....	....	....	....	....	....	....
....	....	....	....	....	....	....	....	....	....	....	....	....

AND SOUTH AMERICA

Habana	Saint Thomas	Port Castries	Demerara	Pernambuco	Bahia	Rio de Janeiro	Montevideo	Buenos Ayres	Punta Arenas (Sandy Point)	
1215	1428	1746	2209	3696	4096	4778	5768	5868	6890	New York
1444	1562	1853	2289	3701	4101	4783	5773	5873	6895	Portland
1392	1516	1808	2253	3666	4066	4748	5738	5838	6860	Boston
2421	2340	2574	2935	4171	4571	5253	6243	6343	7365	Quebec
1612	1613	1873	2279	3575	3975	4657	5647	5747	6769	Halifax
1851	1790	2028	2437	3662	4062	4744	5734	5834	6856	Charlottetown
1137	1437	1762	2225	3746	4146	4828	5818	5918	6940	Philadelphia
1093	1414	1743	2204	3758	4158	4840	5830	5930	6952	Baltimore
967	1287	1617	2086	3622	4003	4780	5750	5853	6826	Newport News
642	1194	1554	1984	3631	4031	4713	5703	5803	6825	Charleston
613	1212	1566	2202	3660	4060	4742	5732	5832	6854	Savannah
1141	853	1134	1724	3037	3437	4119	5109	5209	6231	Bermuda
90	1040	1360	1797	3814	4214	4896	5886	5986	7008	Key West
0	1019	1360	1869	3509	3909	4591	5581	5681	6703	Habana
....	0	346	802	2469	2869	3551	4541	4641	5663	Saint Thomas
....	....	0	461	2155	2555	3237	4227	4327	5349	Port Castries
....	....	....	0	1788	2188	2870	3860	3960	4986	Demerara
....	....	....	....	0	400	1100	2065	2183	3340	Pernambuco
....	....	....	....	....	0	745	1717	1835	2992	Bahia
....	....	....	....	....	....	0	1056	1162	2228	Rio de Janeiro
....	....	....	....	....	....	....	0	104	1312	Montevideo
....	....	....	....	....	....	....	....	0	1386	Buenos Ayres
....	....	....	....	....	....	....	....	....	0	Punta Arenas (Sandy Point)

DISTANT PORTS

PORTS	By Cape of Good Hope				
	Full powered steam vessels	Auxiliary steam N. E. monsoon	Auxiliary steam S. W. monsoon	Sail alone N. E. monsoon	Sail alone S. W. monsoon
New York to Bombay .	11250	12670	11820	13310	12460
" " " Colombo .	10950	11730	11730	12370	12260
" " " Calcutta .	12180	13710	13140	14390	13780
" " " Singapore .	12150	12850	13120	13490	13760
" " " Hongkong .	13590	14750	14560	15430	15200
" " " Shanghai .	14340	15560	15370	16510	16010
" " " Yokohama	15020	16450	16120	16900	16760
" " " Melbourne	12670	12840	12840	13480	13480
" " " Sydney . .	13140	13310	13310	13950	13950
" " " Wellington	13710	14240	14240	14880	14880

PORTS	By Suez Canal			By Panama
	Auxiliary steam N. E. monsoon	Auxiliary steam S. W. monsoon	Full powered steam vessels	Full powered steam vessels
New York to Bombay	8370	8120	8120	15130
" " " Colombo . . .	8610	8610	8610	14230
" " " Calcutta	10460	9830	9830	14300
" " " Singapore . . .	10170	10170	10170	12670
" " " Hongkong . . .	12110	11610	11610	11260
" " " Shanghai . . .	12920	12410	12360	10720
" " " Yokohama . . .	13820	13160	13040	9670
" " " Melbourne . . .	15030	15010	12790	10020
" " " Sydney	14480	14460	13320	9710
" " " Wellington . . .	15680	15660	14230	8530

PORTS	By Magellan Strait		By Cape Horn	By Panama
	Full powered steam vessels	Auxiliary steam vessels	Sailing vessels	Full powered steam vessels
Melbourne to New York . .	12880	13120	13760	10020
Sydney " " " . .	12700	13050	13750	9710
Wellington " " " . .	11500	11850	12550	8530
Valparaiso " " " . .	8460	8680	9400	4640
San Francisco " " " . .	13090	14670	15420	5300
Esquimalt " " " . .	13840	15330	16060	6080
Honolulu " " " . .	13200	14170	14970	6690
New York to Valparaiso . .	8315	9130	9420	4640
" " " San Francisco . .	13090	15350	15660	5300
" " " Esquimalt . . .	13920	15980	16290	6080
" " " Honolulu . . .	13200	14650	15480	6690

INDEX

INDEX

Boll weevil, Peruvian cotton free from, 126

Borax deposits, 132, 325

Brandy, Pisco, 85

Brazil, (tropical) coffee trade, 8 ; (temperate) cattle and wheat industries, 8 ; boundary disputes, 136, 146 ; coffee product, 161, 328 ; controversy over Acre rubber territory, 327, 333

Bronze in Chorolque district, Bolivia, 320

Bryce, Professor James, 164

Buenaventura, 59

Bull-fight, at Lima, 95 ; abolished in Chile, 213

Bulnes, General Manuel, former Chilean president, 233

Business-letter, the terse English, 23

Caballitos, or grass canoes, 79

Cabildo of Quito, resolution adopted by, 66

Cacao, or chocolate, Ecuador's production of, 63

Caceres, President, his plans concerning central highway, 143, 170

Cachipuscana, Lake, 118

Cailloma district, Peru, silver-producing, 132

Caja de Ahorros, or Savings Bank, Santiago, 256

Cajamarca, 80, 132

Calamarca, 306

Calancha, Friar, concerning the South Sea and the Southern Cross, 57

Calca district, Peru, iron production, 133

Calchas, Bolivia, copper deposits, 322

Caldera, 5, 188

Calderon, Mr. and Mrs. Ignacio, of La Paz, 312

Calderon, Señor Manuel Alvarez, Peruvian minister to Washington, 1903, 169

Calderon, Señor Serapio, second vice-president of Peru, 169

Caledonian cross-cut channel projected, 42

Caleta Buena, 222

Caliche, nitrate layer, 220

Callao, 6, 12–14, 83, 84

Camache, suburb of Iquique, 185

Camana district, Peru, copper-producing, 132 ; sulphur beds, 133

Campaign humor, instance of, 240, 241

Campana, J. J., of Iquique, 219

Canal Commission, 52

Canal Zone, 18, 19, 37–56, 364 ; *see* Panama, Isthmus of

Candamo, Señor Miguel, late president of Peru, 166–172

Cane rum, or *aguardiente*, 27, 128

Cangallo district, Peru, sulphur beds, 133

Canning, George, the statesman, 352, 355

Canta district, Peru, coal deposits, 133

Cape Pillar, 197

Capelo, Joaquin, Peruvian engineer of central highway, 143

Capopo district, copper mines in, 228

Carabaya, Province of, gold mines developed by Americans, 119, 120, 132

Caracas, Bay of, 60

Caracoles silver mines, 230

Caracollo, Bolivia, 302

Casapalca smelting-works on Central Railway of Peru, 103

Castilla, Joaquin, Peruvian patriot, 94

Castrovirreyna district, Peru, silver-producing, 132

Cauca, valley of, 13, 59

Caucho, second quality crude rubber, 134

Caylloma district, Peru, coal deposits, 133

Centenarians in San Juan valley, 281

TABLES